MW01012751

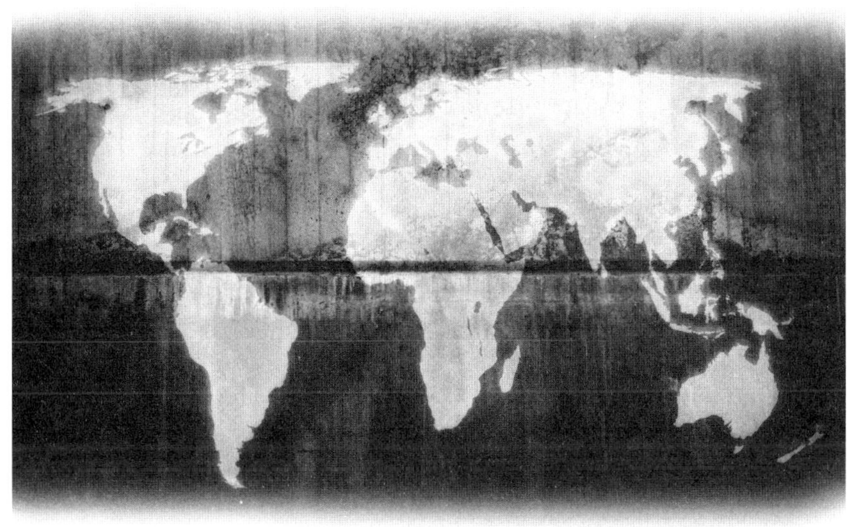

The END of ALL Things Is at HAND

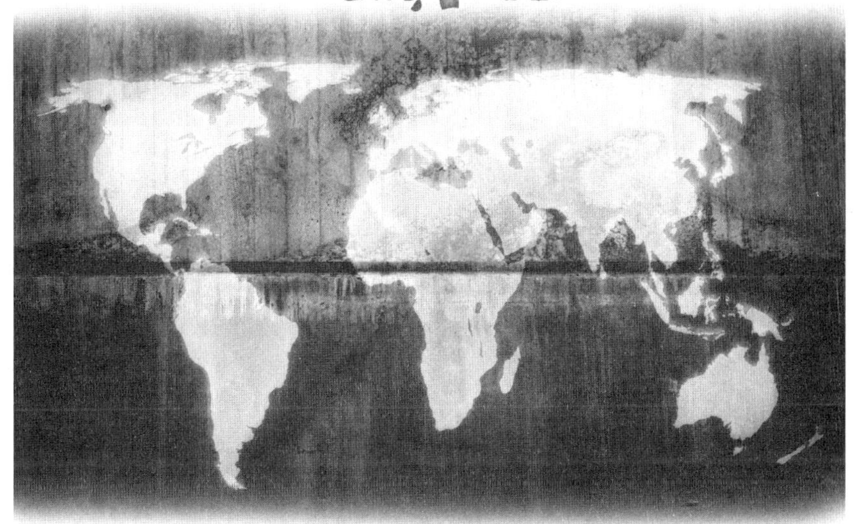

Are You Ready?

Dr. Richard Booker

Bridge-Logos
Alachua, Florida 32615

Bridge-Logos
Alachua, FL 32615USA

The End of All Things Is at Hand: Are Your Ready?
by Richard Booker

Edited by Harold Chadwick

Printed in the United States of America.

Library of Congress Catalog Card Number: 2008939471
International Standard Book Number 978-0-88270-615-3

G218.316.N.m812.35260

Contents

Preface

"What? Another book on Bible prophecy?" This is what I thought when the Lord burdened my heart to write this book. There are so many books on this subject I wondered why another one? As the author of over 30 books, I really wasn't interested in writing another book, particularly one on a subject that already fills the bookshelves. So why another book on Bible prophecy?

As I contemplated this question, I realized that much of what goes under the name of Bible prophecy is really Bible sensationalism. Webster's dictionary defines sensationalism as the use of subject matter to excite temporary superficial interest and emotional response. Unfortunately, this is what many books do that claim to be on Bible prophecy. They are on subjects that appeal to the senses rather than the spirit. They excite and stimulate the emotions but do not touch the heart. They give a temporary "prophecy fix" to the flesh but do not cause a holy change in the life of the reader. While these books may be popular, they are certainly not prophetic.

Furthermore, most books on Bible prophecy are written from a Western cultural worldview rather than from a biblical worldview. This means that the writer interprets the Bible from a Western perspective as opposed to a biblical Hebraic perspective. Our perspective is how we mentally see things. Reading the Bible through Western eyes as opposed to biblical Hebraic eyes can make us think we see things in the Bible that are not necessarily there. The result is an understanding and explanation of Bible prophecy as if the Bible was written in a Western theological seminary rather than in a Middle-East culture.

Since I have written this book from a biblical Hebraic worldview, I do not address typical Western Bible prophecy topics, such as the rapture, the anti-Christ, the meaning of 666. I have tried to write what the Bible actually says rather than what I think it means. Also, some of my explanations may challenge your preconceived ideas. You may not agree with everything I have written, and that is okay. Please ask the Lord to clarify and confirm to your heart what is of Him.

As we look at the conditions of our world, many believe that we are living in the end times. The Lord burdened my heart to write about these end time events with a holy awe of His presence, His plans, and His purposes for the future. Because the God of Abraham, the God of Isaac, and the God of Jacob is outside of time, He knows the end of time from the beginning of time (Isaiah 46:9-10). He has written prophetic events in the Bible to awaken us, alert us, and inform us about the future.

There is a glorious future for believers. The Lord spoke these words through the prophet Jeremiah, "For I know the thoughts that I think toward you, says the LORD, thoughts of peace and not of evil, to give you a future and a hope" (Jeremiah 29:11).

This is a book about our future and our hope. My purpose for writing it is to minister God's word to your spirit, to explain Bible prophecy from a biblical Hebraic context and worldview, and to help you learn practical ways to prepare for the challenging days ahead with faith, hope, and love.

As such, this book is more that just another Western "systematic theology" book on the end times. I not only explain prophetic events, but the book itself is prophetic in its explanations, tone, and urgency. A great spiritual tsunami is coming to our world. This book is a "Watchman's" call to awaken believers to the prophetic season in which we are living, and a spiritual manual on how to prepare for and serve God in the momentous events coming to our world.

The Bible says that the sons of Issachar had understanding of the times and knew what Israel ought to do (1 Chronicles 12:32). May we also understand the times in which we are living, and know what we should do to prepare for the paradigm shift coming to our world as the kingdoms of this world become the kingdoms of our Lord (Revelation 11:15).

May we soon see the time when:

All the ends of the world shall remember and turn to the LORD, and all the families of the nations shall worship before You. For the kingdom is the LORD's, and He rules over the nations (Psalm 22:27-28).

CHAPTER 1

Back to the Future: Ten Prophetic Signs of the Coming of the Lord Part 1

One of the most successful Hollywood movies ever made is called, "Back to the Future." If you saw the movie you remember it was about a time machine where the "mad scientists" and the teenage boy traveled back in time to the 1950's. I particularly enjoyed that movie because I was a teenager in the 1950's.

An interesting part of the movie was when the teenage boy learned that the mad scientist would be harmed when he returned to his own time. He tried to warn his scientist friend not to return because something bad would happen to him. Naturally the boy and the scientist were curious about the future. Fortunately, this was one of those movies where everything worked out for the good. But the movie pointed out something all humans share in common.

We all want to know the future. We all want to know what tomorrow holds. What's just around the corner? What's next! We're like little Johnny who went to school the first day of the first grade. When he came home, he said to his Mom, "OK, now that I've been to school, what's next?" Little Johnny thought that by attending one day of school in the first grade that was all the schooling ever required of him. Did he get a shock when his Mother made him return to school the next day. He didn't realize that he had at least 12-16 more years of school ahead of him. He wanted to know what was next right now.

Young people ask, I wonder what's going to be on the test? As they get a little older they ask, "Is he really the one for me?" "If I ask her to marry me, will she say, "yes?" "Will this marriage work?" With ultrasound we've have taken the guess work out of the question all expecting parents ask, "Is it a boy or a girl?" Then they wonder, "How are we going make ends meet with more mouths to feed?" "How are our kids going to turn out?"

People ask, "Who's going to be the next president?" "What's going to happen to the economy?" "Will I have a job next year?" "Can I pay my bills?" "Is the stock market going to go up or down?" "Is the price of gas going to get higher?" Seniors ask, "Will there be any money left in social security when I retire?"

Most of us would pay someone a lot of money if they could tell us the future. People consult their astrological sign, go to fortune tellers, read tea leaves, have their palms read and do other strange things to try to learn the future. Yes, we all want to know the future.

Only God Knows the Future

But there is only One who knows the future. And that is God. God knows the future because He has already lived it. You see, God is outside of time. He is "the Alpha and Omega, the Beginning and the End, the First and the Last" (Revelation 22:13). Because God is outside of time, He has already lived in the past, present, and future. All of time is contained within Him. Therefore He knows everything that was, is, and is to come. He says in Isaiah:

> "Remember the former things of old, for I am God, and there is no other; I am God, and there is none like Me, declaring the end from the beginning, and from ancient times things that are not yet done, saying, My counsel shall stand, and I will do all My pleasure" (Isaiah 46:9-10).

The Bible says that we must remember the former things of old where God has declared the end from the beginning. In the movie, the characters had to go back in time to learn about the future. And so must we. We must go back to the former things of old written in the Bible to learn about the future. In these first two chapters, we want to go back in time to learn ten prophetic signs of the future "Coming of the Lord."

Prophetic Signs

Now what do I mean by the phrase, "Prophetic Signs"? The word "prophetic" means "foretelling events." God has foretold the future in the Bible. A sign is a signal from God about the future. So prophetic signs are signals from God meant to awaken us, alert us and inform us about the future. Since God lives outside of time, He has written in the Bible prophetic signs for our learning so we can prepare ourselves. When we see the signs, we can know the prophetic season in which we are living. In fact, the Bible says we are responsible to know these prophetic signs.

In Matthew 16:2-3, Jesus rebuked some of the religious leaders because they could discern the signs in the sky to predict the weather but they could not discern the prophetic signs of the times.

In Hebrews 10:24-25, we are told to exhort one another as "we" see the Day approaching." This means we can know the season of the Lord's return by observing the visible prophetic signs happening in our world.

In 1 Thessalonians 5:1-6, Paul says that believers live in the light of God's revelation so we should not be asleep spiritually but should be alert and watching so we will be prepared and not surprised.

In 1 Chronicles 12:32 we learn that the sons of Issachar understand the times in which they were living and knew what Israel should do.

In view of the fact that the Lord has gone to so much effort to tell us these signs, and the fact that He actually holds us accountable to know them, I want to share with you what I believe to be ten of the more visible prophetic signs of our times. We will consider the first three in this chapter that relate to the Jewish people and the modern state of Israel, and the remaining seven in the following chapter. Are your ready?

1. The Return of the Jews to their Homeland

The first and most important and most visible sign is the return of the Jewish people to their ancient homeland—Israel. Isaiah 66:8-

9 reads, "'Who has heard such a thing? Who has seen such things? Shall the earth be made to give birth in one day? Or shall a nation be born at once? For as soon as Zion was in labor, She gave birth to her children. Shall I bring to the time of birth, and not cause delivery?' says the LORD. 'Shall I who cause delivery shut up the womb?' says your God.'"

The Lord says that Zion, the word for Israel and Jerusalem, will be born in one day. And while many would shut up the womb of Zion to stop the delivery, God determined that He would give birth to Zion—that is the State of Israel.

Israel was reborn in one day when David Ben-Gurion read the Declaration of Independence on May 14, 1948. The British High Commissioner was to lower the Union Jack on Friday at midnight. Since that day would begin the Sabbath, the Declaration of Independence was read earlier that afternoon at four o'clock.

The modern-day birth of Israel is a miracle of God and one of the most fascinating stories of history. Many wonderful books have been written about it. I wrote my book on the subject, *Blow the Trumpet in Zion* over twenty years ago. You may order it through my online bookstore at www.soundsofthetrumpet.com.or www.rbooker.com. What makes this story so exciting is that it has happened in our times. And the Bible connects the rebirth of Israel to the coming of the Lord.

Psalm 102:13, 16 reads:

> "You will arise and have mercy on Zion; for the time to favor her, yes, the set time has come.... For the LORD shall build up Zion; He shall appear in His glory."

There are so many places in the Bible that tells us this prophetic signal, it would take months to read and study all of them. I want to share just a few of them.

Isaiah 43:5-6 reads:

> "Fear not, for I am with you; I will bring your descendants from the east, and gather you from the west; I will say to the north 'Give them up!' and to the south, 'Do not keep them back!' Bring my sons from afar, and My daughters from the ends of the earth."

In this and many other Scriptures, we learn that this is an ingathering from all the nations of the world. In fact, it will be such a large ingathering, that the Jewish people will consider it a greater miracle than their deliverance from Egypt. For 3,500 years the Jewish people have celebrated Passover as a memorial to their deliverance from Egypt. But this ingathering will be so great they will see it as even a greater miracle.

Jeremiah 16:14-15 reads this way:

> "Therefore, behold, the days are coming," says the LORD, "That it shall no more be said, 'The LORD lives who brought up the children from the land of Egypt,' but, 'The LORD lives who brought up the children of Israel from the land of the north and from all the lands where He had driven them.' For I will bring them back into their land which I gave to their fathers."

In the late 1980's and 1990's approximately 1,000,000 Jews from the former Soviet Union made *aliyah* (went up) to Israel. I am proud that Christian Zionist organizations such as the International Christian Embassy Jerusalem, Bridges for Peace, The Ebenezer Emergency Fund, Exobus and others had a major role in bringing 100,000's of these Jews back to the land in fulfillment of Bible prophecy. My own organization had a small part helping bus Jews from the Ukraine.

There are about 13 million Jews in the world today. About 5 million live in Israel, 5 million in the U.S. and the rest in Europe, Canada, South Africa, and Central and South America. Ezekiel 39:28 says that God will leave none of them behind in the nations. This means that the remaining Jews in Europe will soon be making *aliyah* followed by the Jews in America who are already beginning the process.

As far as American Jews are concerned, Nefesh B'Nefesh is the primary Jewish organization assisting North American Jews to make *aliyah*. It has received major funding from Christians who desire to help the Jewish people return to their ancient land—Israel. Since its founding in 2002, they have brought 10,000 Jews from America to Israel. While that is a small amount, it represents the first fruits of American Jews to make *aliyah*. Their new goal is to bring 5,000 a year. As Americas problem escalate, the number of Jews making *aliyah* will continue to grow in fulfillment of Bible prophecy. This is a frightening thought for Jews as well as Christians but it is a clear prophetic sign of our times. Everything is beginning to change and this is one of the changes.

One of the most interesting stories of a recent immigrant is that of Sam Habers. Sam was one of the engineers who prepared the Exodus for its 1947 journey. Thousands of Jewish refugees left Europe on the Exodus, which Habers considered a piece of rusted-out junk that never should have made it out of the shipyard. When Habers took the ship on the test run, he actually didn't think it was fit for anything much. He had little or no confidence in the ship. Habers waited 59 years before he would make "*aliyah*."

2. The Jews Repossess Jerusalem

The second most important and most visible sign is that the Jews repossess Jerusalem. In Luke 21:24, Jesus said that Jerusalem would be trampled by the Gentiles until the times of the Gentiles are fulfilled. One of the major prophetic signs that the times of the Gentiles is over is the Jews repossessing Jerusalem. This miracle of God took place in the 6-day war which began on June 5, 1967. Several days later (June 7) the Jews liberated Jerusalem, which came under Jewish control for the first time in almost 2,000 years.

But let's back up 50 years to see the hand of God orchestrating events so this could happen. One of the most important battles in World War I was the battle for control of the wells at Beersheba. It also turns out that this was one of the most important battles in redemptive history that would change the course of history.

You see, without the wells, the British/Australian/New Zealand military would not be able to liberate Jerusalem from the Turks. They needed the water for their horses and men. But Beersheba was protected by thousands of German and Turkish soldiers as well as the desert. It was tactically and humanly impossible to take Beersheba. Impossible, that is, for everyone but God and the 800 Australian Light horsemen who did it on October 31, 1917. You can rent the movie entitled, The Light Horseman" to see this action-packed story on film.

The British General at that time was Edmund Allenby. There is an awesome God-story about Allenby. He was a God-fearing Christian Zionist. When he was a little boy in England, his mother taught him this prayer which he would say every night before going to bed, "And, O Lord, we would not forget your ancient people, Israel. Hasten the day when Israel shall again be your people and shall be restored to your favor and to their land."

There was an eerie silence as Allenby and his troops approached Jerusalem on December 9. They were prepared to fight for the city. But the Turks had already fled so that Allenby was able to take the city without firing a shot. How did this happen?

The name Allenby had a mystical significance in Arabic. When read from left to right in Western style, the name is Allah Nabi, which means, "prophet of God." When read from right to left in Arabic style it means, "Son of God." In Turkish, the name means, "Scourge of God." When the Turks learned that a general named Allenby was coming to fight them, they ran away and no one was left to defend the city.

On December 11, when Allenby entered Jerusalem for the official victory declaration, he dismounted from his horse, bowed his head and humbly walked in through the Jaffa Gate. There was no display of arms, and no pomp and ceremony. As a God-fearing Christian, Allenby felt unworthy to ride into the city of God on his white horse as a great conqueror. He understood that honor was reserved for the Messiah who would enter Jerusalem on His white horse as written in Revelation 19:11. Allenby said he never knew God would give him the privilege of answering his own childhood prayer.

Contrast Allenby's attitude to that of the German Kaiser Wilhelm. The Kaiser had promised Theodore Herzl that he would help him purchase land in Palestine from the Turkish Sultan. But the Kaiser turned his back on Herzl. The Kaiser also went to Jerusalem in 1912, five years before Allenby.

Now the word Kaiser comes from the Roman word for Caesar. Before the Kaiser-Caesar Wilhelm entered Jerusalem, he had a special opening made in the city wall. So when he entered, he did so through the opening with great pomp and ceremony with the German naval choir singing, "Behold the King Cometh Unto Thee."

At the end of the war, Allenby was honored with the title "Earl of Megiddo." And the Kaiser? Well before the war was over he fled to Holland where he remained a self-styled prison for the rest of his life. God's word in Genesis 12:3 is still true. He still promises to bless those who bless the Jews and curse those who curse them.

Now one last God-story about Jerusalem. In Ezekiel 44:1-3, the Lord explained to Ezekiel that He would seal up the Eastern Gate until the time of Messiah who would open it and enter His city in all His power and glory. The reason He would seal the gate is because the Lord Himself had entered the city through this gate (Ezekiel 43:4). And no mere mortal could enter the city where the glory of God had entered.

It was centuries later in 1545 AD when this prophecy was actually fulfilled by Suleiman the Magnificent, the Turkish ruler who built the present wall around the Old City and sealed up the Eastern Gate. Suleiman heard the stories about the Jewish Messiah coming to Jerusalem through the Eastern Gate. So he sealed it shut and put a Muslim cemetery in front of the gate thinking no Jewish holy priest from the tribe of Levi would desecrate himself by walking through the cemetery.

When a special IDF commando group approached the Old City to fight the Jordanians, they had a difficult time getting into the city. Some of the members of the group suggested that they surprise the Jordanians by blowing up the Eastern Gate and entering through it. But as God had orchestrated this event, the leader of the group was an Orthodox Jew. He told his squad the story of Ezekiel and that the Eastern Gate could only be opened by the Messiah. Instead of blowing up the Eastern Gate, they entered through the Lions Gate and captured the Old City in fulfillment of Bible prophecy. Of course the Messiah is not from the tribe of Levi but from the tribe of Judah. So no Muslim cemetery is going to bother Him. I have stood directly in front of that Eastern Gate and touched it while praying for the coming of the Messiah.

When the Lord returns to Zion, He will speak the word of God to the Eastern Gate. His voice, like thunder, will command the Eastern Gate with these words from Psalm 24:7-10:

> Lift up you heads, O you gates! And be lifted up, you everlasting doors! And the King of glory shall come in. Who is the King of glory? The LORD strong and mighty, the LORD mighty in battle. Lift up your head, O you gates! Lift up, you everlasting doors! And the King of glory shall come in. Who is the King of glory? The LORD of hosts, He is the King of glory.

A beautiful and inspiring poem about the Eastern Gate was written by Terry Gibson. In 1987, Terry and his wife, Virginia, accompanied my friend Dr. David Reagan on a pilgrimage to Israel to attend the International Christian Embassy's celebration of the Feast of Tabernacles. On the last day of the celebration, 4,000 pilgrims from all over the world paraded around the city of Jerusalem, and then marched to the top of the Mount of Olives where they sang hymns as the sun set behind the city. Terry wrote the following poem out of that experience. It is called, "The Gate in Waiting."

The Gate in Waiting

A POEM BY TERRY GIBSON

There is a gate in waiting, in the city of the King.
It waits above the valley, and adorns a tranquil scene.

Jerusalem is churning, on the north, south and west.
Yet the Eastern Gate waits quietly, above multitudes at rest.

On Olive Mount, I stood one day, and viewed this Golden Gate.
Amid singing saints and setting sun, in the spirit was my state.

Looking o'er this glorious Gate, from atop that blessed mount.
Two scenes of great events, I saw, and now recount.

The First Coming

One scene took place in ages past, the other is soon to be.
In both there was the Son of God, and the Gate of Destiny.

The first scene was triumphant, they hailed Him as a King.
There were thousands in the valley, and "Hosannas" loud did ring.

Many miracles of greatness, had He done before their eyes.
Giving sight to the blind, calling forth the dead to rise.

His disciples were elated, as they joined this happy throng.
But little did they know, that their hopes would soon be gone.

So long ago the prophet told, that lowly He would come.
Riding on a donkey's colt, unbefitting the Righteous One.

Yet thousands upon thousands, stood in the valley on that day.
And up the path to the Eastern Gate, with Palm branches did array.

"Save us Son of David," the multitudes did cry.
*When suddenly, the *crowd did change, they shouted "Crucify!"*

Oh! What price our God did pay, while sinners yet we were.
The mocking ones—the crown of thorns, pierced hands—what agony!

And so the only Son of God, was hung upon a cross.
He'd come to earth in godly love, to save those that were lost.

(* To clarify, the crowd that shouted "crucify Him" was a different group of people than the ones who greeted Jesus when He entered Jerusalem.)

The Second Coming

Then the scene did fade away, and another scene took its place.
For Jesus had said He would return, to redeem mankind's disgrace.

On Olive Mount I stood again, and viewed the Eastern Gate.

Yet, it was closed, sealed with stone, awaiting a King to coronate.

Ezekiel long ago had said, the Gate would thus be so.
Until the Prince returned to earth, then all the world would know.

Around the city armies stood, from nations of the world.
As smoke and fire were everywhere, the armaments were hurled!

Yet the Golden Gate still quietly stood, while looking upward it seemed.
Suddenly the trump did sound, it was the coming of the King!

And then I saw the Lord of Lords, descending from on high.
With multitudes of Heavenly Hosts, behind Him in the sky.

He came and stood on Olive Mount, and then the earth did shake.
He spoke and all the armies fell, and the evil power did break.

Upon a white and valiant steed, down Olive Mount did ride.
Through Kidron Valley up to the Gate, while the Jewish remnant cried.

They looked upon Him, Whom they had pierced, and grieved as for a son,
So bitterly they wept in shame, yet with grace He did respond.

And all the while the numbers grew of Angels and the Saints.
Millions upon millions, joined Him in the ranks.

They sang "Hosanna to the Son of David," "Hosanna to the King."
Throughout all heaven and the earth, the loud Hosannas ring.

The Gate in waiting trembled, and the stones then blew apart.
And the Holy One did enter, His eternal reign to start.

Oh! What sweetness in that Day, the redeemed of God shall know.
From Mount Zion in Jerusalem, the living waters flow.

Are you yearning for that day, when the Lord of Hosts shall come?
Or do you flee in fear, before the Holy One?

Call upon His name, before that coming day.
Flee into His loving arms, He will wipe all tears away.

3. The Jews will Rebuild the Temple

Wow! I hope you enjoy that poem as much as I enjoy it. This leads us to the third prophetic sign, which is that the Jews will rebuild the Temple. Not all Christian theologians and scholars agree that the Jews will rebuild the Temple. They rightly understand that, as believers, our body is the Temple of God so why would God want to build a literal Temple in Jerusalem. In their mind, God did away with the Jewish rituals when He allowed the destruction of the Temple. These are usually leaders of Christian denominations that teach replacement theology—the teaching that the Church replaced the Jews in God's covenantal plans. If this is true it means that God's covenant words cannot be trusted or that He is impotent to keep them.

Jewish theologians and scholars are also divided on this subject. While they do believe God will rebuild the Temple, some extreme Orthodox believe that only Messiah can do this and that it is blaspheme for Jews to attempt this without the Messiah. Others believe the Hebrew Scriptures (Old Testament) say the Jews should rebuild the Temple in preparation for the coming of Messiah.

So does the Bible talk about a third Temple? The answer is yes. A very familiar Scripture is Isaiah 2:2-3 which says:

> Now it shall come to pass in the latter days that the mountain of the LORD's house shall be established on the top of the mountains, and shall be exalted above the hills; and all nations shall flow to it. Many people shall come and say, "Come, and let us go up to the mountain of the LORD, to the house of the God of Jacob; He shall teach us His ways, and we shall walk in His paths." For out of Zion shall go forth the law, and the word of the LORD from Jerusalem.

In Daniel 9:27, Daniel talks about an evil person who will commit the "Abomination of Desolation," which brings an end to offerings and sacrifices. Some interpret this to be referring to Antiochus Epiphanes who desecrated the Temple at the time of the Maccabean revolt or the Romans when Titus destroyed the Temple in 70 AD. Others believe Daniel is referring to a third Temple build at the end-times. In Matthew 24:15, Jesus referred to Daniel's prophecy and warned the believers to flee Judea when they saw the "abomination of desolation ... standing in the holy place." Again, some believe Jesus is referring to Titus rather than an end-time Temple. Neither of these references could be speaking about Titus because he didn't enter the Temple. He burned it down.

In 2 Thessalonians 2:3-4, Paul refers to the "the man of sin ... the son of perdition," and says that he is the one "who opposes and exalts himself above all that is called God or that is worshipped, so that he sits as God in the temple of God, showing himself that he is God." Titus did not do this.

The apostle John wrote the book of Revelation in the 90s. This was over twenty years after Titus burned down the Temple in 70 AD. So John could not have been talking about that Temple. In Revelation 11:1-2, John talks about "the temple of God" and clearly puts it in the time of the Great Tribulation at the end of the age, prior to the coming of Messiah. When we put all the Scriptures together, it is clear there will be a third Temple built before the coming of Messiah. It is a prophetic sign of the end-times.

Why would God want to rebuild a Temple in Jerusalem? As non-Jewish believers (Christians), we know that when Jesus said, "It is finished" (John 19:30), He meant that He was the once and for all perfect sacrifice for sin. We know that, but Jewish people don't. And this is a Jewish Temple.

The Jewish people are in need of a great spiritual awakening and revival. The Temple will be a great catalyst for this spiritual renewal. It will be like a magnet drawing Jews back to Israel and back to their covenant God. The Temple and the sacrifices offered at the Temple will be an important visual aid for the Jewish people to understand the necessity of a blood covenant sacrifice for sin. It will be a powerful picture of redemption pointing them to Jesus (Yeshua in Hebrew), and His death as the final atoning sacrifice for sin.

This view is not just a Christian understanding. The core prayer of Judaism for thousands of years is called, "The Amidah." In this prayer, the Jewish people connect the rebuilding of Jerusalem and the Temple with the coming of Messiah. The fourteenth blessing says, "And to Jerusalem, Your city, may you return in compassion, and may You rest within it, as You have spoken. May You speedily establish the throne of David within it. Blessed are You, HASHEM, the Builder of Jerusalem."

The seventh blessing says, "Be favorable, HASHEM, our God, toward Your people Israel and their prayer and restore the service to the Holy of Holies of Your Temple. The fire-offering of Israel and their prayer accept with love and favor, and may the service of Your people Israel always be favorable to You. Blessed are You, HASHEM, Who restores His presence to Zion."

God is going to restore His presence to Zion. While most of our Jewish friends do not realize it, and many Christians are ignorant of who Jesus really is, the Jewish Messiah and the Christian Savior and Lord are the same person. He is the Jewish *Yeshua* who is returning to His people in the land of Israel. The rebuilding of the Temple will hasten this glorious event.

As we observe prophetic events, do we see any sign of this Temple being built? Absolutely, yes! Most of the Christian groups that go to Israel today will visit the Temple Institute under the direction of our personal acquaintance, Rabbi Chaim Richman. Rabbi Richman tells us that 80% of all the vessels needed for Temple use have been made. Furthermore, thousands of young men are being trained in the Yeshivas (Jewish Seminaries) in Israel to serves as priests at the Temple when it is built. Those of us who go to the Christian celebration of Succot in Jerusalem see this for ourselves at the Western Wall celebration led by these priests in training, and attended by many thousands of Israelis as well as hundreds, and perhaps thousands, of Christians.

Furthermore, the Lord is preparing for the rebuilding of the Temple by restoring the blue thread needed in the robe of the High Priest and which, eventually, all Jewish men will wear. When God called the Hebrew people into covenant with Him, He intended for the entire nation to be a kingdom of priests. We read in the book of Exodus:

> "Now therefore, if you will indeed obey My voice and keep My covenant, then you shall be a special treasure to Me above all people; for the earth is Mine. And you shall be to Me a kingdom of priests and a holy nation" (Exodus 19:5-6).

After this proclamation, the LORD gave the people His holy commandments, including instructions for making a visual aid that would remind them of His commandments. When the people looked at this visual aid, they would be reminded of their high priestly calling. They were the royal priests of God and were to always remember and keep His commandments.

We find the instructions to make this visual aid in the book of Numbers:

> Again the LORD spoke to Moses, saying, "Speak to the children of Israel: Tell them to make tassels [*tzitziot*] [*tzitzit*, singular] on the corners of their garments throughout their generations, and to put a blue tread in the tassels of the corners. And you shall have the tassel, that you may look upon it and remember all the commandments of the LORD and do them."(Numbers 15:37-39).

In ancient times, the Jewish men wore a four-cornered garment. God instructed the men to put tassels on the four corners with a blue thread in the tassels. As they look at the tassels they would be reminded to keep God's commandments. White is the symbol of purity and blue the color of heaven. The blue thread represented the presence of the Almighty in the midst of His people.

The blue thread was very expensive to make. The dye that was used to color the thread came from the blood of a hillazon snail. It took 12,000 of these snails to make just 1.4 grams of the dye. That's about enough to fill a thimble. In 200 BC, one pound of cloth, dyed blue, cost the equivalent of $36,000. By the year AD 300, that same pound of blue cloth cost about $96,000.

Because it was so expensive, garments made with this blue dye were worn only by royalty and priests. We can see clearly the significance of every Jewish male wearing the blue threaded *tzitziot*. They were the royal priests of God.

As an observant Jewish man, Jesus wore two garments, a *tunic* and a *tallit* with *tzitziot* on the borders of the *tallit*. The *tunic* was the under garment. It was a lighter robe, usually made of linen that extended to just above the ankles. The outer garment (*tallit* or mantle) was a heavier garment draped over the *tunic*. It was usually made of wool. It was a rectangular piece of cloth that, according to Jewish tradition, had to be a hand's breadth shorter in length than the *tunic*. The *tzitziot* were the "hem of His garment" the woman with the issue of blood wanted to touch (Matthew 9:20-21). It was not like the modern Jewish prayer shawl; it was part of the everyday dress of a Jewish man. In fact, it was considered immodest to wear only the *tunic* in public, even though it extended to the ankles.

Some of the Pharisees showed their wealth by the size of their tassels on their *tallit*. Jesus rebuked them because they were enlarging the borders of their garments, not because they love God, but to be seen of men (Matthew 23:5).

In the second century after the time of Jesus, the Roman Emperor Hadrian forbid the Jews to practice their faith. They were no longer allowed to wear the royal blue thread in their *tzitzit*. As time passed, the snails seem to have disappeared and the people no longer had the exact color of blue required for the *tzitziot*. Therefore, they could only use white thread for centuries, until recently.

The Lord has supernaturally called the snails back to Israel. Not long ago, millions of these "lost snails of Israel" made *aliyah [went up to the land]* and washed up on the shores of Tel Aviv. About that same time, a Jewish man also made *aliyah* who claimed to know how to make the blue dye. Today, in Israel, a blue thread has been made that is acceptable by a growing number of rabbis. At the Temple Institute, the blue robe of the High Priest has been made from the dye of these snails. Surely, this cannot all be just a coincidence. Can any honest inquiry truly believe all these happenings are just coincidences? Surely it is the hand of the Almighty moving forward "prophetic history" in preparation for the coming of the Messiah.

When Jesus returns to establish the Kingdom of God on the earth, He will wear a robe that is surely a *tallit*. That robe will have

His name in the position of the *tzitziot*, KING OF KINGS AND LORD OF LORDS (Revelation 19:16). At His return, Jesus will rule from Jerusalem as King Messiah over Israel and the nations. The Jewish men will once again wear their *tallit* with the blue thread to acknowledge that God is in their midst in the person of Jesus (Yeshua). It is a fulfillment of Bible prophecy and it is connected to the Temple. All the nations will seek God's blessing through Messiah Jesus and the Jewish people at the rebuilt Temple in Jerusalem.

Zechariah wrote of this time and said:

> Yes, many peoples and strong nations shall come to seek the LORD of hosts in Jerusalem, and to pray before the LORD. Thus says the LORD of hosts: "In those days ten men from every language of the nations shall grasp the sleeve (wing, corner of a garment, *tzitzit*) of a Jewish man, saying, 'Let us go with you, for we have heard that God is with you'" (Zechariah 8:22-23).

A friend of mine in Jerusalem is Pastor David Decker. David has written a most interesting and thought-provoking book: *Revival from Zion: 50 Reasons why Christians Should Support the Building of the third Jewish Temple.* While you may not necessarily agree with nor fully understand all his reasons, I list them below in order to stimulate your thinking and discussions on this subject.

Reason 1 – God's Not Finished with Israel
Reason 2 – You Are Spiritual Israel
Reason 3 – Both Israel's Are in a Blood Covenant
Reason 4 – What's so "Old" about the Old Covenant?
Reason 5 – Israel's Priestly Destiny (and Our Own)
Reason 6 – It's Why Modern Israel Exists
Reason 7 – The Next Big Thing
Reason 8 – Physical Temple then Physical Return
Reason 9 – It will Mark the End of the Gentile Age
Reason 10 – As Israel Goes, so Goes the Church
Reason 11 – Bringing Jews Back to God
Reason 12 – A Call to Righteousness
Reason 13 – God Demands a Sacrifice
Reason 14 – This is Especially for Natural Israel

Reason 15 – The Original Blueprint Has Always Existed
Reason 16 – Even the Mere Earthly Copies are Blessed
Reason 17 – A Return to Biblical Judaism
Reason 18 – Phasing Out – Phasing In
Reason 19 – All the Temples Are Blessed by God
Reason 20 – Jesus Loved the Temple
Reason 21 – The Disciples of Jesus Loved the Temple
Reason 22 – Answering Solomon's Prayer
Reason 23 – Answering Centuries of Jewish Prayers
Reason 24 – Restoring the Tabernacle of David
Reason 25 – Great Latter Day Call to Holiness
Reason 26 – A Direct Assault on Satan and Anti-Semitism
Reason 27 – Blood Sacrifices Are Still Allowed
Reason 28 – It All Points to Christ
Reason 29 – The Aaronic Priesthood Remains in Effect
Reason 30 – The Greater Priesthood of Christ
Reason 31 – Prophesied Influx of Humanity to Zion
Reason 32 – Confronting Moral Relativism
Reason 33 – New Meaning for All the Jewish Holidays
Reason 34 – Rehearsal for the Millennium
Reason 35 – Supremacy of the God of Israel
Reason 36 – Peace through Moral Strength
Reason 37 – Call for Modern-Day Hirams
Reason 38 – Restoration of God's Shekinah Glory to Jerusalem
Reason 39 – Spiritual Protection for Israel
Reason 40 – Getting the Focus Off Ourselves
Reason 41 – Creating an Awesome Monument to the One True God
Reason 42 – Bringing all the Bible Believers Together
Reason 43 – Public Renewal of an Ancient Bible Covenant
Reason 44 – Ceremonial Law Buttressing the Moral Law
Reason 45 – Ending the Elapsed Time: Daniel's 70th Week
Reason 46 – The Supremacy of Christ
Reason 47 – Behold the Tabernacle of God is with Man
Reason 48 – Fresh Outpouring of the Holy Spirit on Zion
Reason 49 – Revival from Zion
Reason 50 – The Second Coming of Our Lord and Savior

We are certainly living in exciting times. The Lord is fulfilling the many prophecies in the Bible about the return of the Jews to their ancient land. While the Islamic led Arab countries and the nations of the world are doing their best to stop God's prophetic word from happening, God is a faithful, covenant-keeping God. He will fulfill His word as He assures us many times in the Bible.

The prophets declared God's word regarding His final ingathering of the Jewish people and reminded them again and again of God's faithfulness. We see these prophecies happening before our very eyes. As Amos explains:

> I will bring back the captives of My people Israel; they shall build the waste cities and inhabit them; they shall plant vineyards and drink wine from them; they shall also make gardens and eat fruit from them. I will plant them in their land, and no longer shall they be pulled up for the land I have given them, Says the LORD your God (Amos 9:14-15).

Not only does God promise to bring the Jewish people back to their land, He also promises them that He will enable them to live in their ancient capital, Jerusalem, where His presence will be with them. Zechariah writes:

> Thus says the LORD: "I will return to Zion, and dwell in the midst of Jerusalem. Jerusalem shall be called the City of Truth, the Mountain of the LORD of hosts, the Holy Mountain" (Zechariah 8:3).

> "Behold, I will save My people from the land of the east and from the land of the west; I will bring them back, and they shall dwell in the midst of Jerusalem. They shall be My people and I will be their God, in truth and righteousness" (Zechariah 8:7-8).

For those who would want to divide the land God gave to His people, Joel writes:

> For behold, in those days and at that time, when I bring back the captives of Judah and Jerusalem, I will also gather all

nations, and bring them down to the Valley of Jehoshaphat; and I will enter into judgment with them there on account of My people, My heritage Israel, whom they have scattered among the nations; they have also divided up My land (Joel 3:1-2).

CHAPTER 2

Back to the Future: Ten Prophetic Signs of the Coming of the Lord Part 2

When we study the Bible and world history, we see that God has a plan for mankind, and that He is actively moving world events forward to fulfill that plan. He has written these events in the Bible so we can know His plan and see it unfold throughout the pages of world history. It is all there in the Bible if we will just take the time to study it for ourselves. Anyone who will study the Bible and have an open mind and heart to God can see it clearly. God's plans and purposes revolve around an everlasting covenant He made with Abraham and his descendants through Isaac and Jacob. That is why we considered His redemptive acts with the Jews as the first three prophetic signs. We now want to consider the prophetic signs that relate to the Gentiles, beginning with a "New World Order One World Government and One World Religion."

4. One World Government

The fourth prophetic sign is a New World Order consisting of a One World Government and a One World Religion. Ever since the days of Nimrod, world leaders have tried to put together a One World Government. While what I am about to say is certainly not "politically correct," as a Christian minister it is my view that this is an idea inspired by Satan to facilitate his control of the nations and the souls of mankind. Through this one world government and accompanying religious system, Satan believes he will at last achieve his goal to be worshipped like the Most High (Isaiah 14:12-14). While this sounds like nonsense to globalists and secular humanist, it is the clear teaching in the Bible.

The prophet Daniel was given a vision about these world empires and describes a terrible coalition of nations at the end of the age (Daniel 7). In the book of Revelation, chapter 13, the apostle John describes a world leader empowered by Satan who establishes control over the nations. John says that with the exception of the people of God, everyone takes his mark and worships him. This is the false political Messiah that John refers to as the beast rising out of the sea speaking great blasphemies against God and persecuting God's people.

The Babylonians, the Persians, the Greeks and the Romans established huge empires with leaders that believed they were the incarnation of their gods. They controlled much of the world of their time and ruled over the souls of their subjects whom were required to worship the Emperor or Caesar as a god. The leaders of these empires all had their religious sages and priests that promoted Emperor worship to the people. This is how the leader united his empire

After Rome fell in AD 476, the Byzantium Empire centered in Constantinople lasted another one thousand years until the Turks conquered Constantinople in AD 1453. The empire of the Ottoman Turks lasted 400 years from 1517-1917.

Britain had one of the greatest empires in history until they turned their backs to the Jews. At the end of the 19th century and the beginning of the 20th century, many British leaders such as William Gladstone, James Balfour, Edmund Allenby, Orde Wingate, etc, were godly Christians. They believed that the Almighty has raised up the British Empire to spread the gospel and assist the Jews in having their ancient homeland. Today we would call them Christian Zionist. This is one of the reasons why Britain issued the Balfour Declaration in 1917, which favored the establishment of a Jewish state. Later leaders did not have this worldview. When they turned their backs to the Jews in favor of Arab oil, Britain lost its empire and Israel was reborn. Is America next?

World leaders of the past have tried and failed in their attempts to revive the Roman Empire by uniting Europe. Some believe these failed attempts are referenced in the nursery rhyme most of us learned as a child: "Humpty Dumpty sat on the wall; Humpty Dumpty had a great fall. All the Kings horses and all the Kings men, couldn't put Hhumpty Dumpty together again." Now we have radical Islam seeking to establish an Islamic world order of the nations.

Do we see today any prophetic signal of a One World Government? We certainly do. At the end of World War II, Europe was in shambles. They would still be in shambles except for the generosity of the American taxpayers who rebuilt Europe through the Marshall Plan. The fragmented nations of Europe realized their need for one another was greater than their need for their own national sovereignty. They would never survive unless they united.

Two great movements were accelerated out of the ashes of World War II. One was Zionism and the return of the Jews to their ancient homeland. The other was European unity which gave birth to the League of Nations followed by the United Nations and now the European Union (EU).

The EU was formed by people determined to destroy the nation-states that had dominated Europe for centuries. They saw this as the only solution to prevent further wars in Europe. After two World Wars, a number of European leaders became convinced that in order to secure a lasting peace between their countries, the nation-states must unite economically and politically. So the EU, earlier known as the European Economic Community, was formed after WW II to prevent another war in Europe.

The man known as the "Father of the European Union" was Jean Monnet, a Frenchman born in 1888. He believed that more European wars were inevitable as long as Europeans saw themselves primarily as nationals such a British, French, Italian, German, etc., and only secondarily as Europeans.

In 1943, Monnet became a member of the National Liberation Committee, the free French government in Algiers. In an address to the Committee on August 5, 1943, he said:

> There will be no peace in Europe if the States rebuild themselves on the basis of national sovereignty, with its

> implications of prestige politics and economic protection. The countries of Europe are not strong enough individually to be able to guarantee prosperity and social development for their peoples. The States of Europe must therefore form a federation or a European entity that would make them into a common economic unity.

In a later writing, he said, "The sovereign nations of the past could no longer solve the problems of the present; they cannot ensure their own progress or control their own future. And the community itself is only a stage on the way to the organized world of tomorrow." Monnet died in 1979, having seen much of his dream of European unity realized.

While the European Union has had many obstacles and challenges in its formation and development, it has made tremendous progress in convincing member states to surrender their national sovereignty to the European Union. The goal is to convince Europeans to think of themselves as Europeans rather than national citizens of their own countries. The current strategy is to divide the world into three major regions: 1) the European Region, 2) the Asian Region, and 3) the Americas Region. People in these regions will identify themselves as Region citizens rather than national citizens.

While Jean Monnet may be considered the "Father of the European Union," his American counterpart is Robert Pastor. Pastor is an extreme left-wing anti-nationalist political thinker and advisor whose goal in life is to merge the United States, Canada, and Mexico into a North American Union similar to the EU. Of course the result would be that the United States, as well as Canada and Mexico, would no longer be sovereign nations but members of the North American Union.

Dr. Pastor has served in influential political positions where his views are given serous consideration by the highest politicians in the land. He has served as an advisor to every major Democratic presidential candidate since Jimmy Carter. In the Carter administration, he gave policy advice regarding US policy towards Latin America and was influential in giving up US sovereignty over the Panama Canal.

Former President Clinton nominated Pastor as U.S. ambassador to Panama but his nomination failed.

While Dr. Pastor acknowledges that the citizens of the United States are not yet ready to give up their sovereignty, he believes a major crisis such as a financial panic and devalued currency might prepare them for such an idea and advance his North American agenda. His agenda of a One World Government is the same as that planned, promoted, and pushed forward by three of the most powerful groups in the world: 1) the Bilderberg Group, 2) the Council on Foreign Relations, and 3) the Trilateral Commission. While unknown to the average American, some of the most powerful people in America share this globalist agenda and are members of these organizations. This includes a number of American presidents and many members of Congress and the press.

While the unsuspecting, ever-trusting American people go about their lives oblivious to the changes that will threaten our national sovereignty and way of life, the globalists are quietly going about their business of merging the U.S. into a North American Union that will be administratively linked to the European Union.

For example, on March 10, 2008, the Advisory Committee on International Economic Policy (ACIEP), met at the State Department to discuss the progress of integrating the U.S., Canada and Mexico and how to best link this North American Union with the European Union.

Also going unnoticed was a military agreement entered into on February 14, 2008 by the U.S. and Canada in which both countries would allow the armed forces of the other country to support their armed forces in the case of civil disorder. This agreement known as a Civil Defense Plan was made without any debate or approval of Congress.

The great and last obstacle to the globalists plan to surrender U.S. sovereignty is the American people who are constantly being brainwashed by the media and sympathetic politicians to accept this concept. To move the plan along, America has to be weakened to the point of merging our sovereignty into a North American Union that will be part of the European Union. The attack at every sector of America is seen clearly in the decline of the value of the dollar to the

Euro, so that eventually the dollar will collapse and be replaced by a regional currency (the amero?) tied to the Euro.

In 1999, Herbert Grubel wrote in "The Case for the Amero," "that on the day the North Amerian monetary unit is created—perhaps on January 1, 2010—Canada, the US and Mexico will replace national currencies with the Amero."

The leaders who desire a New World Order One World Government see Bible-believing Christians as their biggest threat. This is why we are constantly slandered in the press, movies, and television, and by leaders of organizations that want America to surrender our national sovereignty to the globalist. With the weapons and technology we have today, along with our mass communications and apostate Christianity, a revived One World Government through a united Europe is clearly an achievable goal.

God also has an agenda for a New World Order One World Government. It is called the kingdom of God. When Messiah comes, He will rule over the nations and establish a just government of righteousness and holiness that will usher in the golden age the prophets envisioned. Then we won't need to be concerned about weapons of technology, because nations will beat their swords into plowshares and study war no more. As Isaiah says:

> He shall judge between the nations, and rebuke many people; they shall beat their swords into plowshares, and their spears into pruning hooks; nation shall not lift up sword against nation, neither shall they learn war anymore (Isaiah 2:4).

5. One World Religion

The fifth prophetic sign is a New World Order One World Religion. Those who are working toward a New World Order with a One World Government know that human beings are religious by nature. Therefore, in order to convince people to accept the One World Government, they must provide the people with a One World Religion led by a *globalist religious leader*.

John describes this religious leader in the book of Revelation chapter 13 and17. He is the false prophet who is the religious counterpart to the political leader. He presides over a united New

World Order One World Religion and convinces the people of all nations, except the people of God (Matthew 24:24), to worship the false Messiah as God (2 Thessalonians 2:4). It is this false prophet who comes up with the idea of people taking the mark of the political leader as the sign of allegiance to him and the New World Order One World Government and Teligion. This will be the ultimate personality cult as we saw in Hitler and the Nazis. The German people did not pledge their allegiance to the Nazi party but to Hitler personally. They expressed their allegiance by joining the Nazi party and taking the mark of the swastika.

Is there any prophetic sign or evidence in our world today of an emerging New World Order One World Religion? The answer clearly is yes. Religious leaders of all faiths are being encouraged to lay aside their differences in the name of tolerance. They are promoting the idea that we all worship the same God by different names, that we are all God's children, and that there are many ways to God—and any way is as valid as any other. Therefore, we should all join hands as one big happy religious family. For example, a Catholic Bishop in Europe suggested that Christians should call the God of the Bible "Allah," as a way of seeking peaceful tolerance with Muslims.

Let's be honest: traditional mainline Christian denominations are struggling to survive. Many of them no longer believe or teach the basic doctrines of Christianity. They deny that the Bible is the Word of God and deny the miracles of Jesus. They are dying because they have forsaken God and have nothing to offer their congregants.

There is absolutely no doubt in my mind that this is the apostate Christianity that Paul had in mind when he wrote in 2 Thessalonians 2:3 of the great "falling away," after which the false political Messiah will be revealed. This apostate Christianity will persecute the people of God who believe the Bible, stand with Israel, and refuse to worship the beast and take his mark. We already see this happening today.

While American Christianity and churches are declining, spiritual interest is on the rise. Eastern religions, New Age Spirituality, Scientology, and Islam, to name only a few, are growing rapidly. So while spiritually is on the increase, Christianity or, shall we say "Churchianity," is on the decline. The reason must be that the American public considers the American church to be irrelevant to their needs and life. In my own opinion, this is because much of the traditional church no longer believes and preaches the Bible as the Word of God that can convict people of their sins and turn them to righteousness. We all want revival in the White House. But there won't be revival in the White House until there is revival in the church house.

The good news is that the Bible tells us in many places in both Testaments, that the true Messiah, Jesus of Nazareth in case you don't know, will return to earth and destroy both the political and religious anti-God systems. He will establish the real New World Order—the kingdom of God on the earth, with His people ruling with Him over the nations, and with Israel as the head of nations under the righteous rule of Messiah.

At that time, all nations will worship the one true God as King David promised:

> All the ends of the world shall remember and turn to the LORD, and all the families of the nations shall worship before You. For the Kingdom is the LORD's, and He rules over the nations (Psalm 22:27-28).

6. The Northern Invasion of Israel

The sixth prophetic sign is the *northern invasion of Israel.* In Ezekiel 38 and 39, Ezekiel prophesies that a confederation of nations called Gog and Magog will attack Israel from the far north. This will happen in the latter years, or latter days, when Israel has been reborn. In modern times, most western Christian scholars have identified Gog and Magog as Russia leading a Russian/Turkey/Iranian confederation. Jewish sages view Gog and Magog as generic names for the great Gentile powers who will invade Israel in the latter years prior to the coming of Messiah. When President George W. Bush went to Israel he was greeted by some religious leaders as the "Leader of Gog."

There are four reasons why we believe this is Russia. First, historians and Bible scholars have traced the migration of the people mentioned in the prophecy to the geographic area we know today as Russia/Turkey.

Second, Ezekiel places the time of the invasion in the latter days. Russia, as we know her today, did not even exist before the twentieth century. Even though Russia has been weak, she is recovering economically due to her vast oil and gas reserves. With renewed economic wealth, Russia is able to rebuild her military and she still has nuclear weapons. Furthermore, Russia is aggressively supplying weapons to her client states in the Middle East.

The third reason we believe this to be Russia is their relationship to the state of Israel, which did not come into existence until 1948. Therefore Ezekiel's prophecy of a Russian invasion of Israel could not have been fulfilled until after Israel was reborn in 1948. The fourth reason is the geographic location of the invading coalition coming from the extreme north (Ezekiel 38:15). Russia is the only power to the extreme north of Israel.

From the Ezekiel prophecy, we understand that the allies represent the Muslim nations that hate Israel and the West and are willing to align themselves with Russia in this confederation. Once again we ask ourselves, "Do we see a prophetic sign of this prophecy." We all know the answer is yes!

Russia is beginning to prosper economically from revenues from its vast oil and gas reserves. Russia is rebuilding its military. Russia is now positioning itself to make a move along with its client states, to attack Israel. It is shipping weapons of mass destruction to Iran and Syria. Russia is building a naval base in Syria that will give it a major foothold in the Middle East. Is it just a coincidence or the hand of God that by the year 2015, more than half of the soldiers in the Russian army will be Muslim.

The prophet Ezekiel tells us that God himself will destroy this invading force. Ezekiel predicts that God will fight against the invaders with great earthquakes, plagues, torrential rains, hailstorms, and fire and brimstone (Ezekiel 28:18-23).

Ezekiel informs us that God will destroy the coalition army (Ezekiel 39). The destruction will be so bad that it will take seven months just to bury the dead (Ezekiel 39:12). The result of this war is that God will glorify His name and the people of Israel will once again turn their hearts towards God (Ezekiel 39:21-29).

Not only will the people of Israel return to their God, but God will sanctify His name among the nations as Ezekiel explains:

> So I will make My holy name known in the midst of My people Israel, and I will not let them profane My holy name anymore. Then the nations shall know that I am the LORD, the Holy One in Israel (Ezekiel 39:7).

7. Worldwide Travel and Knowledge

The seventh prophetic sign is an *increase in travel and knowledge*. Daniel 12:4 reads, "But you, Daniel, shut up the words, and seal the book until the time of the end; many shall run to and fro, and knowledge shall increase."

Now we don't have to be awake, alert, or prophetic to see this sign everywhere. The scientific and technological developments in the twentieth century have overwhelmed us. No one can keep up with it.

Barely one hundred years ago, people traveled by horse and buggy. Then along came Henry Ford who made the automobile affordable for the masses. After the automobile, came airplanes that could fly short distances. Later the jet engine made international travel possible for everyone. There are so many people traveling on the airlines that we have dangerously overloaded the ability of our aviation system to maintain the safety of our air transportation.

Anyone who is on social security was born before television, the computer, the internet, and many other wonderful inventions that we take for granted. With television we can watch world events as they unfold. With satellites, I can sit in a television studio and send my programs all over the world. I still marvel when traveling that I can rest in my hotel room while at the same time watch my program on the television.

When I was a professor at a small college in Alabama in the 1960's, the college bought an IBM computer. It was so large, a building had to be built just to house it. We had to have special air-conditioning and huge cables lay on the floor connecting the machines. This computer's memory was only 4K! Now no one who doesn't recognize the name, Thomas Watson, can even imagine a computer with such a small memory. What used to require a building can now sit on our desk at home or in a notebook computer we can carry with us on an international flight while talking to our friend on the cell phone. I can put an entire course including 12-audio tapes and a 150-page syllabus on one CD that people can read and listen to in their computer.

Now with the internet, we can access information from encyclopedias, libraries and data sources from all over the world and never leave our house. We have access to more information that we will ever be able to learn or process. I am still trying to learn how to take pictures, check my e-mail and download data on my cell phone.

The most frightening aspect of all of this advancement is in military weapons. Before World War I, people attacked covered wagons with bows and arrows. Then came the Gatlin gun that kept firing until everyone was dead. Even as late as World War I, weapons were primitive. It was called the "trench war" because neither side had sophisticated enough weapons to have a decided advantage. Then we split the atom so that now we can destroy an entire city by dropping one little bomb or sending one laser guided nuclear tipped missile with or without biological and chemical weapons. We are all on travel and knowledge overload and it is getting worse.

While the forces of evil in our world use modern technology to promote their own agenda, God also uses it to promote His agenda. We are grateful to the Lord that we have the technology to distribute His word through television, satellites, the internet, and even old media like the printed book you're reading. More people are hearing God's word today than anytime in world history. And more are responding than anytime in world history. The greatest spiritual explosion the world has every known is at hand.

8. Rise of False Prophets, Cults, and the Occult

The eighth prophetic sign is the *rise of false prophets, cults, and the occult.* In Matthew 24, the disciples asked Jesus about the prophetic sign of His coming and of the end of the age. Jesus responded by telling them numerous signs that would intensify as His return drew near. There would be religious deception through many false prophets, wars and rumors of wars, natural calamities such as earthquakes and tsunamis, famines and pestilence, an increase of evil, hearts growing cold, persecution of true believers, general lawlessness, and the preaching of the gospel of the kingdom of God. Now we have always had these conditions at various times in the world. But the idea is that they would all come together and intensify in their frequency.

Perhaps the most alarming is the increase in false prophets which often leads to the formation of cults, and ultimately the occult. The reason this is the most alarming is because false prophets, cults and the occult are spiritual deceptions that capture people's souls. Any time there are true prophets of God there will also be false prophets sent by Satan to deceive people. If there is true biblical faith, there will be counterfeit cult faiths. If there are miracles of God and the gifts of the Spirit, there will be counterfeit miracles and demonic manifestations. If there is a true Messiah, then there must be false messiahs.

Since the time of Jesus, there have been many false messiahs in Judaism. They usually appeared in history when the Jews were desperate for hope. When people are desperate for hope, they are very susceptible to following false prophets, false messiahs, cults, and the occult. The false messiahs of Judaism gave the people hope and promise for deliverance from their oppressors, which were either Christian or Muslim rulers, depending on the time in history when the false messiahs appeared. But it was a false hope and a false promise.

The two most famous false messiahs in Jewish history were Simon Bar Kochba in the second century, and Sabbatai Zevi in the seventh century. After the first Jewish revolt, which was crushed by Titus, the people were desperate for someone who could deliver them from the Romans. In AD 132, Rabbi Akiba convinced the struggling Zealots that Bar Kochba was the messiah. Bar Kochba accepted the messianic mantle and led the people in the second great revolt against the Romans. The revolt lasted for three years, but was crushed in AD 135 by the Roman emperor Hadrian. Even though Rabbi Akiba promoted a false messiah, he is considered as one of the greatest of the rabbis and sages of Judaism. He is still honored, even though later rabbinic teaching sought to discredit Bar Kochba.

My question is: How can a Jewish religious leader be so honored and acclaimed when he promoted a false messiah whose rebellion resulted in the death of half a million Jews, the destruction of Jerusalem, the building of a temple to Jupiter on the Temple Mount, and the changing of the name of Israel to Palestine and Jerusalem to Aelia Capitalina? At the same time, Yeshua, the real Messiah, is rejected.

The most successful of all Messianic pretenders in Judaism was Sabbatai Zevi. Zevi was born in Smyrna, Turkey, and lived from 1626-1676. He created the most powerful and widespread of all false Messianic movements in the history of Judaism. He came on the scene when Jews were enduring various calamities and hoping for messianic redemption. In the year 1648, the Kabbalistic mystical Jews were proclaiming Israel's redemption was at hand. And Zevi did what only the Messiah was supposed to do, he pronounced the unpronounceable holy name of God.

A Rabbi Nathan of Gaza declared Zevi to be the Messiah and proclaimed himself as Elijah the Prophet. Together they declared that Zevi would depose the Sultan, return the Ten Lost Tribes of Israel to the land, and usher in the redemption of Israel and the Jewish people. This was to happen on June 18, 1666. There was a tremendous messianic frenzy around Zevi. He had a huge cult following and was widely hailed as the Messiah. Jews prepared themselves for the Messianic Moment when they would all follow him to Jerusalem.

But it didn't happen. Before Zevi could reveal himself to be the Messiah, the Sultan had him arrested in February 1666. When faced with a choice between life or death, Zevi showed himself to be the pretender he really was by converting to Islam (September 16, 1666). While the masses he had deceived returned to their traditional Judaism, his hard core followers invented reasons for the conversion and continued their movement for decades. We see from this story that Jews also have problems with date setting.

Just as there have been many false messianic movements in Judaism, there have been many false cults in Christianity. The number has increased in recent times along with the occult. From a Christian view, a cult is any religious organization that presents itself as Christian or pseudo-Christian but denies the fundamental teachings about Jesus.

Christianity teaches that Jesus is God in human flesh, and that His death on the Cross was the necessary and all-sufficient sacrifice for our sins. True Christians can and usually do disagree on practically everything except these two beliefs. A religious organization that presents itself as Christian or pseudo-Christian can have some very good qualities about it, but if it denies the person of Jesus and His redemptive work, it is not a Christian organization.

The most successful cult in New Testament times was Gnosticism. Gnostics taught that all matter was inherently evil. Therefore, Jesus could not have been God; He was either a spirit being or just a great prophet. Gnosticism was the greatest threat to early Christianity and one of the main reasons why John wrote his first two letters in the New Testament. Gnostic writings discovered in Egypt were used as the basis for the popular movie, *The De Vinci Code*.

Gnosticism is still with us today. It is the source of numerous modern-day cults that speak of Christ as the divine idea of God, but not God in human flesh. This deception is attractive to people who do not know the Bible and do not want to face the reality and consequences of sin.

While there has been an explosion of false prophets and their cults in our time, the most successful ones are Joseph Smith (Mormonism), Charles Russell (Jehovah's Witnesses), Sun Myung Moon (The Unification Church "Moonies"), Victor Paul Wierwille (The Way International), Mary Baker Eddy (Christian Science), and Charles and Myrtle Fillmore (Unity).

In addition to an increase in false prophets that lead to cults, the Bible also warns against the occult that will ultimately merge with pseudo-Christianity as part of the end-time one world religion. Revelation 9:20-21 reads, "But the rest of mankind, who were not killed by these plagues, did not repent of the works of their hands, that they should not worship demons, and idols of gold, silver, brass, stone, and wood, which can neither see nor hear nor walk. And they did not repent of their murders or their sorceries or their sexual immorality or their thefts."

The Greek word translated into English as "sorceries" is the same root word for the word "pharmacy," and refers to the place where you get your drugs. The occult has always mixed drugs with religion as a way to open up people to mind control and demonic possession.

In the 1960's, during the Vietnam war, the baby boomers were just coming of age. They were looking for the meaning and purpose of life. They were looking for truth, reality, and relationships. Instead of offering them meaning and purpose, our society offered them materialism and performance as the standard of happiness. Instead of offering them a relationship with the Almighty, the American church offered them dead religion.

While what society and the church was offering young people could not meet their needs, Timothy Leary was offering them something else that tempted them to tune in, turn on, and drop out. That something else was drugs and make love not war. And so began the drug and sexual revolution of our young people.

Do we see prophetic signs today regarding false prophets, cults, drugs, and the occult? Unfortunately, the answer is yes. These things are glorified on television and in the movies. Drugs have destroyed the lives of thousands of American young people. Drugs are easily available to anyone who wants them. Satan is using drugs to condition the next generation of young people to accept the end-time one world religion which will mix religious indoctrination and the occult with drugs and satanic signs and wonders.

As Christians, we can protect ourselves against deception by studying the Bible, being in a submitted relationship with mature, godly believers, recognizing those who labor among us (1 Thessalonians 5:12), and realizing that character is more important than charisma.

Christian parents can best protect their children against cults, drugs, and the occult by teaching them the Bible, praying with them, living a godly example before them, spending quality time with them and helping them find God's plan for their lives. Isaiah says, "When the enemy comes in like a flood, the Spirit of the LORD will lift up a standard against him" (Isaiah 59:19b).

9. The Apostate Church

The ninth prophetic sign is the *end-time apostate church*. In 2 Thessalonians 2:1-4 we read, "Now, brethren, concerning the coming of our Lord Jesus Christ and our gathering together to Him, we ask you, not to be soon shaken in mind or troubled, either by spirit or by word or by letter, as if from us, as though the day of Christ had come. Let no one deceive you by an means; for that Day will not come unless the falling away comes first, and the man of sin is revealed, the son of perdition, who opposes and exalts himself above all this is called God or that is worshiped, so that he sits as God in the temple of God, showing himself that he is God."

Paul talks about the great apostasy or falling away. He says it will come before the anti-Christ, the false Messiah, is revealed. In fact, the great apostasy will pave the way for the false Messiah to be revealed because the apostate church will embrace him.

One of the major prophetic signs that will contribute to this falling away is that the traditional mainline denominations will no longer teach sound biblical doctrine. Paul writes in 2 Timothy 4:2-4, "Preach the word! Be ready in season and out of season. Convince, rebuke, exhort, with all longsuffering and teaching. For the time will come when they will not endure sound doctrine, but according to their own desires, because they have itching ears, they will heap up for themselves teachers; and they will turn their ears away from the truth, and be turned aside to fables."

Paul adds in 2 Timothy 3:5 that the religious leaders and organizations will have a form of godliness while denying its power. He warns us to turn away from them.

What Paul describes is a form of religious Christianity that neither believes nor teaches the Bible and the gospel of Jesus. The two most important distinctions of Christianity is that the Bible is the Word of God and that the gospel of Jesus is the power of God to save us from our sins and give us a new life transformed by the Spirit of God. When traditional mainline Christian denominations no longer believe and teach these core elements of Christianity, they lose their identity and can easily merge with other religions.

Are we seeing this prophetic sign? Unfortunately, the answer is yes. In the 1920's a number of theologians and scholars in Germany developed what they called the "School of Higher Criticism of Scripture." Their purpose was to study the Scriptures, not for the purpose of knowing God, but to analyze and dissect the Scriptures for the purpose of finding fault, as if the Bible was like any other book.

In the arrogance of their learning and knowledge, they put themselves above the Bible and decided that it was not the Word of God but was written by man. Therefore, the Bible was filled with legends, superstitions, and myths that could not be believed as literal truth. While the Bible might contain something of the Word of God, these scholars decided they would use their own reasoning and better judgment to decide what, if anything written, was actually from God.

Unfortunately, this approach to the Bible crossed the ocean to America and infiltrated our theological seminaries. The result is that, for the most part, the theological seminaries of the traditional mainline denominations do not teach the Bible as the Word of God. They don't believe the miracles in the Bible actually happened. They neither believe nor teach the virgin birth of Jesus. They don't believe that Jesus actually performed miracles. They don't even believe that Jesus actually said the words attributed to Him in the gospels. They just don't believe the Bible. In their arrogance, they even hold seminars to pass on their brilliant discoveries to those who are not as enlightened as they are.

Naturally, the seminary students accept what their professors tell them. When they graduate and start pasturing a local church, they pass on what they learned to their congregants who don't know the Bible and accept what they are told. The result is a local congregation and a denomination filled with professing Christians who don't know the Bible, don't believe the Bible, and have no personal relationship with Jesus. Consequently, these "professing Christian church-goers" will easily embrace the one world religion.

When traditional mainline Christian denominations no longer believe the Bible, they lose their moral compass of right and wrong. They no longer believe in absolutes. They deny the power of the gospel to save people from their sins. When the ministers no longer preach about sin and righteousness, the church goers have no conviction that leads them to live a godly live. Because of this, they are able to accept and embrace any and all lifestyles, no matter how abhorrent, except those of Bible-believing Christians.

The professing Christian denominational leaders who have lost their biblical faith promote inter-faith tolerance and dialogue on the basis that we all worship the same God just by a different name. This is how the apostate church can easily become part of the end-time one world religion. Because they no longer believe the Bible, they also become anti-Semitic and anti-Israel, which we see happening in these denominations today. And there is no doubt they will persecute true believers who they consider as obstacles to their noble goal of obtaining world peace through their one world religion.

This is the "MYSTERY, BABYLON THE GREAT" religion in the book of Revelation (17:5) that works in partnership with the new world order political system. Now just so we all understand God's mind about true Christians and this apostate Christianity, Revelation 18:4-5 says, "Come out of her, my people, lest you share in her sins, and lest you receive of her plagues. For her sins have reached to heaven, and God has remembered her iniquities."

While God will judge the apostate church, He gives the following assuring promise to His own people:

> Behold, I am coming quickly! Hold fast what you have, that no one may take your crown. He who overcomes, I will make him a pillar in the temple of My God, and He shall go out no more. I will write on him the name of My God and the name of the city of My God, the New Jerusalem, which comes down out of heaven from My God. And I will write on him My new name. He who has an ear, let him hear what the Sprit says to the churches (Revelation 3:11-13).

10. Moral Breakdown of Society

The tenth prophetic sign is the moral breakdown of society. The apostasy of the church is the main reason for this moral collapse. When the church no longer preaches and teaches about righteousness and sin, people no longer are convicted about the way they live. It only takes one generation for the moral breakdown to be manifested.

Paul write in 2 Timothy 3:1-5:

> But know this, that in the last day perilous times will come: for men will be lovers of themselves, lovers of money, boasters, proud, blasphemers, disobedient to parents, unthankful, unholy, unloving, unforgiving, slanderers, without self-control, brutal, despisers of good, traitors, headstrong, haughty, lovers of pleasure rather than lovers of God, having a form of godliness but denying its power. And from such people turn away!

Paul gives a similar list in Romans 1:22-32.

If we think the moral conditions in America are bad, consider Europe, which is now the "Spiritually Dark Continent." For example, in the Netherlands, godless leaders of some segments of the society want to form a political party for the purpose of legalizing child pornography, bestiality, and complete sexual freedom for all ages including children. According to the Catholic news outlet *Zenit*, brothel owners in Germany have access to official databases of the unemployed. Women under 55 who are unemployed must be willing to work as a prostitute or risk losing unemployment benefits. This total moral collapse is rampant throughout Europe.

Do we see this prophetic sign in our society today? Unfortunately, the answer is clear. America is on the verge of a political, financial, social, moral, and religious collapse. Our society is crumbling so fast it is in an accelerated decline that could only be reversed by a direct intervention from God. We don't have to review the sins of our society, because Paul just listed them. These are characteristics of a society that is collapsing. We see it all around us. But we live in denial, as if America is God's favorite nation and that somehow things will continue as they are because we sing "God Bless America," while removing Him from all areas of our society.

Our parents and grandparents would be absolutely shocked at the shameful behavior of our country today. They could not even imagine what we see everyday on the television and in the movies. We are so inundated with wicked, immoral, behavior, our conscience is hardened to it.

The founders of our nation said that our form of government was written for a moral people who would govern themselves based on our Judeo-Christian laws that came from the Bible. They said that our nation could not survive otherwise. As just one example, President John Adams said in a speech on October 11, 1798:

> We have no government armed with power capable of contending with human passions unbridled by morality and religion. Avarice, ambition, revenge, or gallantry, would break the strongest cords of our Constitution as a whale goes through a net. Our constitution was made only for a moral and

> religious people. It is wholly inadequate for the government of any other.

One of Satan's greatest deceptions has been the false statement that our founding documents call for a separation of church and state, as if God was not to be part of our public institutions. Our founding documents wisely declare that there should be no national state church as there had been in England. This is what the colonists were running from. They did not want an American State Church. When they said that the institutions of the government and religion should be separated, they did not mean that the government and God should be separated.

When the government kicked God out of our public institutions, God was no longer responsible for providing His covering of protection and blessing over America. We have been in a decline ever since, and the decline is accelerating so fast one wonders how much longer the United States will survive as it is today. While God is a God of mercy, He is also a God of judgment. While He alone knows when we have crossed the line of no return, the characteristics of our society are the same as those given in the Bible of a nation that is under the judgment of God. American believers love our country and are grateful to be Americans, but our first love is to God and His kingdom, which abides forever.

The prophetic signs are a mixture of good news and bad news. For the people of God, it is an awesome privilege to see God at work in our times fulfilling Bible prophecy. But it is disheartening to see Israel's enemies constantly attacking the Jewish people, whom God is bringing back from the nations. It is heartbreaking to see the moral collapse of the nations. It is to frustrating to see evil increase seemingly unabated. We struggle with how to deal with these issues to make our world a better place. Don't lose hope. There is a physical analogy.

A woman in labor has birth pains just before delivering her baby. Her suffering is only for a short time and then she gives birth. When she holds that new born, she knows all her suffering and pain was worthwhile.

Likewise, both the good news and the bad news of the prophetic signs of our times are birth pains of the coming of the Messiah. As with the woman giving birth, they will become more frequent and intense as we get closer to the time when Messiah Jesus, our Lord and Savior, will deliver the kingdom of God on the earth. Our struggle to establish righteousness in our world will all be worthwhile when we see the Lord and His kingdom fully born on the earth.

While the Lord will continue to judge the nations for their evil, He will give full birth to His kingdom on the earth and God's people will reign with Him. The prophet Daniel assures us with these words:

> I was watching in the night visions, and behold, One like the Son of Man, coming with the clouds of heaven! He came to the Ancient of Days, and they brought Him near before Him. Then to Him was given dominion and glory and a kingdom, that all peoples, nations, and languages should serve Him. His dominion is an everlasting dominion, which shall not pass away, and His kingdom the one which shall not be destroyed. ... But the saints of the Most High shall receive the kingdom, and possess the kingdom forever, even forever and ever (Daniel 7:13-14, 18).

As a woman receives the strength and love to give birth, so the Lord will give strength and love to His people to endure the birth pains of the Messiah. As Paul wrote:

> Yet in all these things we are more than conquerors through Him who loved us. For I am persuaded that neither death, nor life, nor angels nor principalities nor powers, nor things present nor things to come, nor height nor depth, nor any other created thing, shall be able to separate us from the love of God which is in Christ Jesus our Lord (Romans 8:37-39).

CHAPTER 3

The Nations in Prophecy

What I'm going to share in this chapter is absolutely critical in order for us to understand the times in which we are living. If we believe that we are living in what the Bible calls "the last days," we certainly want to know what is going to happen in our world in those days.

Secular people who don't believe the Bible and don't know anything about "the last days," also want to know the future. They spend their money and their time trying to prepare for an uncertain future. It is a natural desire for humans to want to know what lies ahead. What's going to happen next? What does the future hold? The difference between believers and non-believers is that we believers look to the Bible for answers about the future. For believers, this is the subject of Bible prophecy.

When Christians study Bible prophecy as it relates to the last days, or end times, we usually study what the Bible says about the Church and Israel. This is certainly understandable because prophecies about the Church and Israel are the priority of our interest.

As the people of God, we are the Church—that is, the community of the living God—and we are part of the commonwealth of Israel. Our destinies are linked through our Judeo-Christian faith in Messiah. Whether you believe Messiah is coming the first time or the second time, He is coming. It is this shared faith in His coming that connects believing Jews and Christians. So naturally we study the prophecies that relate to our shared destiny.

But there is a third subject of Bible prophecy that we need to study because it also relates to the church and Israel. While the Bible says a lot about this subject it is not a subject we have spent much time learning about. That is the subject of the nations in Bible prophecy. Now since we all live in nations, and since we believe we are living in the latter days, we should certainly want to know what the Bible says about the nations in prophecy.

While the Lord revealed much about the nations to the prophets, the one person He gave the most information to was the prophet Daniel. We learn in Daniel 10 that Daniel was praying and fasting for 21 days for divine insight to some of His visions about the future of the nations (Daniel 10:3). Finally, an angel appeared to Daniel and said that the Lord had sent him to Daniel on the first day that Daniel began to pray and fast. But powerful spiritual forces hindered him from getting to Daniel. Seeing the difficulty the angel was having, the Lord had Michael, the guardian angel of Israel, help the angel break through to Daniel. When the angel finally reached Daniel, he said these words to Daniel, "Now I have come to make you understand what will happen to your people in the latter days" (Daniel 10:14).

The Lord wants us to know what the future holds. He wants us to know what lies ahead. He wants us to be prepared and ready for the latter days of the Christian world, the Israel-Jewish world, and the nations. Since Daniel is the man to whom the Lord most revealed His plan for the nations, it is important to learn what he has to say. But first we need some background to understand the beginning of the nations. We really can't understand Daniel without this background.

The Beginning of the Nations

The most important prophecy of the beginning of the nations was given to Noah. You recall that Noah has three sons, Shem, Ham, and Japheth. After the flood, these three sons and their wives repopulated the world (Genesis 9:19).

After Noah planted a vineyard and drank too much wine, he became drunk, and in his drunken state, was in his tent passed out and naked. His son, Ham saw his father in this condition and mocked him and ridiculed him to his brothers. Ham was not embarrassed for his father. His attitude and actions showed his true character. While I'm sure they were embarrassed, Shem and Japheth did not join Ham in his mockery. They showed the proper respect to their father, went into the tent with their eyes turned away and properly covered their father. (Genesis 9:20-23)

Noah's Prophetic Word of the Nations

It is obvious that Ham did not love his father. When Noah awakened and sobered up, he realized what Ham had done and how Shem and Japheth responded. Noah pronounced a curse on Canaan, Ham's son, and blessings on Shem and Japheth. Genesis 9:25-27 reads:

> "Cursed be Canaan; a servant of servants he shall be to his brethren." And he said: "Blessed be the LORD, the God of Shem, and may Canaan be his servant. May God enlarge Japheth, and may he dwell in the tents of Shem; and may Canaan be his servant."

It is sometimes hard for modern Western folk to understand the idea of blessings and curses. But in Bible times, people related to one another on the basis of a covenant. For example, God related to Noah and his three sons based on the covenant of the rainbow. A covenant relationship included blessings and curses. If the person honored the covenant relationship, they benefited by the agreed blessings. If they dishonored the covenant relationship, they would incur the curses. (See Deuteronomy 28:2, 15.)

The most important covenantal relationship was the family. So it would not be a surprise to the Hebrews that one of the Ten Words or Commandments from the Lord said, "Honor your father and your mother, that your days may be long upon the land which the LORD your God is giving you" (Exodus 20:12).

The Jewish apostle Paul referred to this verse when he wrote to the believers in Ephesus, "Honor your father and mother, which is the first commandment with promise: that it may be well with you and you may live long on the earth" (Ephesians 6:2-3).

When the Lord was preparing the people to enter the land, He said, "Cursed is the one who treats his father or his mother with contempt" (Deuteronomy 27:16).

Since God had already pronounced a blessing on all three sons, Noah did not curse Ham but instead cursed Canaan, Ham's son. Due to this unfortunate act of disrespect, Canaan and his descendants would inherit a generational curse of contempt for authority, wickedness, and moral corruption. Some sages believe that it was actually Canaan who first saw Noah in his condition and went and told Ham.

The bottom line is that Noah's prophecy of blessings and curses laid the foundation for the future of all the nations of history even to our own times. So how can we understand our own times, if we do not understand the nations in prophecy?

Shem's Blessing

Shem would be the father of the Hebrews—the people God chose to bring a renewed revelation of the one true God to the world, write the Holy Scriptures, and give us the Messiah. Because Shem's descendants would bring redemption to the world, Noah recognized that the LORD would be the "the God of Shem" (Genesis 9:26).

From a biblical standpoint, Shem would be the most important of the three sons because his descendants would be the chosen people of God. This does not mean Shem's descendants would be better than the descendants of Ham and Japheth, it simply means they were the ones God chose for His redemptive purposes. They had a higher calling and purpose than the Gentiles. They were not to seek the things of this world but the things of God. They were to be a light to the nations bearing witness to the one true God.

Japheth's Blessing

Noah's blessing to Japheth was that God would enlarge him and that his descendants would dwell in the tents of Shem. Noah's prophetic word of blessing to Japhetic proved accurate in that the descendants of Japheth were many more in number than those of Shem and Ham. And as we will see, Japheth's descendants have and will dwell in the tents of Shem through their relationship with one of Shem's descendants.

Canaan's Curse

The curse of Canaan was that his descendants would serve Shem and Japheth. This Scripture has been taken out of context and twisted by Europeans and Americans to justify slavery. I want to emphasize that this is not what this Scripture says and it is not what it means. It does not say that Ham's descendants would be servants to Shem and Japheth but that Canaan's descendants would serve them. As we will see in the Bible in Joshua 9, Noah was pronouncing a curse on one family line of descendants in a specific place and at a specific time.

The Table of Nations

In Genesis 10, we have a table of nations showing the genealogy of Shem, Ham, and Japheth. This record shows how Noah's general prophecy would be fulfilled in the division of the human race. It is an amazing prophecy that has proven itself in the history of nations. Only the Almighty could have revealed this development of the nations to Noah and orchestrated the outworking of the prophecy in history.

The table of nations is important, not only because of the genealogical records but it also helps us understand Bible prophecy to know who these people are and where they lived. After the flood and the subsequent confusion of languages and scattering of the people at the Tower of Babel, the descendants of Shem, Ham, and Japheth scattered to the north, south, east and west (see Genesis 11:1-9).

The table of nations helps us learn where these people went and their role in both Bible and secular history. Since all of these people originated in the Middle East, many of those who scattered stayed in that general area while others went farther away.

There are 70 primary nations recorded in the Scriptures that developed from Noah's three sons. There is a connection to the number of nations and the number of sacrifices the Lord told the Hebrews to make during the Feast of Tabernacles (see Numbers 29).

The Feast of Tabernacles is the one feast where all the nations are commanded to celebrate in Jerusalem (see Zechariah 14:16).

In Numbers 29, the Lord commanded the Hebrews to sacrifice 70 bulls on the seven days of the Feast. The Jews have always understood these as sacrifices on behalf of the nations. So from the very beginning of the call of the Hebrews, God showed that He also cared for the Gentiles.

Shem's Descendants (Genesis 10:21-31)

Shem had five sons mentioned in Genesis 10:22. The genealogy that follows lists 26 nation descendants of Shem. Two important descendants of Shem were Asshur, whose descendants settled in Assyria, and Aram whose descendants settled the area that would be known as Syria. Jacob's wives were from this area and were called Syrians. By marrying these women, Jacob himself is referred to as a Syrian by marriage in Deuteronomy 26:5.

Most importantly, Shem's descendants included both the Hebrews/Jews and the Arabs. One of his descendants was named Eber. Eber had two sons. One son, Peleg, was the father of the Hebrews. The other son, Joktan, was the father of the Arabs. Obviously Eber's descendants are the primary focus of Bible prophecy for the end times.

Generally speaking, Shem's descendants populated a broad area in the Middle East and Asia.

Ham's Descendants (Genesis 10:6-20)

Ham had four sons. The genealogy lists 30 nation descendants of Ham. Generally speaking, Ham's descendants populated the Middle East and North Africa, and south Asia. Ham's descendants are very important in biblical history because they lived in close physical approximation to the descendants of Shem.

Ham's son Mizraim is the father of the Egyptians and also the ancestor of the Philistines. His son Phut or Put, is connected with both Egypt and Libya. His son, Cush, is identified with Ethiopia, modern Yemen, and Southwest Arabia.

Canaan

As far as Bible prophecy is concerned, Ham's most important son is Canaan, the one Noah cursed. Canaan had eleven sons listed in Genesis 10:15-18. You will recognize some of these names because they are the people who were living in the land that God promised to Abraham, Isaac, and Jacob, and to their descendants. It was these descendants of Canaan who were living in the land when Joshua led the children of Israel into battle to conquer the land.

When God entered into covenant with Abraham in Genesis 15, the Lord said to Abraham, "to your descendants I have given this land" (Genesis 15:18). Then in verses 19-21, He identifies the tribal groups who were in the land, including the Amorites, Canaanites, Girgashites and Jebusites. These were all descendants of Canaan.

When Joshua prepared the people to cross the Jordan River and enter the land, he said to them:

> By this you shall know that the living God is among you, and that He will without fail drive out from before you the Canaanites and the Hittites and the Hivites and the Perizzites and the Girgashites and the Amorites and the Jebusites (Joshua 3:10).

The Jebusites are particularly interesting to us because they were the ones who lived in Jerusalem, when David conquered it and made Jerusalem his capital. Jerusalem would become the city of God and the most important city in the world.

As I mentioned earlier, Noah's prophetic curse was not on Ham but on Canaan. His words were fulfilled for a specific people at a specific time in history. This happened with Canaan's descendants when Shem's descendants conquered them.

We see this clearly in Joshua 9 with one of Canaan's sons, Hivite. His descendants were living in Gibeon. When they heard that the Lord had given the land to the Hebrews, and their great victories, they deceived Joshua so he would not kill them. They pretended to be foreigners who came to enter into covenant with Joshua in order to have his protection. Joshua made a mistake by not seeking the Lord regarding this. He accepted their word and made covenant with them to let them live. When their deception was exposed, Joshua said to them:

> Now therefore, you are cursed, and none of you shall be freed from being slaves—woodcutters and water carriers for the house of my God (Joshua 9:23).

Without knowing the history, we could get the idea that God was unjust to the Canaanites by giving the land they occupied to the Hebrews. But we learn in Genesis 15:16, that one reason God allowed the Hebrews to be slaves in Egypt was to give the descendants of Canaan four more generations to repent before driving them from the land.

The point is that God, in His mercy, gave Canaan's descendents hundreds of years to turn from their wicked ways before He judged them. Would you have given them that long? At a point in time, God's mercy was satisfied so He executed His judgment on them in fulfillment of Noah's prophecy. This is how God works His will and ways with all nations and people groups throughout history. He still works this way today.

Nimrod

Ham's most famous descendant is a son of Cush named Nimrod. We learn about the infamous Nimrod in Genesis 10:8-10 who began his kingdom in Babel in the land of Shinar (modern day Iraq). Nimrod was the first person we know of in the Bible who started a war. He wanted to conquer his neighbors for the purpose of establishing an empire with him as the ruler. His first conquest was Babel, which later became Babylon and the great Babylonian Empire of the days of Nebuchadnezzar. Babylon was one of the greatest cities of the ancient world. He also built Nineveh, another great city, which became the capital of the Assyrian Empire. We know that Jonah preached at Nineveh.

As the centerpiece of his empire, Nimrod built what we call the Tower of Babel (Genesis 11). It was a ziggurat or temple built in the form of a pyramid for the purpose of worshipping the sun and exalting Nimrod as the high priest of the sun. Nimrod was a great promoter who presented himself as the human incarnation of the sun god. This was the beginning of sun worship and emperor worship and all pagan religions.

At this time, all the people spoke the same language. God saw that this powerful idolatry would seduce all the inhabitants so He confused their languages and scattered the people.

When Nimrod died, his wife, Semiramis, claimed she was impregnated by the sun god and miraculously gave birth to a son named Tammuz. She also was a great promoter. She told the people that Tammuz was the reincarnation of Nimrod. Since she was perceived as the mother of God, she and Tammuz were worshipped as the mother-son cult. She was the mother of God and queen of heaven and her son was the reincarnation of the father.

When the people scattered, they took their sun worship and worship of the queen of heaven with them. As they formed new empires and civilizations, this became their form of worship. The names were changed to the new languages the people spoke and there were local adaptations of the worship, but it was basically the same sun worship that began with Nimrod.

The Chaldean/Assyrians called the sun god by the name of Bel. The Egyptians called him Osiris. Nebuchadnezzar and the Babylonians worshiped the sun god as Bel-Merodach. The Persians called him Mithra. The Greeks called him Zeus (Adonis). The Romans called him Jupiter. This was the religion of Constantine when he established Christianity as the official religion of the Roman Empire. In a similar manner, mother-child worship was also an integral part of sun worship and passed from one empire to the next with only the names and local practices differing.

We learn in the Bible that even God's people were influenced by this all-pervasive religion. Ezekiel 8:14 tells us that the women were at the temple in Jerusalem "weeping for Tammuz." Jeremiah 7:18 says the women were making cakes to the "queen of heaven."

Scholars believe that Nimrod's sun worship religion was the origin of all pagan religions, that it was passed down to succeeding empires, and is still with us today in various forms. We learn in the book of Revelation 17-19 that this will be the final form of religion that will continue to seduce the world until God finally judges it at the coming of the Lord. It will contain all the elements of ancient and modern religions synergized into a one world political-economic-religious system. This will certainly include apostate Christianity and Judaism.

Revelation 17:5 connects the ancient paganism of Nimrod with the last days world religion with these words, "And on her forehead a name was written, "MYSTERY, BABYLON THE GREAT, THE MOTHER OF HARLOTS AND OF THE ABOMINATIONS OF THE EARTH."

In Revelation 18:4-5, God warns His people with these words, "Come out of her, my people, lest you share in her sins, and lest you receive of her plagues. For her sins have reached to heaven, and God has remembered her iniquities."

Japheth's Descendants (Genesis 10:2-5)

Finally, we want to learn about Japheth's descendants. They are listed in Genesis 10:2-5. Japheth had seven sons and fourteen nation descendants. You will recognize some of these names such as Gomer, Magog, Tubal, and Meshech, and his grandson, Togarmah, as they are listed in Ezekiel 38-39. They are the invaders of Israel from the north in the latter days.

Noah's prophetic blessing over Japheth was that God would enlarge Japheth and that he would dwell in the tents of Shem. Japhetic's descendants were much more numerous than those of Shem and Ham. They scattered to the areas today known as Russia, Greece, Turkey, Armenia, Europe; and then from Europe to North America. They became the major part of Gentile nations and the major part of secular world history. They will have a major role in the end times as the one world system that will unite against Israel and Jerusalem. At that time, the "times of the Gentiles" (Ezekiel 30:3) will come to an end at the coming of a Jewish Messiah and Lord to establish the descendants of Shem through the Lion of the tribe of Judah as the head of nations (Revelation 5:5).

The Nations

As followers of Jesus from among the nations, we are most interested in the part of the prophetic blessing that says that Japhetic will dwell in the tents of Shem. The Bible tells us that God loves the Gentiles and has always planned for Gentiles to share in the redemptive blessings promised to Shem, as we see in the following Scriptures.

Psalm 22:27-28, "All the ends of the world shall remember and turn to the LORD, and all the families of the nations shall worship before You. For the kingdom is the LORD's, and He rules over the nations."

Psalm 67:1-4, "God be merciful to us and bless us, and cause His face to shine upon us, that Your way may be known on earth, Your salvation among all nations. Let the peoples praise You, O God; let all the peoples praise You. Oh, let the nations be glad and sing for joy! For you shall judge the people righteously, and govern the nations on earth."

Micah 4:1-2, "Now it shall come to pass in the latter days that the mountain of the LORD's house shall be established on the top of the mountains, and shall be exalted above the hills; and peoples shall flow to it. Many nations shall come and say, 'Come, and let us go up to the mountain of the LORD, to the house of the God of Jacob; He will teach us His ways, and we shall walk in His paths.' For out of Zion the law shall go forth, and the word of the LORD from Jerusalem."

Isaiah 56:7, "My house shall be called a house of prayer for all nations."

Zechariah 2:11, "Many nations shall be joined to the LORD in that day, and they shall become My people. And I will dwell in your midst."

Zechariah 8:22-23, "Yes, many peoples and strong nations shall come and seek the LORD of hosts in Jerusalem, and to pray before the LORD. Thus says the LORD of hosts: 'In those days ten men from every language of the nations shall grasp the sleeve of a Jewish man, saying, 'Let us go with you, for we have heard that God is with you.'""

Isaiah 9:1-2, "In Galilee of the Gentiles. The people who walked in darkness have seen a great light; those who dwelt in the land of the shadow of death, upon them a light has shined."

Isaiah 11:10, "And in that day there shall be a root of Jesse, who shall stand as a banner to the people; for the Gentiles shall seek Him, and His resting place shall be glorious."

Isaiah 49:6, "I will also give You as a light to the Gentiles, that You should be My salvation to the ends of the earth."

Isaiah 60:3, "The Gentiles shall come to your light."

The New Testament tells us that the Gentiles would be given the opportunity to find redemption through Jesus of Nazareth. Luke tells us that Jesus was given as a "light to the Gentiles" (Luke 2:32). Matthew informs us that Jesus preached in "Galilee of the Nations" (Matthew 4:12-16). After His resurrection, Jesus told His disciples to preach His message to all the nations (Matthew 28:18-20).

Righteous Gentiles (Christian believers) serve a Jewish Lord and are grafted into the Jewish people. They become part of the commonwealth of Israel. In this way, they dwell in the tents of Shem. The sons of Japheth who believe do not replace the sons of Shem, they are joined to them and become one with them in Messiah.

Jesus said, "many will come from east and west, and sit down with Abraham, Isaac, and Jacob in the kingdom of heaven" (Matthew 8:11).

Once again we turn to Daniel:

> I was watching in the night vision, and behold One like the Son of Man, coming with the clouds of heaven! He came to the Ancient of Days, and they brought Him near before Him. Then to Him was given dominion and glory and a kingdom, that all peoples, nations, and languages should serve Him. His dominion is an everlasting dominion, which shall not pass away, and His kingdom the one which shall not be destroyed (Daniel 7:13-14).

Judgment of the Nations

While the one true God has made a way for Gentiles to enter His covenant and be one with the Jewish people, He will also judge those who reject Him and them. This judgment is recorded in Matthew 25:31-46. It is known as the "Sheep and Goat Judgment."

The Bible makes it clear that this judgment will take place on the earth. It will be at the end of the final tribulation and the coming of

Jesus to reign for a thousand years on the earth (Revelation 2):4-6). Matthew 25:31 says, "When the Son of Man comes in His glory, and all the holy angels with Him, then He will sit on the throne of His glory."

There will obviously be people alive at the coming of the Lord. Most of these are Gentiles. Some are believers and some are not believers. The purpose of this judgment is to separate the believing righteous Gentiles from the non-believing unrighteous Gentiles. Those deemed righteous are allowed to live and enter into the Kingdom of God that will also be the Kingdom of David. Those who are deemed to be unrighteous will not be allowed to live and enter God's kingdom. This means that God's kingdom on earth will be inherited by righteous believers only.

Jeremiah looked forward to this event and wrote:

> "Behold, the days are coming," says the LORD, "that I will raise to David a Branch of righteousness; a King shall reign and prosper, and execute judgment and righteousness in the earth. In His days Judah will be saved, and Israel will dwell safely, now this is His name by which He will be called: THE LORD OUR RIGHTEOUSNESS" (Jeremiah 23:5-6).

This is a judgment of the Gentiles. The English wording says this judgment will be of the nations (Matthew 25:32). But the Greek word that is translated as nations is *ethne*, from which we get the English word, "ethnic." This word is the common word in the Bible that refers to non-Jews. It is really a racial term meaning Gentiles of and from the nations. We can best understand this judgment as being on the non-Jewish population of the world who survive the tribulation period and are alive at the coming of the Lord. The people being judged are clearly distinguished from another group of people Jesus calls, "My brethren," meaning the Jewish people.

What should certainly get our attention is the basis of this judgment. Jesus says the basis of this judgment is how these Gentiles treated the Jewish people during the tribulation period which Jeremiah calls, "the time of Jacob's trouble" (Jeremiah 30:7). During this time, there will be great anti-Semitism unleashed against the Jewish people. Satanic hatred of the sons of Shem will fill the hearts of the leaders of the nations. They will unite in their efforts to destroy Israel and finish what Hitler left undone. It will be the final solution to the Jewish problem.

The Jews will be making Aliyah under great persecution. They will need help from their Gentile neighbors. Anyone who helps the Jewish people during this time will do so to the peril of their own life—much like the family of Corrie ten Boom and other righteous Gentiles during the Holocaust.

By standing with the Jewish people in their great time of need, these Gentiles prove that they are true believers in the God of Shem; the God of Abraham, the God of Isaac, and the God of Jacob; the God of Israel. They are followers and servants of the Messiah of Israel, who is also Savior of the Gentiles. It is not their creeds, but their deeds that prove they are righteous.

This judgment brings to a final close the period of time in history Jesus refers to as the "times of the Gentiles" (Luke 21:24). Israel will be the head of the nations and finally fulfill her destiny to be a light to the nations.

Noah's prophetic words over his three sons are ultimately fulfilled at this time. The God of Shem is worshipped by all the nations. The righteous descendants of Japheth and Ham will dwell in Shem's tents with Shem's people in Shem's Promised Land under the rule of Shem's descendant, Messiah Yeshua-Jesus—the King of the Jews, the King of Kings and Lord of Lords.

Blessed be the LORD, the God of Shem.

CHAPTER 4

World Empires in Prophecy

An unknown student of world history has rightly noted that "History is HIStory." In other words, the Lord, who is outside of time, has foretold for us what would happen in time. This is what we call Bible prophecy. One aspect of Bible prophecy is the foretelling of the national aspirations of people groups. God is particularly interested in telling us the prophetic outline of world empires of the Bible as they relate to Israel and God's people.

While there have been empires in modern times, such as England, the Bible focuses on empires geographically located in the Middle East and the Mediterranean because of their proximity to Israel. In this chapter, I want to share with you what the Bible says about those empires to understand both their historical and prophetic significance.

The Early Pre-Israel Empires

Nimrod and Babylon

There are three pre-Israel empires in the Bible. The earliest attempt to build an empire was by Nimrod who united the people and built the Tower of Babel, as recorded in Genesis 11. Nimrod wanted to establish what we would call today, a *one world system*, with Nimrod as the *one world dictator*. They were already united in language. His goal was to unite them politically, economically, and religiously with him being worshipped as god. It was the first attempt at emperor worship.

This was in the "land of Shinar" (Genesis 10:10), which was called Babel, because it was there that the Lord confused their languages. Babel later became known as Babylon. Babylon is one of the more important future empires related to Israel. But the Lord frustrated Nimrod and Babylon's earliest attempt to establish an empire when He confused their languages and scattered the people. As we know in the Bible from Genesis to Revelation, Babylon as a symbol of the end-time one world order, plays a very important role in prophecy. Modern Iraq is geographically located in the area of ancient Babylon.

Egypt

The next ancient empire established long before Biblical Israel was Egypt. Egypt was one of the greatest civilizations of the ancient world. We don't know exactly when Egypt was established, but it probably dates back to 3500 BC, which makes it the oldest known country in the world.

Egypt is first mentioned in the Bible under its ancient name of Mizraim, who was one of the sons of Ham (Genesis 10:6). The first mention of the name Egypt is in Genesis 12:10, where we learn that Abraham went to Egypt because of a famine in the land of Canaan. This decision by Abraham would eventually set the course of much of history, because when he returned from Egypt he brought the Egyptian woman Hagar with him. Of course we know that Hagar gave birth to Ishmael and, as they say, "the rest is history."

Because of the Hebrews stay in Egypt and subsequent deliverance, as well as being close neighbors, relationships between Israel and Egypt form a large part of the written story in the Hebrew Bible, what Christians call the Old Testament. There are more than 700 references to Egypt in the Hebrew Bible. But Egypt is not just an empire of the past. While the Bible says that God will judge Egypt, Egypt will continue as a sovereign country, with the end-time presence mentioned in Isaiah 19 and Zechariah 14.

Assyria

The third pre-Israel empire is Assyria. Shem's son, Asshur, is considered the father of the Assyrians (Genesis 10:22). This means that the Assyrians were blood kin to the Hebrews. Since Assyria was located just north of Babylonia, the Assyrians intermarried with the Babylonians. Like the Babylonians and the Egyptians, the Assyrians were also an ancient people. Early Assyrian settlements date as far back as 3000 BC. The Assyrians began to establish themselves in 1700 BC and increased in power in later centuries. Assyria is mentioned 140 times in the Hebrew Bible. Its capital city, Nineveh, is mentioned more than twenty times. Nineveh is the place where Jonah went and preached.

We learn in the Bible (2 Kings 18) that the Assyrians conquered the Northern Kingdom of Israel in 721 BC, took many of the children of Israel as captives and scattered them throughout the Assyrian empire. This was the beginning of what became known as the "Lost Ten Tribes of Israel." However, not all of the Israelites were taken captive. Many remained in the land and moved south to be with their brethren in Judea (1 and 2 Chronicles). Archaeologists have uncovered the chronicles of the Assyrian King Sargon who conquered the Northern Kingdom. In his writings, he says that he carried away only 27,290 people and 50 chariots. And the ones taken captive were not lost. they were scattered. Recently the scattered descendants of Manasseh were discovered in India and made *Aliyah* (gone up) to Israel. I have personally met some of them in Israel.

The Assyrians also tried to capture the Southern Kingdom of Judea. But the Bible tells us that the angel of the Lord destroyed the Assyrian army and they returned to Nineveh (2 Kings 19). When the Babylonians increased in power to the south, they conquered the Assyrians and destroyed Nineveh in 612 BC. Thus the Assyrian empire came to an abrupt end.

However, as with Babylon and Egypt, Assyria also has an end-time presence. Isaiah 19:23-25 reads, "In that day there will be a highway from Egypt to Assyria, and the Assyrian will come into Egypt and the Egyptian into Assyria, and the Egyptians will serve with the Assyrians. In that day Israel will be one of three with Egypt and Assyria—a blessing in the midst of the land, whom the LORD of hosts shall bless, saying, 'Blessed is Egypt My people, and Assyria the work of My hands, and Israel My inheritance.'"

The Empires of Daniel

When Nineveh fell, Babylonia became the first of the empires of Bible prophecy. The person in the Bible that the Lord gave most of this understanding was the prophet Daniel. Daniel was a young man when Babylon conquered the Southern Kingdom of Judah and took some of the people captive. This was in 606 BC. In 605 BC, Nebuchadnezzar had defeated the Egyptians, leaving Babylonia as the sole superpower of its day.

Nebuchadnezzar's Dream

Because of his knowledge and wisdom, Daniel and his friends were assigned to serve as advisors to King Nebuchadnezzar (Daniel 1). Now that Nebuchadnezzar had conquered all his enemies, he pondered what he would do next. It was in this state of mind that Nebuchadnezzar had a prophetic dream (Daniel 2:1).

When he awoke, the dream troubled him. So he called for his advisors to interpret the dream for him. When they asked him the dream, Nebuchadnezzar refused to tell them the dream but insisted they give him the interpretation. He knew they would make up something and tell the king what he wanted to hear.

The advisors were shocked. They had no idea what the king dreamed. When they protested that it was impossible for them to give the king an interpretation without knowing the dream, the king became angry. He gave a command to kill all his advisors, including Daniel and his friends, who were unaware of the circumstances. When they told Daniel what was happening, he asked the king for time to interpret the dream (Daniel 2:1-16). When the God of Israel revealed the dream to Daniel, Daniel blessed the Lord with these words, "Blessed be the name of God forever and ever, for wisdom and might are His. And He changes the times and the seasons; He removes kings and raises up kings; He gives wisdom to the wise and knowledge to those who have understanding. He reveals deep and secret things; He knows what is in the darkness, and light dwells with Him. I thank You and praise You, O God of my fathers; You have given me wisdom and might, and have now made known to me what we asked of You, for You have made known to us the king's demand" (Daniel 2:20-23).

Daniel Reveals Nebuchadnezzar's Dream

When Daniel made it known that he knew the dream, he was brought to Nebuchadnezzar. Daniel gave credit where credit was due and acknowledged that the God of heaven revealed the dream to him. He said:

> The secret which the king has demanded, the wise men, the astrologers, the magicians, and the soothsayers cannot declare to the king. But there is a God in heaven who reveals secrets, and He has made known to King Nebuchadnezzar what will be in the latter days, Your dream, and the visions of your head upon your bed, were these (Daniel 2:27-28).

Now that the one true God has been properly honored, Daniel reveals the dream. He says:

> You, O king, were watching; and behold, a great image! This great image, whose splendor was excellent, stood before you; and its form was awesome. This image's head was of fine gold, its chest and arms of silver, its belly and thighs of brass, its legs of iron, its feet partly of iron and partly of clay. You watched while a stone was cut out without hands, which struck the image on its feet of iron and clay, and broke them in pieces. Then the iron, the clay, the bronze, the silver, and the gold were crushed together, and became like chaff from the summer threshing floors; the wind carried them away so that no trace of them was found. And the stone that struck the image became a great mountain and filled the whole earth (Daniel 2:31-35).

Daniel Gives the Interpretation

Now without pausing to take a breath, Daniel gives the interpretation. He says:

This is the dream. Now we will tell the interpretation of it before the king. You, O king, are a king of kings. For the God of heaven has given you a kingdom, power, strength, and glory; and wherever the children of men dwell, or the beasts of the field and the birds of the heaven, He has given them into your hand, and has made you ruler over them all—you are the head of gold (Daniel 2:36-38).

But after you shall arise another kingdom inferior to yours; then another, a third kingdom of bronze, which shall rule over all the earth. And the fourth kingdom shall be as strong as iron, inasmuch as iron breaks in pieces and shatters everything; and like iron that crushes, that kingdom will break in pieces and crush all the others (verses 39-40).

Whereas you saw the feet and toes, partly of potter's clay and partly of iron, the kingdom shall be divided; yet the strength of the iron shall be in it, just as you saw the iron mixed with ceramic clay. And as the toes of the feet were partly of iron and partly of clay, so the kingdom shall be partly strong and partly fragile. As you saw iron mixed with ceramic clay, they will mingle with the seed of men; but they will not adhere to one another, just as iron does not mix with clay (verses 41-43).

And in the days of these kings the God of heaven will set up a kingdom which shall never be destroyed; and the kingdom shall not be left to other people; it shall break in pieces and consume all these kingdoms, and it shall stand forever. Inasmuch as you saw that the stone was cut out of the mountain without hands, and that it broke in pieces the iron, the bronze, the clay, the silver, and the gold—the great God has made known to the king what will come to pass after this. The dream is certain, and its interpretation sure (verses 44-45).

The Explanation

Babylon

Daniel predicts four great empires of the Bible, with a fifth empire being the Kingdom of God coming to the earth. (See Daniel 7:17.) In man's eyes, these empires of men are great and glorious kingdoms, as represented by the image in the dream. But in Daniel chapter 7 they are seen from God's perspective as beasts. Their beastly description characterizes their empire. Let's briefly review these empires in Biblical history and prophecy.

The first is Babylon. Daniel tells Nebuchadnezzar that his empire of Babylon is the head of gold (verse 38). In Daniel 7:4, the head of gold is referred to as a lion with eagle's wings which is the ancient symbol of Babylon. The Babylonian empire was at its peak from 606–536 BC.

As I have mentioned, Nimrod was the first to seek to establish a world empire from Babylon. But the God of heaven put an end to Nimrod's dream. However, the religious worship Nimrod established was passed down as the dominant pagan worship to the successor empires. Elements of this religion were forced on the Christian world from Rome by Constantine.

The geographic area known as Babylon is one of the oldest areas of human civilization, with a history dating back to early human existence on the earth. We know that Abraham lived in this area in Ur in southern Babylon. At that time, Babylon was an advanced society, although very pagan. As city-states in the region fought each other for supremacy, Babylon's fortunes rose and fell.

With the defeat of Assyria and Egypt, Babylon was the new superpower in the time of Daniel. Isaiah prophesied about the rise and fall of Babylon about one hundred years before Babylon rose to power. He even names the Medes as the power who will defeat them (Isaiah 13:17-22). (See Isaiah 13, 14, and 47.)

Jeremiah lived during the time when Babylon was as its peak, yet he also predicted their ultimate defeat. Jeremiah was not politically correct. For 23 years he preached to the people of Judah to repent or else God would use Nebuchadnezzar as judgment against them. He prophesied that Judah would be in Babylon captivity for 70 years and then God would judge Nebuchadnezzar for his cruel treatment of the people (Jeremiah 25:1-14; Jeremiah 50 and 51).

For Jeremiah's good service to the people, they ignored his warnings, burned his prophecies, threw him in prison, and took him to Egypt against his will. Nebuchadnezzar attacked Jerusalem in 606 BC (Jeremiah 36-44). The city fell on July 18, 586 BC, the ninth of Av on the Hebrew calendar (Jeremiah 52:5-6; 2 Kings 25:2-3; 2 Chronicles 36).

According to Jeremiah 52:30, the Babylonians took captive 4,600 of the people of Judah. Daniel would be one of these captives. Jeremiah also prophesied that the people of Judah would be captive for 70 years, because for 490 years they failed to keep the seven year Sabbath (Jeremiah 25:11; 29:10). In Daniel 9:2, we learn that Daniel was reading Jeremiah's prophecy about the 70 years captivity, which caused Daniel to pray for the return of the people to their land.

The splendor of Babylon made it one of wonders of the ancient world. Historians and archeologists give us the following description of the city which was about 14 miles square. The Euphrates River ran through the city dividing it north and south, with a magnificent bridge connecting the two parts of the city. There were two sets of inner and outer walls protecting the city. The walls were 350 feet high and 87 feet thick. There were additional walls lining each side of the river with 150 gates of solid brass protecting the entrances. There were 250 watchtowers on the outer wall, and a deep water moat about 30 feet wide. The city was so well defended; no one thought it could ever be penetrated. But they were wrong.

In the Bible, Babylon represents the spiritual mother of pagan religions. It will be prevalent in the end-time religion of "Mystery Babylon" as described in the book of Revelation. It seems that where Nimrod failed, the anti-Christ false Messiah and his false prophet will be able to establish the one world political, economic, religious system of worship in the end times. Revelation 17:5 speaks of this religious system with these words, *MYSTERY, BABYLON THE GREAT, THE MOTHER OF HARLOTS AND OF THE ABOMINATIONS OF THE EARTH.* Revelation 18 describes the fall of "Babylon the great," which seems to describe the one world political, economic, and military system in place at the coming of the Lord. The same God of heaven that put an end to Nimrod's Tower of Babel will also put an end to the latter day tower of the new world order.

Medo-Persia

The second part of the image in Nebuchadnezzar's dream was the chest and arms of silver. We learn in Daniel 5:22-31; 8:1-7; 11:1-2 that this new empire of the Bible would be the Medo-Persian Empire, which was at its peak from 536 to 333 BC. In Daniel 7:5, the Medo-Persian Empire is likened to a bear, and in Daniel 8 to a ram.

The Medes were descendants of Noah's son, Japheth (Genesis 10:2; 1 Chronicles 1:5). The Persians were descendants of Shem (Genesis 10:22 [Elam]). Both Isaiah (13:17) and Jeremiah (51:11) predicted the rise of the Medes who would destroy Babylon. The Medes lived in the area south of the Caspian Sea, which today would be northern Iran. The Persians lived in the area of central and southern Iran, which was known as Persia until 1935 when the government specified that it should be called Iran.

After the Babylonians and Medes defeated the Assyrians, the Medes were the regional power, second only to the Babylonians. But by the time of King Nebuchadnezzar, the Persians had become the stronger of the two and defeated the Medes. They combined their regional empires and became known as the Medo-Persian Empire.

After Nebuchadnezzar died in 562 BC, his empire began to weaken. It would come to an end under the reign of Belshazzar. Daniel 5 tells the story of Belshazzar having a drunken orgy, which was nothing unusual except for one unforgivable action. Belshazzar had the sacred cups and vessels, which Nebuchadnezzar took from the temple in Jerusalem, brought to the party. And they drink their wine and toasted their gods from these vessels.

That was more than God would allow. God manifested human fingers of a hand that wrote strange letters on the wall. Belshazzar was not so drunk that he didn't immediately sober up. When no one could interpret the strange writings, they sent for Daniel. Daniel interpreted for the king and stunned the party goers with this interpretation:

> God has numbered your kingdom, and finished it ... You have been weighed in the balances, and found wanting;...

> Your kingdom has been divided, and given to the Medes and Persians (Daniel 5:25-28).

That very night the Medes and Persians dug a canal which diverted the water that flowed under the city wall. This enabled them to slip undetected into the city by way of the empty water bed. Imagine the surprise of Belshazzar and his drunken guests when the Medes and Persian fighters crashed their party. They killed Belshazzar and took the undefeatable city without firing a shot. Much to the surprise of the citizens of Babylon, when they awakened the next morning they were no longer Babylonians, they were Medo-Persians.

About one hundred years before Cyrus was born, Isaiah prophesied there would be a ruler named Cyrus (Isaiah 44:28; 45:1), and declared that this Cyrus would allow the rebuilding of the temple and Jerusalem. The Persians were tolerant of the religions of the people they conquered. The Lord, who raises up kings and puts them down, used the tolerant King Cyrus of Persia to issue a proclamation allowing the people of Judah to return to the land of Israel and rebuild their temple (2 Chronicles 36:22-23).

As far as end-time prophecies, Ezekiel 38:5 mentions Persia, along with Ethiopia and Libya, as one of the allies with Gog and Magog (Russia?) in their attack on Israel. This is most interesting since Iran wants the Islamic nuclear bomb to destroy Israel, and Russia is Iran's major suppler of weapons and technical support.

Greece

The third empire in the dream was represented by the belly and thighs of bronze (Daniel 2:32, 39; 8:1-7, 21; 11:3). We learn in Daniel 8:21, and in history, that this was Greece. In Daniel 7:6 Greece is likened to a leopard with four wings and four heads and 8:1-7 to a goat with the large horn that destroyed the ram. In Daniel 11:3-4, he is called a mighty king.

Daniel also prophesied that, at the height of its power, the large horn would be broken and succeeded by four horns. He further says that one horn will arise out of the four horns. This horn would be a fierce and cruel leader who would invade Israel, stop the Jews from practicing their religion, and challenge the one true God.

The Greeks were descendants of Japheth's son, Javan (Genesis 10:2). A young man arose who had the dream and zeal to challenge the Persian Empire. Alexander the Great defeated the Persians and established the Greek empire, which was at its peak from 333 to 323 BC. As a young man, Alexander was tutored by Aristotle. Under Aristotle's mentoring, Alexander came to believe that Greek culture was superior to all other cultures. He believed his mission in life was to spread Greek civilization, culture, and language to the rest of the world.

When Alexander conquered a city, he populated it with Greek citizens who colonized the area with the Greek way of life, the Greek language, Greek gods, and pagan Greek culture. Alexander believed himself to be the son of Zeus. But his untimely death of a fever in Babylon in 323 BC, at the young age of thirty-three, proved him to be mortal like the rest of us.

When Alexander died, his kingdom was divided between his four generals. The two most important of these generals was Ptolemy and Seleucus. Ptolemy ruled in Egypt and Seleucus ruled in Syria. They warred for the control of the empire, and the little land of Israel was caught right in the middle. In Daniel 11, Daniel refers to Egypt as the King of the South and Syria the King of the North. Daniel describes their battles in Daniel 11.

The cruel little horn Daniel mentioned was Antiochus Epiphanes who sought to destroy the covenant faith and practices of the Jewish people in the period between the Testaments. His cruel actions led to the pious Maccabees revolting against Antiochus. Against all odds, the God of Israel gave them a great victory so that they were able to rededicate the temple and renew their worship of the one true God. The Festival of Hanukkah came about as a result of this victory.

While Greece does not seem to be an important country in end-time events, Alexander did have two great accomplishments that affect our world today. First, he established a "Greek worldview" that became the worldview of the Roman Empire, which was then transmitted through Constantine to the Christian world and elements of Christian theology. The Greek worldview was based on the concept of duality which to them meant that physical matter was bad and that only spirit was good. In their way of thinking, the only way to be delivered from the physical was to die and go to the next world.

Our Christian emphasis of going to heaven rather than changing our world and a false separation of the sacred from the secular (what we do with God is sacred while the rest of our life is secular) came directly from Plato. Second, Alexander established Greek as the universal language of his day, which enabled the gospel and the letters of Paul to be transmitted to the world. Amazingly, we still study Paul's letters in Greek.

Rome

The fourth empire is represented by the legs of iron. While Daniel does not name this empire, we know from history that he was prophesying about the Roman Empire. This fourth empire is described as fiercer than all the others, which certainly fits the character of the Roman Empire. They enslaved the nations they conquered and showed them no mercy. It has been said that the glory of Rome was built on the misery of its conquered peoples.

Rome began to expand her powers several centuries before the birth of Jesus. Before she finished, she controlled much of the known world. As far as Rome's connection to Israel, the Roman General Pompey established Roman control over Israel in 63 BC. The life and ministry of Jesus and the Apostle Paul took place in the Roman Empire. Titus destroyed the Temple and Jerusalem in AD 70, and then a generation later, in AD 132-135, Hadrian crushed the second Jewish revolt.

The Romans rendered the land of Israel inhabitable and scattered the Jews among the nations. They forbade the Jews to live in Jerusalem and renamed Israel "Palestine." I might point out that when I teach in Israel, I explain different Roman ruins where the Romans were, while we watch the Israelis shop in the Jewish Quarter of the Old City. The Romans are gone but the Jews have returned. The God of Israel has defeated the gods of the Romans.

As the image is divided by its two legs, Daniel says that the fourth empire will also be divided (Daniel 2:41). Daniel does not say the empire will be conquered. He says it will be divided. Many scholars have interpreted his words to mean that it will be revived in some form in the end times, at which time God Almighty will destroy it.

The Roman Empire was divided in AD 364 into the western and eastern divisions. Rome was the capital of the western division and Constantinople the eastern capital. The western division fell to the invaders in the middle of the fifth century. The eastern division lasted another 1,000 years until finally in AD 1453 it was defeated by the Turks .

The longest lasting empire in history finally came to an end. But it was already divided before it fell to the invaders. And it was not destroyed by the Almighty as Daniel prophesied. This has caused scholars to believe that the Roman Empire would be revived in some form in the end times.

Most of us are familiar with the nursery rhyme, "Humpty Dumpty sat on a wall; Humpty Dumpty had a great fall. All the kings horses and all the Kings men couldn't put Humpty Dumpty together again."

Some see a parallel of this nursery rhyme to the quest of world leaders and emperors of times past that have tried, but failed, in their attempt to revive the Roman Empire. But there will be one last attempt before the coming of the Lord at the end of the age.

In Daniel 7, we learn that ten horns will arise from this empire. The ten horns are the beastly equivalent of the 10 toes that symbolize the last of the four great Gentile empires which will be ruling the world at the time of the coming of the Lord. Daniel says that the ten horns are ten kings or rulers. Daniel further says that one horn will rise up out of the ten horns (Daniel 7:7-8, 23-25). Daniel says this little horn will establish himself as the world leader and persecute the saints of God for three and half years (Daniel 7:21-25).

Students of Bible prophecy recognize this little horn as the anti-Christ, the false Messiah in the book of Revelation. It is believed that he will be able to fulfill Nimrod's vision of a one world system and rule as dictator over the world, which will worship him as God. He will be promoted by a false prophet. The two will merge the political and the religious in order to control the souls of people. This is how BABYLON THE GREAT is revived as the one world religion (2 Thessalonians 2:1-4; Revelation 13:1-8, 17:5).

This could only happen in modern times with our technology of jet airplanes, television, computers, internet, globalization, etc. Today we have in place a developing European Union that seeks to de-emphasize national identities and encourage people to think of themselves as Europeans rather than according to their nationality.

This is clearly their vision for America. They desire to merge the United States, Canada, and Mexico into an American region where we will think of ourselves not as citizens of the sovereign United States but as citizens of the Americas. The Americas will be one of the administrative regions of the one world system. It does not take much imagination to see the desire to put together a one world system of government, economics, military, and religion.

The short-lived empire of this little horn will last for seven years. The Bible refers to this time as the Tribulation which will come upon all the earth. Jesus referred to the last three and half years as Great Tribulation. As predicted about the little horn, the false Messiah will establish himself as the head of the New World Order. He too will persecute the saints of God. Jesus said unless those days are shortened for the elects sake, the whole world would perish (Matthew 24:22). While the Hebrew Bible speaks about this time period, the book of Revelation provides the terrible details.

When you compare what Daniel says about the little horn with what John says about the false Messiah in the book of Revelation, you get the impression that they are talking about the same person and the same terrible events. It is man's last desperate attempt to rule the world without God. Needless to say, it will end in disaster for those who do not want to live under God's rule. But the end will be glorious for the people of God.

The Kingdom Cut out of the Mountain

Daniel says that in the days of this last world empire of man, the God of heaven is going to establish His own empire on the earth. He describes this kingdom as a stone cut out of a mountain made without hands. In other words, this will be God's kingdom established by His own sovereign power over the nations. Daniel says that this mountain or kingdom will smash the ten toes of the image, which will bring an end to the empires of man. God's mountain or kingdom will fill the whole earth.

Daniel explains:

> I was watching; and the same horn was making war against the saints, and prevailing against them, until the Ancient of Days came, and a judgment was made in favor of the saints of the Most High, and the time came for the saints to possess the kingdom (Daniel 7:21-22).

Daniel saw the God of heaven destroying the empire of the beast and establishing God's empire on the earth. I quoted Daniel at the end of the last chapter but it is important to hear his words again:

> I watched till the beast was slain, and its body destroyed and given to the burning flame. As for the rest of the beasts, they had their dominion taken away, yet their lives were prolonged for a season and a time.
>
> I was watching in the night visions, and behold, One like the Son of Man, coming with the clouds of heaven! He came to the Ancient of Days, and they brought Him near before Him. Then to Him was given dominion and glory and a kingdom, that all peoples, nations, and languages should serve Him. His dominion is an everlasting dominion, which shall not pass away, and His kingdom the one which shall not be destroyed (Daniel 7:11-14). (See also Daniel 7:22-28.)

The book of Revelation gives the same account with more detail. Revelation 17-18 describes the destruction of the one world system in place at the coming of Messiah Jesus. He is the chief cornerstone who will establish the fullness of God's empire on the earth. He is the governor of the nations. Of the increase of His government there shall be no end. He is the King of kings and Lord of Lords.

Revelation 19:11-16 reads:

> Now I saw heaven opened, and behold, a white horse. And He who sat on him was called Faithful and True, and in righteousness He judges and makes war. His eyes were like a flame of fire, and on His head were many crowns. He had a name written that no one knew except Himself. He was

> clothed with a robe dipped in blood, and His name is called The Word of God. And the armies in heaven clothed in fine linen, white and clean, followed Him on white horses. Now out of His mouth goes a sharp sword, that with it He should strike the nations. And He Himself will rule them with a rod of iron. He Himself treads the winepress of the fierceness and wrath of Almighty God. And He has on His robe and on His thigh a name written: KING OF KINGS AND LORD OF LORDS.

In Revelation 19:17-21, John describes the destruction of the armies of the beast. It is the great Battle of Armageddon He writes:

> Then I say an angel standing in the sun; and he cried with a loud voice, saying to all the birds that fly in the midst of heaven, "Come and gather together for the supper of the great God, that you may eat the flesh of kings, the flesh of captains, the flesh of mighty men, the flesh of horses and of those who sit on them, and the flesh of all people, free and slave, both small and great."
>
> And I saw the beast, the kings of the earth, and their armies, gathered together to make war against Him who sat on the horse and against His army. Then the beast was captured, and with him the false prophet who worked signs in his presence, by which he deceived those who received the mark of the beast and those who worshiped him image. These two were cast alive into the lake of fire burning with brimstone. And the rest were killed with the sword which proceeded from the mouth of Him who sat on the horse. And all the birds were filled with their flesh.

Then in Revelation 20:1-6, John gives the comment regarding God's empire. We learn it will last 1,000 years, after which God will create a new heaven and a new earth for God and His people to live together in eternity. John says:

> Then I saw an angel coming down from heaven, having the key to the bottomless pit and a great chain in his hand. He laid hold of the dragon, that serpent of old, who is the Devil

> and Satan, and bound him for a thousand years; and he cast him into the bottomless pit, and shut him up, and set a seal on him, so that he should deceive the nations no more till the thousand years were finished. But after these things he must be released for a little while.
>
> And I saw thrones, and they sat on them, and judgment was committed to them. Then I saw the souls of those who were beheaded for their witness to Jesus and for the word of God, and had not worshiped the beast or his image, and had not received his mark on their foreheads or on their hands. And they lived and reigned with Christ [Messiah] for a thousand years (Revelation 20:1-4).

In Daniel 2:45, when Daniel finished explaining the dream to Nebuchadnezzar, he said, "The dream is certain, and its interpretation is sure."

It certainly seems that we are living in the times that Daniel and John wrote about. Everything in our world is about to change. As world leaders seek to establish their authority without God, this will bring much chaos and suffering to all of us. For a while it will seem like evil will prevail. But comfort one another with the words of Daniel, "The dream is certain, and its interpretation is sure." The one true God of the Bible is going to establish His righteous empire on the earth.

As Isaiah wrote:

> Now it shall come to pass in the latter days that the mountain of the LORD's house shall be established on the top of the mountains, and shall be exalted above the hills; and all nations shall flow to it. Many people shall come and say, "Come, and let us go up to the mountain of the LORD, to the house of the God of Jacob; He will teach us His ways, and we shall walk in His paths." For out of Zion shall go forth the law, and the word of the LORD from Jerusalem. He shall judge between the nations, and rebuke many people; they shall beat their swords into plowshares, and their spears into pruning hooks; nation shall not lift up sword against nation, neither shall they learn war anymore (Isaiah 2:2-4).

CHAPTER 5

Israel in Prophecy

One of the most important verses in the Bible is Genesis 12:1-3 where God makes certain covenantal promises to Abraham. It reads, "Now the LORD had said to Abraham: 'Get out of your country, from your family and from your father's house, to a land that I will show you. I will make you a great nation; I will bless you and make your name great; and you shall be a blessing. I will bless those who bless you, and I will curse him who curses you; and in you all the families of the earth shall be blessed.'"

In these verses, God promised Abraham and his descendants through Isaac and Jacob a land of their own, that they would be a great nation, and that the Messiah would come through them to be a blessing to the whole world. This was a sacred blood covenant that was literal, everlasting, and unconditional.

These promises were never fulfilled in ancient history to the degree God intended. While it is true that God brought the Hebrews out of Egypt into the land, they never fully controlled it as God promised Abraham. They also became a great nation under King Solomon, but they perished from the land and were dominated by the Gentile world powers. Jesus did come as their Messiah. He did establish the new covenant, but the Jews as a nation rejected Him.

In spite of their failure to honor the covenant, God must honor His commitment to Abraham. He must keep His promises. He must do whatever is necessary to bring the covenant promises to fulfillment. As we look at world events, we see clearly that the Almighty is moving them around the Jews and the nation of Israel to bring His covenant promises to pass.

Renewing the Covenant

When God made His covenant with Abraham, He told him that his descendants would be slaves in a strange country, but that He would deliver them with great wealth (Genesis 15:13-14). We learn from the Bible that this strange country was Egypt. We all know the story of God delivering the Hebrews from Egypt and their forty years of wandering in the desert because they refused to enter the land God promised them.

When the long desert journey finally came to an end, it was time for the new generation of Jews who were born during the forty years to enter the land. They had not been alive when God renewed His covenant with their parents, so it was necessary that God confirm the covenant with them.

Moses called them together for one last time before he died. He reminded them of how God entered into covenant with their father Abraham. He spoke of blessings if they obeyed God, but warned of judgment and curses if they disobeyed (Deuteronomy 28).

Before Moses handed over the leadership to Joshua, he spoke to the people about their future. He said:

> Take heed to yourselves, lest you forget the covenant of the LORD your God which He made with you, and make for yourselves a carved image in the form of anything which the LORD your God has forbidden you. For the LORD your God is a consuming fire, a jealous God.
>
> When you beget children and grandchildren and have grown old in the land, and act corruptly and make a carved image in the form of anything, and do evil in the sight of the LORD your God to provoke Him to anger, I call heaven and earth to witness against you this day, that you will soon utterly perish from the land which you cross over the Jordan to possess; you will not prolong your days in it, but will be utterly destroyed. And the LORD will scatter you among the peoples, and you will be left few in number among the nations where the LORD will drive you. And there you will

serve gods, the work of men's hands, wood and stone, which neither see nor hear nor eat nor smell. But from there you will seek the LORD your God, and you will find Him if you seek Him with all your heart and with all your soul. When you are in distress[tribulation], and all these things come upon you in the latter days, when you turn to the LORD your God and obey His voice (for the LORD your God is a merciful God), He will not forsake you nor destroy you, nor forget the covenant of your fathers which He swore to them (Deuteronomy 4:23-31).

Moses further predicted:

Now it shall come to pass, when all these things come upon you, the blessing and the curse which I have set before you, and you call them to mind among all the nations where the LORD your God drives you, and you return to the LORD your God and obey His voice, according to all that I command you today, you and your children, with all your heart and will all your soul, that the LORD your God will bring you back from captivity, and have compassion on you, and gather you again from all the nations where the LORD your God has scattered you. If any of you are driven out to the farthest parts under heaven, from there the LORD your God will gather you, and from there He will bring you. Then the LORD your God will bring you to the land which your fathers possessed, and you shall possess it. He will prosper you and multiply you more than your fathers. And the LORD your God will circumcise your heart and the heart of your descendants to love the LORD your God will all your heart and with all your soul, that you may live (Deuteronomy 30:1-6).

A Ten-Point Prediction

In this incredible sermon, Moses looked far into the future and made a prediction about the future of the Jewish people. His prediction was based on God's covenant with Abraham. It included ten statements that accurately describe the past, present, and future of the Jews. It was a sweeping declaration of God's plan for Israel.

This is one of the most profound sermons we will ever read. Moses gave it before the Jews even got into land, yet he tells what will happen to them afterward. As we study world history, we see his sermon has been fulfilled just as he predicted. The only possible explanation is that the Almighty rules over His world and revealed the future to Moses. Let's briefly go over these ten points and see how they have been fulfilled in prophecy, are now being fulfilled, and will be fulfilled. The information presented in this chapter is taken from my book, *Blow the Trumpet in Zion*, which is available from my Internet bookstore: www.rbooker.com/html/online_store.html.

1. Breaking the Covenant

The first point Moses makes is that the Jews will break the covenant. The first and most important command God gave the Jews was that they were not to worship idols. The LORD said:

> You shall have no other gods before Me. You shall not make for yourselves any carved image—any likeness of anything that is in heaven above, or that is in the earth beneath, or that is in the water under the earth; you shall not bow down to them nor serve them. For I, the LORD your God, am a jealous God. (Exodus 20:3-5).

God told the Jews to destroy all the idols of the nations in the land or else they would be tempted to worship them (Exodus 34:13-16). Obedience to this instruction was necessary for them to stay in the land.

After Moses died, Joshua led the people into the Promised Land. As long as Joshua and the elders who served with him were alive, the people were outwardly faithful to God (Joshua 24:31). But afterwards, they began to worship heathen gods and live immorally. This was during the period of the judges.

God then raised up Samuel to guide the Jews during the transition period from the time of the judges to the time of the monarchy. Samuel was a true prophet of God who persuaded the people to repent and turn back to God (1 Samuel 7:3-4).

Before Samuel died, the people demanded that he appoint a king to rule over them. The first king, Saul, was proud and disobeyed God. But because of Samuel's influence, Saul did not lead the people away from God.

During Saul's rule, God chose David as his king to succeed Saul. Although David would fail God, he loved God and sought to please Him (Acts 13:22). Just before David died, he appointed his son Solomon to succeed him as king.

Solomon brought disaster on the nation. Contrary to God's instruction (Deuteronomy 7:1-5), Solomon took many foreign wives who led him and the nation into idol worship from which they never recovered (1 Kings 11:1-13). In order to support his many wives and finance their idol worship, Solomon oppressed the people with excessive taxes and forced labor. They finally revolted at Solomon's death and the kingdom was divided into north and south (1 Kings 12).

The northern kingdom was called Israel. It consisted of ten tribes, with Samaria as its capital. It had nineteen kings who were of nine different families. All of these kings were evil and led the people into idol worship.

The southern kingdom was called Judah. It consisted of the two tribes of Judah and Benjamin, with Jerusalem as its capital. It had nineteen kings and one queen, all from the line of David. Although Judah honored the covenant more so than brothers to the north, they, too, eventually turned away from God.

2. Driven From the Land

The second point is that Abraham's descendants will be driven from their land. Because of their idol worship, Moses declared that God would drive His chosen people from their land. While God's covenant is unconditional, the benefits or blessings of the covenant are conditional, based on obedience. Any one generation of Hebrews could break the covenant by worshipping idols. That generation would miss the benefits of the covenant, but their disobedience could not annul the covenant itself. It would still be in force for the next generation, if they chose to honor it.

3. Scattered Among the Nations

The third point is that the Hebrews/Jews would be scattered among the nations. God used Assyria and Babylon to drive the Jews from their land and to begin this scattering among the nations. The Assyrians conquered the northern kingdom in 721 BC (2 Kings 17:5-23), and the Babylonians conquered the southern kingdom in 606 BC (Jeremiah 25:4-11; 2 Chronicles 36:14-20). The Abrahamic covenant, though still in force, had come to a standstill.

God had decreed that the Jews would be captive in Babylon for seventy years (2 Chronicles 36:21; Jeremiah 25:12). At the end of the seventy year period, God used the Persian Empire for the purpose of allowing the Jews to return to their land. King Cyrus defeated the Babylonians in 536 BC and gave the Jews permission to return to the land (2 Chronicles 36:22-23).

Comfort in Babylon

There were three expeditions from Babylon to the land of Israel. The first of these was led by Zerubbabel in the year 536 BC. But only about 50,000 Jews accompanied him (Ezra 2:64-65).

Ezra led the second return in 458 BC, but only 1,750 men plus women and children accompanied him (Ezra 8). The last expedition was led by Nehemiah in the year 445 BC (Nehemiah 2:1-8).

Although some exiles from the northern kingdom also returned during this time, apparently there was no organized return from Assyria. The ten "lost tribes" were never lost; they were scattered.

Jews and Greeks

The next great Gentile power was Greece established by Alexander the Great. The Jews fared will under the Greeks and assimilated into Greek culture. Alexander ruled from 333-323 BC. When he died, his empire was divided among his generals who constantly warred against each other for territorial control. The land of Israel was geographically located between the warring factions. These battles continued until 63 BC when the Roman general Pompey established Roman rule over Israel.

The Great Scattering

The Romans completed the great scattering of the Jews. This began in AD 70 when the Romans, under the leadership of Titus, burned Jerusalem, destroyed the Temple, slaughtered over one million Jews, and sold the survivors as slaves to foreign merchants who carried them off to the various nations of the world.

The final scattering took place a generation later after the failure of Simon bar Kochba to overthrow the Romans in AD 132-135. Once again, the Romans, this time under the Emperor Hadrian, slaughter the Jews unmercifully.

The famine in Israel was so bad that the Jews ate the flesh of their own family members, just as God said they would (Leviticus 26:29; Deuteronomy 28:53-57; Jeremiah 19:9; Ezekiel 5:10). The glut of Jews on the slave market was so great that many of them were not even bought as God predicted in Deuteronomy 28:68.

Jerusalem was declared off-limits to the Jews. As a further insult, Emperor Hadrian renamed the land of Israel after their ancient enemy the Philistines. He called it Palestine.

4. Few in Number Among the Nations

The fourth point is that the Jews would be few in number among the nations. Abraham is the father of both the Jews and the Arabs. He is the father of the Jews through Isaac and the Arabs through Ishmael. Abraham fathered these children around the year 2,000 BC. The present population of Arab people is around 150 million. You would expect the same for the Jews, but it's not. The total Jewish population in the world is only about 13 million and it is getting smaller while the Arab population is getting larger.

The explanation for such a huge difference in the population of Jews and Arabs can only be because of God's judgment upon the Jews for dishonoring the covenant. From the scattering in AD 70 and again in AD 135 to 1948 when Israel became a nation, the Jews have lived in exile at the mercy of God and their Gentile masters.

5. Serving Other Gods

The fifth point in the Moses' sermon is that the Jews would serve other gods. While the Jews were in Egypt, they were tempted to serve the Egyptian gods. A considerable number of the Jews never put away these Egyptian idols (Ezekiel 20:7-8). For the most part, the people did not repent of their idolatry (Ezekiel. 20:16). Even though they sacrificed to the LORD, they desired to go back to Egypt and their Egyptian gods (Ezekiel 20:24; Amos 5:26-27; Acts 7:39-43).

Except for a brief period under Samuel and King David, and other brief revivals, the people worshipped idols most of the time they were in the land.

While the exile did cause the Jews not to worship physical idols, they assimilated into the culture of the Gentile nations that ruled over them. When the Jews came under Greek rule, Alexander showed favor to them. The Greek culture made major inroads into Jewish life.

As previously noted, Alexander's dream for world conquest went beyond the sphere of the military. He desired to spread Greek philosophy and culture throughout the world. He wanted his subjects to think Greek, talk Greek, and act Greek.

Greek philosophy and culture influenced the Jews' language, manners, and customs. They began to speak the Greek language, take Greek names, and practice Greek ways. It wasn't long before Jewish attitudes, morals, and religious views were also being influenced by Greek thinking and practices. Sadly the majority of Jews in the world today have assimilated and profess to be secular.

6. God Will Preserve a Remnant of the Jews Throughout History

The sixth point in this prophetic sermon is that God will preserve a remnant of Jews throughout history. No other people group in all of history has suffered like the Jews. No other ethnic people have survived a long-term period of exile from their own country. They were either killed off by their conquerors or assimilated into their culture, with the loss of their identity, never to be heard from again. The Jews are the one exception.

Every Jew alive today is a living testimony and witness to the truth of the Scriptures and the faithfulness of God to keep His covenant. In fact, when Queen Victoria asked her Jewish Prime Minister to give her just one verse in the Bible to prove that it is true, he replied, "I can give you one word, the Jew!" He went on to explain how the history of the Jewish people is overwhelming proof that the Bible is the inspired Word of God. There is simply no other explanation for the existence of the Jews today.

Ancient Foes

God allowed the Assyrians and Babylonians to bring about the Jews' first exile. Their armies crushed the Jews, but many survived and were taken captive. Yet even though Cyrus allowed them to return to their land, most remained scattered throughout the Persian Empire. It was during the Persian rule that the king's Prime Minister, Haman, conceived a wicked plot to exterminate all the Jews. He surely would have succeeded except for divine intervention as recorded in the book of Esther.

Alexander was kind to the Jews. But when he died, his kingdom was divided among his four top generals who constantly fought each other for supremacy. Every time they had a war, their armies marched right through Israel. During these wars, the Jews could have been easily annihilated. God, however, protected them in fulfillment of His covenant word.

We learned earlier that a descendant of one of these generals was named Antiochus Epiphanes. To review, Antiochus took control of the land of Israel, and in the year 176 BC, he decreed that all of his subjects were to erect statues of the Greek gods, as well as himself, and worship him as an incarnation of Zeus—Jupiter to the Romans. Some of the Jews went along with this decree while the pious resisted.

Antiochus was determined to wipe out this resistance. He cruelly massacred tens of thousands of Jews and forbade them to practice their religion. When he found a baby boy who had been circumcised, he killed the boy and hung him around the neck of his mother, whom he then crucified.

To make matters worse, he erected a statue of Zeus in the temple at Jerusalem and sacrificed a pig on the altar. This pushed the Jews beyond their limit. A pious group rebelled. Although greatly outnumbered and once again threatened by annihilation, God gave the Jews a great military victory, thus saving them from extinction.

Next came the Romans. The Roman army was the most powerful the world had ever known. They could easily crush any foe. As we have learned, the Romans devastated the Jews in AD 70 and again in AD 135. Over a million Jews were killed. Those who were not killed in battle were sold into slavery, forced to fight wild beasts in Roman arenas, or tortured in other ways. Hundreds were crucified every day. The dead bodies were left to rot in the streets as a warning to any other group who was thinking about rebelling.

Every Jew the Romans could find was either killed, enslaved, or exiled. From that time until 1948, when Israel became a state, the Jews have been wandering in exile and persecution, with only the hand of God miraculously preserving them.

Christendom and the Jews

In the second and third centuries, both Jews and Christians alike were persecuted by the Romans. But something happened that changed this, at least for the Christians. In the year 312, the Roman Emperor Constantine declared Christianity to be the official religion of the Roman Empire. Except for a brief period under Julian the Apostate (360-363), this brought an end to the persecution of the Christians by the powerful Roman government.

This was certainly a welcome change for the Christians. It had, however, a devastating effect on the purity of the Church. The newly established official Roman Church embraced Greek philosophy, Roman pagan practices, and became flooded with nonbelievers who embraced the Christian faith but never received Jesus personally as their Lord and Savior. They outwardly professed to be Christians in order to gain favor with the Emperor and advance themselves in the Christian-Roman world. They were Christians in name only, as many are today. These nonbelievers brought their hate against the Jews with them into this new Christian faith.

Furthermore, Constantine established anti-Semitism and Replacement Theology as official church policy Replacement theology is the teaching that the Christian Church has replaced the Jewish people in God's covenant. This false teaching has always led to the Church persecuting the Jews. Constantine enforced this teaching with the Roman sword. That same anti-Semitism and teaching of Replacement Theology is still the dominant attitude and theology in the Church today.

The Crusades

One of the darkest hours for the Jews was during the period of the Crusades. The Crusades were military expeditions conducted under the authority and with the blessings of the church for the purpose of recovering the Holy Land from the Muslims. These "Christian" crusades took place during the eleventh, twelfth, and thirteenth centuries.

As I shared in a previous chapter, some of these Crusaders were probably sincere (but misguided) Christians, but many more were these same evil-hearted men who were Christian in name only. They were seeking an opportunity to kill, rape, and plunder with impunity. They not only hated the Muslims, the also hated the Jews.

Recall that during their conquest of the Holy Land, the Crusaders savagely butchered thousands of Jews. When the Crusaders arrived in Jerusalem, the forced all the Jews into a synagogue and burned it while singing, "O Christ we adore Thee." This was all done under the banner of the cross and in the name of Christ [Messiah].

The Inquisition

Americans remember 1492 as the year that Columbus discovered our great country. But something else happened that year which you may not have learned about in school.

The Spanish Inquisition (15th and 16th century) was one of the most terrible periods in all of church history. During this period, the leaders of the Roman Catholic Church tortured and murdered tens of thousands of true believers who were falsely accused of being heretics. In their thirst for blood, the inquisitors also insanely killed thousands of Jews. Again, this was all done in the name of Christ [Messiah].

The inquisition was especially perilous for the Jews in Spain and Portugal. While Columbus was discovering America, Ferdinand and Isabella, at the insistence of the Roman Catholic Church, began a systematic scheme which brought great suffering on the Jews.

Ferdinand and Isabella gave the Jews the choice of forced baptism (which is no baptism at all) or exile. If the Jews refused to be baptized, their property was confiscated and sold to the highest bidder. It was these funds which Ferdinand and Isabella used to finance Columbus' trip. The Jews were either then killed or forced to leave the country in conditions only the hardiest survived.

The Russian *Pogrom*

As we continue on is this broad sweep of Jewish history, we come to the latter period of the 19th century. The setting is in Eastern Europe. Millions of Jews had earlier fled there to escape on-going persecution from Western Europe. Poland became a refuge for them. They found favor with the Polish rulers who gave them some measure of autonomy and enabled them to live without the constant threat of persecution. The Jews felt safe. Old fears began to wane.

But their time of suffering and persecution was not over. Russia began to flex her muscles and conquer border states including parts of Poland, Rumania, and other eastern European countries were there were large Jewish communities. Russia suddenly found herself with an unwanted population of millions of Jews.

Following the example of previous nations, Russian leaders used the Jews as a scapegoat for their internal difficulties. Their solution to this Jewish problem was forced conversion for a third of them, emigration for another third, and starvation for the last third.

The Holocaust

"The final solution of the Jewish problem!" That's what Hitler called it. The Jews call it the *"holocaust!"* This was Hitler's plan for mass murder as the means to completely exterminate the Jews from the face of the earth. He almost did it. But God promised to preserve a remnant of the Jews for the end of the age when Israel will be the head nation on the earth through the rule of King Messiah.

Germany had been devastated by World War I. They needed someone to blame for all their problems. Hitler pointed to the Jew. He knew that European Christendom would not hinder his plan to destroy the Jews. He began organized persecution against them immediately after he took office in 1933. True believing Christians and Jews alike were herded into concentration camps. In 1939, these concentration camps became death camps.

The Jewish population in Europe in 1939 was about nine million. Hitler reduced it to about three million. Six million Jews who contributed immensely to European life were exterminated. Now Europe has 20 million Muslims that are contributing to its death. As a result of the Holocaust, observers of world events have pointed out that Europe died at Auschwitz.

The horror of the holocaust finally awakened the Jews to the fact that the world did not want them. There was no place safe for them to live except in their own homeland. As horrible as this demonic-inspired torture was, God used it to put the desire in Jewish hearts to return to their ancient land in fulfillment of Bible prophecy and God's plan for Israel.

7. God will Bring the Jews Back to Their Land

Perhaps the most significant event of modern times is the rebirth of the nation of Israel. After all these centuries, the Jews are back in their own land. There is no other possible explanation for this incredible fact except the biblical one.

The man whom God used to promote this return was Theodore Herzl. Herzl was born in 1860 in Budapest. He was the son of a wealthy banker. Herzl studied law but later became a journalist. He was well assimilated into the Gentile world in which he lived and felt very comfortable in it. He believed that modern man had become so civilized and tolerant of his fellowman, that Gentile prejudices against Jews would soon disappear.

In 1894, Herzl had an experience that showed him the foolishness of his thinking and his total ignorance of men's hearts. The experience that changed his thinking was the "Dreyfus Affair."

Alfred Dreyfus was a captain in the French army. He was also a Jew. He was falsely accused of giving French military secrets to the Germans and was humiliated and sentenced to life imprisonment. This guilty verdict was passed even though there was little evidence to support it.

During the trial, the public demanded justice. There demands were not so much because they thought Dreyfus was a traitor, but because he was a Jew. Herzl was in Paris covering the story. Herzl heard the angry mobs scream, "Kill the traitor, kill the Jew." His eyes were opened to the fact that Gentile hate of the Jews would never disappear, and, given the opportunity, they would again try to wipe them off the face of the earth.

The Birth of Zion

Herzl's attitude had now changed. He saw the Jews would never be safe outside of their own land. In 1896, Herzl wrote *The Jewish State*. In this little book, Herzl stated the problem and challenged the Jews to work toward the establishment of their own nation. In 1897, he called together the first meeting to lay the groundwork for what would later become known as "Zionism." At this meeting held in Basil, Switzerland, Herzl predicted that within fifty years the Jews would have their own state.

There was only one problem with his prediction. The land of Palestine was under control of the Turks. They had ruled over this land since 1517 and were certainly not interested in giving it to Jews. But something happened that dramatically changed the situation. That something was World War I.

In this terrible war, Turkey and England fought each other for control of the Middle East. England won. Ironically enough, a Jewish chemist named Chaim Weizmann made a major contribution to the war effort for England. He developed a means for improving the making of explosives, which England vitally needed in the war effort.

The Prime Minister of England publicly recognized Weizmann's contribution and desired to reward him. Instead of seeking personal gain, Weizmann asked that England grant the Jews a national homeland.

The Prime Minister agreed, and in 1917 the British Foreign Secretary, James Balfour, prepared a declaration that established the mandate for the Jews to once again live in their ancient land. As horrible as the war was, God used it to bring the Jews back home for the final and complete fulfillment of the covenant promise He made to Abraham 4,000 years earlier.

The newly formed League of Nations gave its stamp of approval to the Balfour Declaration. But except for a few religious zealots and political idealists, the Jews were not too thrilled with the idea of returning to the land. They were comfortably assimilated in the Gentile world. They had not been in Paris with Herzl. They had not seen what he had seen. It had been too long since they had heard, "Death to the Jews!" World War II woke them up. Hitler's death camps opened their eyes to the stark reality of what Herzl saw at the Dreyfus trial. Thus the Jews began a mass exodus back to their land.

8. The Jews Will Go Through Tribulation

The persecution the Jewish people have experienced the last 2,000 years has been tragic. And as much as we would like to think that is all behind us, unfortunately it is not. There is more trouble ahead.

We would have to have our heads in the sand, or be completely naive, not to realize the nations are preparing for the battle for Jerusalem. They want to take Jerusalem from the Jews, and will fight them to the end if necessary to achieve their goals. The United States, led by our own anti-Semitic State Department, is no exception. The Bible is clear that all nations will fight against Israel for control of Jerusalem as we read in Zechariah 12:2-3; 14:2, Joel 3:2; Micah 4:11-12; Zephaniah 3:8.

Moses predicted that the Jews would go through tribulation in the latter days. He says, "When you are in distress [tribulation], and all these things come upon you in the latter days." (Deuteronomy 4:30).

Jeremiah speaks of this period as the time of Jacob's trouble. It will happen in the latter days after the Jews are back in their land. God will save the Jews from destruction but destroy the nations that fight against Israel. Jeremiah writes:

> "For behold, the days are coming," says the LORD, "that I will bring back from captivity My people Israel and Judah," says the LORD. "And I will cause them to return to the land that I gave to their fathers, and they shall possess it. ... Alas! For that day is great, so that none is like it; and it is the time of Jacob's trouble, but he shall be saved out of it" (Jeremiah. 30:3, 7).

> "For I am with you," says the LORD, "to save you; though I make a full end of all nations where I have scattered you, yet I will not make a complete end of you. But I will correct you in justice, and will not let you go altogether unpunished" (Jeremiah 30:11).

Jeremiah adds, "In the latter days you will consider it" (Jeremiah. 30:24).

Both Hosea and Daniel confirm that this tribulation will take place in the latter days.

Hosea writes:

> For the children of Israel shall abide many days without king or prince, without sacrifice or sacred pillar, without ephod or teraphim. Afterward the children of Israel shall return and seek the LORD their God and David their king. They shall fear the LORD and His goodness in the latter days (Hosea 3:4-5).

Daniel adds, "Now I have come to make you understand what will happen to your people in the latter days, for the vision refers to many days yet to come (Daniel 10:14).

Some would like to believe the Holocaust was the fulfillment of the time of Jacob's trouble. It certainly was the most horrific suffering the Jewish people have experienced in their long struggle of survival among the Gentiles. However one views the timing of this difficulty, it should be clear to everyone that Israel is in a fight for its very survival. This struggle will bring great suffering to not only the Jewish people but to all of God's people.

Traditionally, it is believed that this time of tribulation is the last seven years of our world as we know it prior to the coming of Messiah Jesus to earth in power and glory. The Bible says this will be a time of suffering such as the world has never known. The last three and one-half years of this period will be so bad that Jesus referred to it as "great tribulation" in Matthew 24:21.

9. The Jews will Return to God

For now, God is bringing the Jews back to their land in their state of unbelief. The prophet Ezekiel said this would happen when he spoke about the Jews returning to their land with no breath in them (Ezekiel 37:8). By this he meant the Spirit of God.

Orthodox Jews do not recognize and accept the modern restoration of the state of Israel. They believe Scripture teaches that the Messiah will be the one to gather the Jews back to their land (Deuteronomy 30:3-6). This is true.

However, both the present restoration, which is political, and the orthodox view, which is religious, is scriptural. God is bringing the Jews back to their land in unbelief as Ezekiel predicted.

God's Providence Revealed

As we read about what is taking place in Israel today, we learn that even now the Jews are beginning to experience a renewed awareness of God's protection over them. As of this writing, the Jews have fought four wars since becoming an independent nation. They have also been involved in the crisis in Lebanon.

In all of these wars, the Jews have been completely outnumbered by their hostile Arab neighbors whose stated intention is to destroy them all. Yet against enemies that it seemed could easily overwhelm them, the Jews have won each war. How can this be? There's only one answer. God is miraculously interceding on their behalf, and the Jews are beginning to figure that out.

God's providential care will become even more clear to the Jews when He defeats Russia. It is inconceivable to think that the little nation of Israel could win a war against Russia. Humanly speaking, it is impossible. But with God all things are possible. God overrides man's evil and uses it for His glory and the good of those He has called to be His own. In this instance, He will destroy the Russian army and her allies, with the result being the Jews will realize it was God who saved them. The whole world will also realize it.

Ezekiel wrote:

> So I will make My holy name known in the midst of My people Israel, and I will not let them profane My holy name anymore. Then the nations shall know that I am the LORD, the Holy One in Israel (Ezekiel 39:7).
>
> I will set My glory among the nations; all the nations shall see My judgment which I have executed, and My hand which I have laid on them. So the house of Israel shall know that I am the LORD their God from that day forward (Ezekiel 39:21-22).

10. God will Remember His Covenant

We now come to the last of Moses' ten-point prediction. As we've learned in the previous lessons, God's covenant with Abraham was the most sacred of all compacts. It was a literal, unconditional, everlasting covenant that absolutely cannot be broken. And although any one generation of Hebrews could dishonor the covenant, the covenant itself remained in force.

The three particular covenant blessings God promised Abraham and his descendants were a land, a nation, and spiritual blessings through the Messiah. These blessings were conditional, based on the Hebrews obeying God. Tragically, the Hebrews were not obedient. They worshipped other gods in spite of God's continuous warnings from the prophets. As a result, the Jew were driven from their land, banished as a nation, and missed the blessings offered to them by Messiah Jesus.

Yet God has not forgotten His covenant people. He has preserved a remnant throughout history and brought them back to the land where He is going to make them a great nation and turn their hearts back to Him. Then, as we've seen, Jesus (Yeshua) will come and rule, not only as King of the Jews, but as King of kings and Lord of lords (Revelation 19:16).

When Messiah Jesus returns, He will rule over the nations from Jerusalem (Isaiah 2:2-4). Israel will be the head nation of the world (Deuteronomy 28:13; Zechariah 8:23). They will live in peace among their neighbors in the land God promised them (Isaiah 2:4). The blessings of Messiah Jesus will be enjoyed by all. It is at this time that God's three covenant promises to Abraham will find their complete fulfillment. Then Israel will fulfill her prophetic destiny to be a light to the nations.

> For the earth shall be full of the knowledge of the LORD as the waters cover the sea. And in that day there shall be a Root of Jesse, Who shall stand as a banner to the people; for the Gentiles shall seek Him, and His resting place shall be glorious (Isaiah 11:9-10).

CHAPTER 6

Jerusalem in Prophecy

Without a doubt, the most famous city in the world is not Washington, New York, London, Paris, Moscow, Rome, or some other capital city of the nations. The most famous city in the world does not have a deep water port. It is not a city by the bay with a Golden Gate Bridge. It does not have a Statute of Liberty beckoning the tired and poor. There is no Eiffel Tower, Big Bend, or famous Coliseum. Yet, there have been more books written, more poems penned, more songs sang, and more wars fought over this city than any other city in the world. It has been estimated that more than 50,000 books have been written about this city. While this city is called the City of Peace, it has not known much peace. In its 3,000 year history, this city has been destroyed 16 times and rebuilt 17 times.

This small city sits on a barren hilltop and basically has no natural resources that would attract people to it or make it a great city. Yet millions of people around the world call it home. The most famous city in the world, of course, is Jerusalem.

So what makes Jerusalem so special? Why do people want to go there? Why have the nations fought over it? Why do Jews, Christians, and Muslims want to control it? Why, after centuries of being a forgotten, desolate place, has Jerusalem, once again, become the center of the world's attention?

Jerusalem: God's Hometown

Jerusalem is the most famous city in the world because it is God's hometown. God has chosen Jerusalem as His residence on the earth.

In 2 Chronicles 6:6, the Lord says, "Yet I have chosen Jerusalem, that My name may be there."

Where but to God's hometown would people from around the world send letters addressed to "God, the Western Wall, Jerusalem."

Jerusalem has approximately 70 names in the Bible. It is called the City of David, the City of God, the City of Truth, Joyful City, Faithful City, Ariel (meaning Lion of God), and many other names. The most common name is Zion.

Psalm 135:21 reads, "Blessed be the LORD out of Zion, who dwells in Jerusalem."

Psalm 132:13-14 reads, "For the LORD has chosen Zion; He has desired it for His dwelling place: this is My resting place forever; Here will I dwell, for I have desired it."

Psalm 50:2, "Out of Zion, the perfection of beauty, God will shine forth."

Psalm 87:2-3, "The LORD loves the gates of Zion more than all the dwellings of Jacob. Glorious things are spoken of you, O city of God!"

Psalm 102:21 says that we are, "To declare the name of the LORD in Zion, and His praise in Jerusalem."

Psalm 122:6 says we are to "Pray for the peace of Jerusalem."

Jeremiah 3:17 says that Jerusalem shall be called "The Throne of the LORD."

Zechariah 1:17 says, "The LORD will again comfort Zion, and will again choose Jerusalem."

Zechariah 1:14, the Lord says, "I am zealous for Jerusalem and for Zion with great zeal."

Zechariah 8:3, the Lord says, "I will return to Zion, and dwell in the midst of Jerusalem. Jerusalem shall be called the City of Truth, the Mountain of the LORD of hosts, the Holy Mountain."

In Matthew 5:35 Jesus calls Jerusalem the "city of the great King."

The book of Revelation talks about a heavenly Jerusalem coming down out of heaven to the earth (Revelation 21). It is the final home for the people of God.

Jerusalem is mentioned 811 times in the Bible. There are 657 references in the Hebrew Bible and 154 references in the New Testament. Furthermore, Zion is mentioned 152 times in the Hebrew Bible and 7 times in the New Testament. Together Jerusalem and Zion are mentioned 963 times in the Bible. With all of the controversy over Jerusalem, it is interesting that Jerusalem is not mentioned a single time in the Koran.

Because of centuries of teaching on Replacement Theology, Christians of past times have only thought of Jerusalem as a spiritual place in heaven, not a real place on the earth. The stories in the Bible were allegorized so that Christians didn't believe the events and places were real. This separated the heavenly-minded Christian world from the real world of the real Jerusalem in a real land called Israel.

When Golda Meir was Prime Minister, she traveled around the world speaking on behalf of Israel. She tells the following story about her trip to Liberia.

> We traveled for miles in Liberia. I talked to hundreds of people and answered thousands of questions about Israel, many of them about Israel as the land of the Bible. A very nice young woman from the Liberian Foreign Office accompanied us, and I remember that on the last day of my visit she said very bashfully to me, "I have an old mother to whom I explained that I would be busy all week with a visitor from Jerusalem. My mother just stared at me. 'Don't you know,' she said, 'that there is no such place as Jerusalem? Jerusalem is in Heaven.' Do you think, Mrs. Meir, that you could possibly see her for a minute and tell her about Jerusalem?"
>
> Of course, I went to meet her mother that day and took with me a little bottle of water from the Jordan River. The old woman just walked around and around me, though she never actually touched me. "You come from Jerusalem," she kept on saying. "You mean, there's a real city, with streets and houses where real people live?"
>
> "Yes, I live there," I answered, but I don't think she believed me for a moment. It was a question that I was asked all over Africa, and I used to tell the Africans that the only thing that was heavenly about Jerusalem was that it still

existed! (Golda Meir, *My Life,* G.P. Putnam's Sons, NY, 1975, pp. 322-323)

Yes, there is a real Jerusalem. And it is a miracle of heaven that it still exists. Since Jerusalem is the most famous city in the world, since it is God's hometown, and since it is the final destination for believers, it is most important that we have an understanding of Jerusalem in prophecy.

Ancient Canaanite Period

19th - 14th Centuries BC

Jerusalem is an ancient city. The oldest know reference to Jerusalem is an Egyptian text dated to 1800-1900 BC. It was referred to by the name "Urusalim." The first biblical reference to Jerusalem is in Genesis 14:18 where Abraham is greeted by Melchizedek, who is identified as the King of Salem, which was the name of Jerusalem at that time.

The first mention of the city by the name of Yerushalayim in the Hebrew Bible is in Joshua 10:1 where the King of Yerushalayim makes an alliance to attack Joshua's army. In English, Yerushalayim is spelled as Jerusalem.

13th Century BC

In Joshua 18:28 the city is called, "Jebus" or Jebusalem. It was named after the Jebusites who lived there at the time Joshua and the Hebrews showed up to claim their promised land. The city was in the territory allotted to Benjamin. We learn in Judges 1:21 that the Benjaminites could not drive out the Jebusites. This was around 1400 BC.

The First Temple Period

King David (1010-970 BC)

Four hundred years would pass before King David conquered the city around 1010 BC (2 Samuel 5). Because David conquered the city and ruled from there as king for 33 years, Jerusalem became known as the "City of David." It was also called the stronghold of Zion.

David not only ruled from there but he also brought the Ark of the Covenant to Jerusalem where he established 24 hour daily worship to God. Jerusalem became David's political and spiritual capital. His political rule and his spiritual worship would be known as the "Tabernacle of David." We learn in 1 Kings 2:10 that David was buried in the City of David, which at that time was the southeastern ridge below the Temple Mount.

It didn't seem right to King David that he lived in a nice palace while the Ark of the Covenant was in a tent. So before he died, he decided to build a temple for the Ark (2 Samuel 7; 1 Chronicles 17). While it seemed like a good idea, the Lord said "No." Because David was a warrior king, he had a lot of blood on his hands. The Lord did not want David's blood-stained hands to build a temple of worship (1 Chronicles 22:8).

King Solomon (970-930 BC)

But God did agree that David's son, Solomon, could build the Temple (1 Chronicles 22). Even though David was not allowed to build the Temple, he did buy the threshing floor which would become the Temple Mount (2 Samuel 24:24). Furthermore, David did make most of the preparation for the Temple and give to Solomon the divine plans the Lord had given to him for building of the Temple.

Because David had defeated Israel's enemies, Solomon ruled in times of peace. With peace and great wealth, Solomon was able to build the Temple in only seven years. He not only built the Temple, Solomon became the earth's richest and greatest king. Under his reign, Jerusalem prospered and was one of the richest and greatest cities of its time. His rule was from about 970-930 BC.

A Divided Kingdom (930 BC)

Unfortunately, Solomon disobeyed God and married many foreign women who led Solomon into idolatry. He built temples to house the gods of his pagan wives and had to tax the people beyond what they could bear. When Solomon died, there was a civil war and Israel was split between the north and the south. The northern kingdom was called Israel and consisted of ten tribes. Its capital was Samaria. The northern kingdom had nineteen kings who were from nine different families. All these kings were evil and led the people away from their covenant God. The Lord finally judged them by allowing the Assyrians to conquer the northern kingdom in 721 BC and exile many of the Jews.

The southern kingdom was called Judah and consisted of the two tribes of Judah and Benjamin. Jerusalem remained the capital. The southern kingdom had nineteen kings and one queen, all from the line of David. Some were good and some were evil. The southern kingdom eventually rebelled from the Lord.

Babylonian Rule (606-536 BC)

God finally judged them by allowing the Babylonians to attack Jerusalem in 606 BC. They completely destroyed Jerusalem in 586 BC (2 Kings 25; 2 Chronicles 36). At this time, many of the prominent Jews were killed or taken to Babylon to serve the king. Jeremiah had prophesied that the Jews would be in captivity in Babylon for seventy years (Jeremiah 25). At the end of that captivity, God would judge Babylon and allow the Jews to return to the land.

The Second Temple Period

Persian Rule (536-333 BC)

In 536 BC, Persia defeated Babylon. The Persians established a great empire throughout the ancient Near East, including the land of Israel. It was a benevolent rule whose subjects enjoyed a reasonable amount of freedom and peace.

As a result of their tolerance, King Cyrus allowed the Jews to return to their homeland and rebuild the Temple (2 Chronicles 36:22-23; Ezra). Zerubbabel led the first group of 50,000 returning to the land. The people didn't have the wealth and labor Solomon had so they became discouraged. The Lord sent the prophets Zechariah and Haggai to encourage the people to get busy building the Temple. It took about twenty years to complete the rebuilding of the Temple which was finished in 516 BC. Compared to Solomon's Temple, this second Temple was rather plain. In 458 BC, Ezra led a second group of about 2,000. In 445 BC, King Xerxes allowed Nehemiah to return to rebuild Jerusalem itself.

Greek Rule (333-323 BC)

Like other mighty empires, it seemed like the Persian Empire would last forever. However, it would soon succumb to one of the greatest military leaders of all time, Alexander the Great. Alexander (356-323 BC) was only in his twenty's when he defeated the mighty Persian army in 333 BC. He believed he was the son of Zeus. But his untimely death in 323 BC at the age of thirty-three proved him to be a mortal like all the rest of us. In his brief time, Alexander conquered much of the known world. It is said that when Alexander looked at his empire, he wept for there was nothing more to conquer.

During his military campaigns against Persia, Alexander passed through Israel on his way to conquer Egypt. Jewish traditional writings (Talmud – Yoma 69a) as well as the writing of Josephus (Antiquities XI, 321-347) record an interesting legend when Alexander came to Jerusalem. Both accounts tell that when Alexander came to Jerusalem, the High Priest, fearing that Alexander would destroy the city, went out to meet him. According to the story, when Alexander saw the High Priest, he dismounted and bowed to him. Now Alexander didn't normally bow to anyone. When his general inquired why he did this, Alexander replied that he did not bow to the High Priest, but to the God who honored him with the position of High Priest. Alexander then explained that he has seen the High Priest in a vision. Because he considered this a good omen, he spared Jerusalem and Israel from devastation.

Alexander did not normally destroy cities. Instead, he "Hellenized" them. That means he established a Greek colony, Greek culture, Greek language, Greek philosophy, Greek gods, and Greek practices in the cities he conquered. So while he did not physically destroy Jerusalem, he did something worse. He began to destroy the soul of Jerusalem by Hellenizing the city to be a Greek city. God was going to have to do something or Jerusalem would be lost as His hometown.

Ptolemy Dynasty (King of the South, 301-198 BC)

When Alexander died, he did not have a successor. His kingdom was divided among his generals who fought over control of his empire. The Greek generals who succeeded Alexander and ruled from Egypt were called the "Ptolemies." They established a dynasty in Egypt from 301-198 BC. In Daniel 11, they are called the "King of the South."

Seleucid Dynasty (King of the North, 198-164 BC)

The Greek generals who succeeded Alexander and ruled from Syria were called the "Seleucids." This is the King of the North mentioned in Daniel 11. Their dynasty was from 198-164 BC.

The Kings of the South in Egypt and the Kings of the North in Syria fought five major battles during their era. The little land of Israel and Jerusalem was caught in the middle. It was only a miracle of God that Jerusalem was not destroyed as they moved their armies back and forth through the land of Israel and God's hometown.

One of these Syrian kings was Antiochus Epiphanes (175-164 BC). Antiochus sought to Hellenize all the territories under his rule, including Israel and Jerusalem. He forbade the Jewish people to practice their ancient faith. They could not practice circumcision, observe the Sabbath, celebrate the feasts, keep their dietary laws, study the *Torah*, or in any way, worship their God.

Antiochus erected a statue of Zeus in the Temple bearing his own image. He built a new altar to Zeus on which he offered a sacrificial pig. He then poured the pig's blood over the *Torah*.

Antiochus erected shrines and altars throughout the land and forced the people to make sacrifices as tokens of their acceptance of the Greek gods. Those who disobeyed were tortured or killed. Their bodies were mutilated, and while still alive and breathing, they were crucified. The wives and the sons whom they circumcised were strangled. The mothers were then crucified with the dead bodies of their children hung around their necks.

The Maccabean Era (164-63 BC)

Unfortunately, many of the leaders in Israel embraced Hellenism. The lovers of God, however, rebelled. The revolt started in 167 BC when one of the king's officers erected a pagan altar and commanded the people to sacrifice a pig as a show of loyalty to Antiochus.

The king's officers ordered an aged priest named Mattathias to be the first to obey in order to set an example for the rest of the town. But he refused. When a local Jew stepped forwarded to make the sacrifice, Mattathias killed him and the king's officer. He and his five sons fled into the hills and began their revolt against Antiochus. The family which led the revolt was given the name "Maccabees."

Although they did not have a chance, in the natural, to be victorious, God helped them to defeat Antiochus. With fighting going on in and around Jerusalem, it was only divine intervention that saved the city from destruction. In 164 BC, exactly three years after the altar to Zeus had been set up, the Temple in Jerusalem was cleansed, and the daily sacrifices and religious ceremonies resumed. That rededication of the Temple is still commemorated each December as *Hanukkah*, the Festival of Lights.

The Maccabees and their descendants, also known as the Hasmoneans, reestablished Jewish sovereignty over Israel, with Jerusalem as the capital of the independent Jewish state. They maintained their independent rule for approximately 100 years, from about 164 BC to 63 BC. It was during this time that the Sadducees and the Pharisees emerged, along with other factions and groups that would influence events recorded in the New Testament. We learn of these factions and groups in the Apocryphal books of 1 and 2 Maccabees.

The Hasmonean descendants did not have the religious zeal of the earlier Maccabees. They wanted power and wealth. Over time, they began to fight among themselves for control over the land, the people, and the resources. Their constant warring among themselves weakened their position at the same time the Romans were expanding their power in the region.

Roman Rule (63 BC-312 AD)

This civil conflict provided just the opportunity for the Roman general Pompey to establish Roman presence in Judea and Jerusalem. It was on the Sabbath in the Hebrew month of Sivan (June), 63 BC, when Pompey's soldiers broke through the walls of Jerusalem and entered the city. Pompey entered the Holy of Holies in the Temple, expecting to plunder the Temple treasures. Instead, he found an empty Holy of Holies. While Pompey did not harm the actual city of Jerusalem he did establish Roman rule that would last for approximately six hundred years until the Muslim period.

Herod (37-4 BC)

Instead of ruling directly, the Romans appointed Herod as their puppet king. The gospel of Matthew (Matthew 2:1-2) tells us that Jesus was born in Bethlehem when Herod was king of Judea. Herod ruled from 37-4 BC. From all we know about Herod, we can best describe him as a charming, clever, cruel, paranoid, evil genius.

Herod was a good administrator who was totally loyal to Rome. He built numerous monuments to Caesar and held festivals throughout the land, which he dedicated to Caesar. Herod is best known for expanding the Temple in Jerusalem. This was a major building project. It was started in 20 BC and not finished until AD 64, many years after Herod had died. Herod's expanded Temple was a magnificent structure and one of the wonders of the ancient world.

In connection to the Temple, Herod appointed the High Priest regardless of his ancestry or character. As a result, Temple administration and worship in the time of Jesus was very corrupt, having been sold to the highest bidders. The Sadducee priests in Jerusalem made a fortune from the Temple activities. When Jesus became a threat to their power and position, they schemed to put him to death.

Before Herod died in 4 BC, he divided his kingdom among three of his sons. Archelaus (4 BC-6 AD) was given the most important rule in that it included Judea and Samaria. This means he had to administer Jerusalem. Unfortunately, he was not up to the task. He was an incompetent and unwise man who sought to rule by cruel force. This explains why Matthew tells us that Joseph and Mary decided to live in Nazareth rather than Bethlehem whey they returned to the land from Egypt (Matthew 2:19-23). They knew Jesus would be in danger if they lived in the territory governed by Archelaus.

Archelaus was so bad that two bitter enemies, the Jews and the Samaritans, joined forces and appealed to Augustus to have him removed. When Augustus saw how much they hated Archelaus, he know Archelaus could never keep the peace. He banished him in AD 6 and established direct Roman rule in the form of Roman governors.

The most famous of these Roman governors was Pilate, who was governor from AD 26-36. According to historical records, as well as the New Testament, Pilate was a cruel, cold-blooded, weak administrator. He executed prisoners without trials, slaughtered any group that he perceived as a threat, robbed the treasury of the Temple, greatly oppressed the residents of Jerusalem, and mocked everything Judaism considered sacred.

Pilate was just the right cruel Roman authority, with just the right Roman appointed evil High Priest, at just the right time and place when God ordained that Jesus would be crucified, buried, and resurrected in fulfillment of God's eternal plan to bring redemption to the world. While God uses human beings to further His purposes, it was God's divine plan from eternity past that Jesus would die for the sins of the world.

Before He was arrested, Jesus anticipated Jerusalem's future and gave this warning, "But when you see Jerusalem surrounded by armies, then know that its desolation is near. Then let those who are in Judea flee to the mountains, let those who are in the midst of her depart, and let not those who are in the country enter her. For these are the days of vengeance, that all things which are written may be fulfilled. But woe to those who are pregnant and to those who are nursing babies in those days! For there will be great distress in the land and wrath upon this people. And they will fall by the edge of the sword, and be led away captive into all nations. And Jerusalem will be trampled by Gentiles until the times of the Gentiles are fulfilled" (Luke 21:20-24).

Roman and Byzantine Period

First Jewish Revolt (66-73 AD)

While the times of the Gentiles began with Nebuchadnezzar and Babylon, it was the Romans that would scatter the Jews to the nations and establish Gentile domination of Jerusalem for centuries. In the gospel of Luke, we learn of the census for tax purposes that caused

Joseph and Mary to go to Bethlehem to register for the census (Luke 2:1-7). This census caused an uprising that would eventually lead to the First Jewish Revolt which took place from 66-73 AD.

The revolt brought the Roman armies into Israel to crush the uprising. When Titus attacked Jerusalem in 70 AD, he burned the city, burned down the Temple, slaughtered over one million Jews, and sold the survivors as slaves to foreign merchants who carried them off to the various nations of the word. This was on the ninth of Av, the same date Nebuchadnezzar destroyed Jerusalem in 586 BC. As was the Roman custom, Jerusalem was ploughed up with a yoke of oxen, as Jesus prophesied in Matthew 24:1-2. The final victory for the Romans was in AD 73 at Masada, where 960 Jewish zealots took their lives rather than fall into the hands of the Romans.

Second Jewish Revolt (132-135 AD)

The second Jewish Revolt took place a generation later when Rabbi Akiba pronounced that Simon bar Kochba was the Messiah. Bar Kochba attempted to overthrow the Romans in AD 132-135. Once again, the Romans, under the Emperor Hadrian, slaughtered the Jews unmercifully and scattered them throughout his empire. Hadrian renamed the land of Israel after the Jews ancient enemy the Philistines. He called it Palestine. Jerusalem he renamed after himself and called it "Aelia Capitalina." Hadrian built a temple to Jupiter on the Temple Mount and did everything he could to make Jerusalem a pagan city. The Jews were not allowed to enter the city, and Jerusalem remained in the hands of Gentiles for the next 1832 years—until 1967.

Pre-Christian Rome (AD 135-312)

Between the time of Hadrian and Constantine, pagan imperial Rome ruled Palestine and Jerusalem through various governor-generals. Their provincial capital was in Caesarea. But everything was about to change with Constantine.

Byzantine Roman Rule (AD 312-638)

When Constantine (288-337) became the Emperor of Rome, he claimed that the Christian God helped give him his victories. As a result, Constantine issued decrees (Edict of Milan, 313) favoring Christianity. Constantine sent his mother, Helena, to Palestine to build church structures in the Holy Land in honor of his new Christian religion. Helena (250-330?) traveled the 1400-plus miles from Rome to Palestine at the age of 80. She built the basilica in Bethlehem, the Church of the Holy Sepulture in Jerusalem, and a basilica on the Mount of Olives honoring the Lord's ascension. Legend is that Helena found the true cross of Jesus and other Christian relics. In the next generation, the Empress Eudocia traveled to Jerusalem in 438 and contributed to the building of Christian structures around Jerusalem.

As the Roman Empire in the west began to crumble, Constantine moved his capital to Byzantium in the east (331). The empire then became known as the Byzantine Empire. Constantine rebuilt Byzantium into a Christian city and called it Constantinople. Later it would be conquered by the Turks and renamed Istanbul.

Constantine encouraged pilgrimages to Jerusalem and the Holy Land. As a result, many Christian pilgrims went to Palestine and built churches and monasteries throughout the land on sites believed to be important according to New Testament events. While the Christian population increased, Jews were not permitted to enter Jerusalem without special permission. While there was always a small Jewish presence in the land, Jews were not permitted to pray in Jerusalem except on the ninth of Av, the day that memorialized the destruction of the First and Second Temples.

In 614, the Persians invaded Palestine, and with the help of the Jews defeated the Byzantines. As a thank you for their help, the Persians allowed the Jews to live in Jerusalem. The Byzantines returned in 629 and defeated the Persians. They reestablished Jerusalem as a Christian city and, once again, forbade the Jews from living there. This situation lasted until 638 when the Arabs defeated the Byzantines and captured Jerusalem.

Almost all of the Christian churches were destroyed by the Persians and Moslems. Some were rebuilt by the Crusaders and again destroyed by the Muslims.

Muslim Period

The next drama in the history of Jerusalem was the Muslim Period. When Mohammed was alive, his travels and conquests were limited to Arabia. He certainly never went to Palestine, contrary to Muslim legend. There was no Islam or Mosque in Jerusalem until after Mohammed's death.

When Mohammed died in 632, he had not appointed a successor. This almost always causes rivalries to fight for control of the movement or organization. Islam was no exception. Mohammed was succeeded by four warlords called caliphs (meaning successors). The first three caliphs were not related to Mohammed. The fourth caliph, Ali, was Mohammed's cousin and son-in-law. Ali was assassinated in 661. This action caused a split in the Muslim world that is still with us today. One group, the Sunnis, follows the teaching that the caliphs were legitimate successors to Mohammed. The other group, the Shiites, believe that the leader must be a descendant of Mohammed, and therefore recognize only Ali and his descendants as the legitimate successors to Mohammed.

This split can be compared to the split between the Catholics and Protestants in the 1500's and the wars and brutality that followed as best exemplified by the Inquisition against the Jews and true Christians. While the Catholics and Protestants have stopped fighting each other for the most part, the struggle between the Sunni and the Shiites has been going on for 1400 years and continues today.

Umayyad Arabs (638-750)

The first successors to Mohammed were the Umayyad Arabs. They were Sunni. They expanded Islam beyond the borders of Arabia, and in a short time, conquered all of the Middle East, including Jerusalem. They ruled from their capital in Damascus from 638-750. During their rule, Caliph Abed al-Malik built the Dome of the Rock in 692. His son built the Al Aska mosque in 711-712.

Abbasids Arabs (750-1099)

The Shiite Muslims were called the Abbasids. They revolted against the Umayyads and defeated them. They ruled the Middle East from Baghdad from 750-1099. They expanded Muslim rule to North Africa and Spain all the way to France until they were defeated by Charles Martel in the Battle of Tours outside Paris in 732. This was one of the most important battles of history as it stopped the Muslim advance in the Christian West.

While conditions for the Jews in Palestine under Muslim rule were not good, it was better than under the rule of the Byzantines. A small Jewish community was allowed to develop in Jerusalem and the Jews were allowed to pray at the Western Wall. But situation for Jews in Jerusalem would soon go from bad to worse as the Crusaders were preparing to liberate the Holy Land from the infidels. This desire to expel the infidels became more urgent when an Egyptian leader named Al-Hakim fought over Jerusalem with a Turkish group known as the Seljuks. The Seljuks captured Jerusalem in 1091 and held it until 1098 when the Egyptians took control of it in 1098.

The Crusader Period

Crusaders (1099-1291)

One of the darkest hours for Jerusalem and the Jews was during the period of the Crusades. The Crusades were military expeditions conducted under the authority and with the blessing of the Roman Catholic Church. Their purpose was to recover the Holy Land from the Muslims and stop the spread of Islam. Although some of the Crusaders were sincere (but misguided) Christians, many more were evil-hearted men who were Christian in name only. The Crusades gave them an opportunity to kill and plunder with impunity in the name of God while having their sins forgiven by the Pope.

The Crusaders not only hated the Muslims, they also hated the Jews. During their conquest of the Holy Land, which turned out to be a failure, they savagely butchered thousands of Jews. This was all done under the banner of the cross and in the name of Christ. When the Crusaders reached Jerusalem, their swords were already bathed in blood. They killed the Muslims and herded the Jews into a synagogue. As they sang, "O Christ, We Adore Thee," they set fire to the synagogue and burned the Jews alive who were inside.

Saladin the Kurd (1187-1193)

Fortunately, this brutal misguided religious jihad would soon come to an end. While it seems almost sacrilegious for a Christian to make the following comment, it was better for the Jews that the Muslims defeated the Christians and eventually drove them from Jerusalem. Whereas the Crusaders banished the Jews from Jerusalem, Saladin invited them to return to the city.

Saladin, a Kurd from Iraq, defeated the Crusader army at the Horn of Hittin in July 1187. This was the beginning of the end of the Crusader rule of Jerusalem. Saladin conquered Jerusalem in October 1187, at which time the Crusader army withdrew to a small defensible area along the coast. They were finally driven from the Holy Land in 1291 when they surrendered Acco (Acre) to the Mamelukes. To this day, Saladin is considered a great hero and inspiration to the Muslims in their quest to defeat the "Crusader West" led by America and their proxy, Israel.

Mameluke Period (1291-1517)

The Mamelukes were not a people or a nation. They were soldier slaves the Egyptians had imported from Asia. The Egyptians converted them to Islam and trained them from childhood to serve in their personal armies. Eventually they rose up against the Egyptians and overthrew them. They established their own rule in the Middle East with their capital in Cairo. We can liken their situation to that of the legendary Spartacus who led a slave army rebellion against Rome. While Spartacus lost, the Mamelukes were victorious.

Under their rule, Jews and Christians suffered greatly. The Mamelukes were extremely cruel and fanatical. They destroyed synagogues and forced Jews to wear a distinctive yellow turban and other degrading clothing and practices. Jews in Jerusalem were constantly harassed and most had to leave Jerusalem for fear of the lives. The land suffered greatly from neglect, and only a small minority of Jews and Christians survived the cruel conditions they were made to live under. Jerusalem was almost abandoned. While the land was laid to waste, the Mamelukes did build extensively in and around Jerusalem as a way of establishing a Muslim presence in the land.

The Mameluke Empire and rule over Jerusalem began to crumble in 1453 when the Turks invaded and conquered Constantinople, thus ending a 1000 year Byzantine capital and presence. The Turks renamed Constantinople, Istanbul, and established it as the capital of their empire. They then gained control of what had once been the Byzantine Empire. By 1517, they defeated the Mamelukes and ruled the entire Middle East, including Palestine and Jerusalem.

Ottoman Turkish Period (1517-1917)

The Ottoman Turks got their name from a Turkish warlord named Uthman or Othman who established a military dictatorship that grew into a great empire. He was the first Sultan and was succeeded by the Sultan Salim (1512-1520), who conquered the Holy Land and Jerusalem in 1517. His son, Suleiman the Magnificent (1520-1566), was a strong leader. Under his rule, the empire was greatly extended to encompass all of the Middle East, North Africa, and Eastern Europe. Twice they nearly conquered Vienna, which would have opened up all of Western Europe to Turkish Muslim rule. There were no independent nation-states in the Middle East during the Ottoman Empire as all the peoples were simply considered part of the territories of the Empire.

In Palestine and Jerusalem, Suleiman treated the Jews with benevolence and living condition in the land greatly improved, which encouraged Jews to return. Suleiman rebuilt Jerusalem and the walls around the Old City that exist today. This was around 1545.

Later rulers were not as wise as Suleiman and returned to the old attitudes and harassments against the Jews. They also neglected the land and taxed the people beyond what they could bear. When they taxed the trees, the people cut down the trees, which led to a further desolation of the land that made it almost uninhabitable.

The Ottoman Empire lasted 400 hundred years. When its power began to diminish, it was known as the "sick man of Europe." In World War I, Turkey sided with Germany and lost the war. The British and the French divided Turkey's former Middle East territorial empire between them and artificially created five independent nation-states. These were Iraq, Syria, Lebanon, Israel, and Transjordan. Britain was given the mandate to govern Iraq, Palestine, and Transjordan, while France took Syria and Lebanon.

British Mandate (1917-1948)

The world changed forever on November 2, 1917 when British Foreign Secretary James Balfour issued the Balfour Declaration giving British support for the Jewish people to have their own state in Palestine. On December 9 of the same year, British Christian Zionist, General Edmund Allenby liberated Jerusalem from the Turks without firing a shot. On December 11, as a show of humility, he entered Jerusalem by foot. For the first time since the Crusades, Jerusalem was in the hands of a Christian power. At the San-Remo Conference held on April 25, 1920, the newly formed League of Nations assigned Britain the mandate to administer Palestine and create a national home for the Jews.

On November 29, 1947, the newly formed United Nations approved a resolution to partition the land between the Jews and the Arabs. On May 14, 1948, thirty years of British rule and the mandate of Palestine ended. The United Nations also declared that Jerusalem would be an international city.

Jordan (1948-1967)

When Israel declared itself a state, five Arab neighbors attacked her. While Israel survived the attacks, Jordan took control of the Old City of Jerusalem. Jordan issued decrees severely limiting Christian worship and access to Christian holy sites. Jews were forbidden to enter the city. The Jordanian army destroyed all 58 synagogues in the Old City and desecrated the Jewish cemetery on the Mount of Olives. It is interesting to note that during these 19 years when Jordan controlled the Old City, they did not think it important to proclaim an Arab state or Jerusalem as an Arab capital.

Israel (1967-?)

In May 1967, the Egyptian ruler, Abdul Nasser, provoked Israel to war by blocking the Israeli port of Eilat. He also ordered the United Nations peace-keeping force to leave the Sinai while massing his army to attack Israel. Left with no choice, the Israelis retaliated with a pre-emptive strike on June 5, 1967. The Israeli air force destroyed 450 Egyptian planes and took control of the Sinai. They also defeated the Syrians and took control of the Golan Heights. But most important, they defeated the Jordanian army and liberated the Old City of Jerusalem. This was all done in six days. Jews had control of the Temple Mount for the first time since the Romans destroyed the Temple in AD 70.

Israel will have to fight to hold Jerusalem, as the Bible predicts a time when all the nations will attack Israel in the last great battle for God's hometown. (Some obvious Scriptures that speak of this final unleashing of anti-Semitic-anti-Zionism are Isaiah 66:18; Micah 4:12; Zephaniah 3:8; Zechariah 14:2). The entire chapter of Zechariah 14 describes this battle and states that the Lord Himself will fight on behalf of Israel. While there will be much suffering and destruction, the God of Israel will defeat the enemies of Israel and make "Jerusalem a praise in the earth" (Isaiah 62:7).

The New Jerusalem

The Lord says He will return to Zion and dwell in the midst of Jerusalem, at which time Jerusalem will be called "The Throne of the Lord" (Jeremiah 3:17, Psalm 132:13-14; Zechariah 1:16-17; 8:3). This is referring to New Jerusalem, which is the destiny and eternal home of all believers.

New Jerusalem is presently in heaven. But Revelation 21-22 tells us that it will come down from heaven to earth as the home of the redeemed. Our eternal hometown seems to be in the shape of a cube. It is 1500 miles high, 1500 miles wide and 1500 miles long (Revelation 21:15-16).

A city this size would be 2,250,000 square miles. To give you and idea of how big this is, the city would be 15,000 times bigger than London, 40 times bigger than England, 20 times bigger than New Zealand, 10 times bigger than Germany and France combined, and over one half the land size of the continental U. S. It would stretch from Maine to Florida, and from the Atlantic Ocean to the Midwest.

John tells us that the city is pure gold, like clear glass (Revelation 21:18). The glory of God is the light of the city that permeates throughout the city (Revelation 21:23). The city is designed to transmit the light of God's glory without hindrance so that all the inhabitants will see His glory wherever they are in the city. The street of the city is pure gold, like transparent glass, to reflect the glory of God everywhere (Revelation 21:21).

The wall around the city is 216 feet high—a cubit is approximately 18 inches, or 1.5 feet, and the wall is 144 cubits high (Revelation 21:17). It is made of jasper (Revelation 21:18). The wall has 12 gates each attended by an angel, and the names of the 12 tribes of Israel are written on the gates (Revelation 21:12-13). Each gate is made of a single pearl (Revelation 21:21).

The wall of the city has 12 foundations made of precious stones. Each foundation is named after one of the 12 apostles of Jesus who brought the gospel of the kingdom to the nations. The foundations are designed to reflect the glory of God in a dazzling spectrum of brilliant colors (Revelation 21:19-20).

Because the glory of God illuminates it, and the Lamb is the light of the city, there is no need for the sun (Revelation 21:23). There is no temple in the New Jerusalem because the Lord's presence is the temple. Because all evil and sin is purged from the earth, the gates of the city will always remain open and there is no night (Revelation 21:25). The nations shall walk in the light of God's brightness and bring their glory and honor to Him in our hometown on the earth (Revelation 21:24).

There is a pure river of life, clear as crystal, flowing from the throne of God. Trees of life grow on both sides of the river bearing 12 kinds of fruit, yielding a new crop each month. The leaves of trees are for the health of the nations.

John concludes his description of our hometown with these words:

> And there shall be no more curse, but the throne of God and of the Lamb shall be in it, and His servants shall serve Him. They shall see His face, and His name shall be on their foreheads. There shall be no night there: They need no lamp

> nor light of the sun, for the Lord God gives them light. And they shall reign forever and ever (Revelation 22:3-5).

John adds these words of hope and comfort for all residence of this indescribable city:

> And I heard a voice from heaven saying, "Behold, the tabernacle of God is with men, and He will dwell with them, and they shall be His people. God Himself will be with them and be their God. And God will wipe away every tear from their eyes; there shall be nor more death, nor sorrow, nor crying. There shall be no more pain, for the former things have passed away" (Revelation 21:3-4).

CHAPTER 7

The Arabs in Prophecy

As believers in the one true God, we understand that God has given us a revelation of himself in the Bible. One of the things that He reveals about himself is that He transcends time and space. This means that all of time and space is contained within God. In other words, He is outside of time. This is what the Bible means when it says that God is the Alpha and Omega, the Beginning and the End, the One who was and is and is to come.

Because God lives outside of time, He knows from the beginning of time what events would transpire in the history of time and how history would conclude at the end of time. In His sovereign power and all knowledge of time, God has both caused and allowed some events to happen in time, while not causing or allowing other events that could happen but won't happen, because God did not or will not allow them to happen.

In a Scripture worth repeating, God informs us, "Remember the former things of old, For I am God, and there is no other; I am God, and there is none like Me, declaring the end from beginning, and from ancient times things that are not yet done, saying, 'My counsel shall stand, and I will do all My pleasure'"(Isaiah 46:9-10).

The prophet says that God declares the end from the beginning. His declaration is His counsel and His pleasure. God has written this down in the Bible so we can know what He has declared. We can know His counsel and pleasure. By reading God's word we, who live in time, can know what the One who lives outside of time has declared. We call this Bible prophecy.

Now since the Almighty has chosen the Jewish people as the ethnic group through whom He would bring redemption to the world, most Bible prophecy is about Israel and the Jewish people. But since the Jewish people live with all the rest of us, there is also Bible prophecy about the Messiah, about the nations, about the Kingdom of God, about the grafted in Gentiles we refer to as the Church, about the Arabs, about the end times, about the coming of the Lord, about the Messianic Kingdom, the New Heaven and the New Earth, and whatever else God thought important for us to know about.

In this chapter we want to learn what God has said about the Arabs in Bible prophecy.

The Beginning of the Nations

We learn in Genesis 9-10 that Noah had three sons: Shem, Ham, and Japheth. Noah prophesied to Shem that God would be identified to the world with Shem. One of Shem's grandsons was named Eber. Eber had two sons: Peleg and Joktan. The name Peleg means division because it was during his life that God confused the people's languages and divided them. Based on the names of their descendants and the geographic locations where they lived, we understand that Peleg was the ancestor of the Hebrews and Joktan the ancestor of the Arabs (Genesis 10:22-32; 1 Chronicles 1). Joktan has thirteen sons who fathered the people later known as the Arabs. God's prophecy to Shem would be fulfilled through the line of Peleg.

Peleg and his brother Joktan would give birth to different ethnic groups, the Hebrews and the Arabs. Their descendants would fight each other for supremacy in a sibling rivalry that would eventually engulf the whole world, even to our times today.

The history of this family feud can be traced through the Book of Genesis. The conflict began around the year 1848 BC. The God of the Bible promised that He would give one of the descendants of Peleg a land that would be his forever. God would make this man's descendants a great nation and from his descendants would come One who would bless the whole world. This descendant was a man named Abram, later known as Abraham.

The Call of Abraham

> Now the LORD had said to Abram: "Get out of your country, from your family and from our father's house, to a land that I will show you. I will make you a great nation; I will bless you and make your name great; and you shall be a blessing. I will bless those who bless you, and I will curse him who curses you; and in you all the families of the earth shall be blessed" (Genesis 12:1-3).

God also promised to give Abraham a son as heir to the promises. When God spoke these things to Abraham he was 85 years of age, and his wife, Sarah, who was elderly, had never conceived.

It was the custom in those times for a barren wife to offer her bondwoman or slave to her husband in the hope that she might bear them a son. The child would be considered the offspring of the barren woman. Sarah, despairing of her age and infertility, did just that. She offered Abraham her Egyptian slave Hagar. Abraham accepted Sarah's proposal, and soon Hagar conceived and gave birth to a son. She called the child, Ishmael.

In what seems to be a prophecy about his character, Ishmael is described in Genesis as a "wild man" whose hand would be against every man. The Angel of the LORD says to Hagar:

> Behold, you are with child, and you shall bear a son. You shall call his name Ishmael, because the LORD has heard your affliction. He shall be a wild man; his hand shall be against every man, and every man's hand against him. And he shall dwell in the presence of all his brethren (Genesis 16:11-12).

In Genesis 17:20, God promised to bless Ishmael, but in Genesis 17:18-21 He made it clear to Abraham that the heir to His promises would be a son born to Sarah. God supernaturally enabled Sarah to conceive, and she gave birth to a son, whom she named, Isaac.

God made what the Bible describes as an everlasting covenant with Abraham. In this covenant, God promised to give the land of Canaan to Isaac (not Ishmael) and his descendants. God said to Abraham:

> "And I will establish My covenant between Me and you and your descendants after you in their generations, for an

> everlasting covenant, to be God to you and your descendants after you. Also I give to you and your descendants after you the land in which you are a stranger, all the land of Canaan, as an everlasting possession; and I will be their God" (Genesis 17:7-9).
>
> And Abraham said to God, "Oh, that Ishmael might life before You!" Then God said: "No, Sarah your wife shall bear you a son, and you shall call his name Isaac; and I will establish My covenant with him for an everlasting covenant, and with his descendants after him.
>
> "And as for Ishmael, I have heard you. Behold, I will bless him, and will make him fruitful, and will multiply him exceedingly. He shall beget twelve princes, and I will make him a great nation. But My covenant I will establish with Isaac, whom Sarah shall bear to you at this set time next year" (Genesis 17:18-21).

This covenant promise God made to Abraham is still in effect today. The conflict between these two sons of Abraham and their descendants continues to our times. The world sees it every day on the evening news.

The Mother of all Family Feuds

Isaac married a woman chosen by his father. Her name was Rebecca. Rebecca was a descendant of Shem through his son Aram (Genesis 10:22). By marrying Rebecca, Isaac is staying within the promised covenant family of the God of Shem. Rebecca bore twin sons named Jacob and Esau. According to the Bible, God selected Jacob as heir to the promises He had made to Abraham and Isaac. God later renamed Jacob. He called him Israel.

When Jacob was at Bethel, not far from Jerusalem, he dreamed about a ladder reaching from earth to heaven. The LORD stood above the ladder and spoke to Jacob the promised blessing He had given to Abraham and Isaac.

> And behold, the LORD stood above it and said: "I am the LORD God of Abraham your father and the God of Isaac; the land on which you lie I will give to you and your descendants.

> Also your descendants shall be as the dust of the earth; you shall spread abroad to the west and the east, to the north and the south, and in you and in your seed all the families of the earth shall be blessed. Behold, I am with you and will keep you wherever you go, and will bring you back to this land; for I will not leave you until I have done what I have spoken to you" (Genesis 28:13-15).

Isaac married a woman of Shem chosen by Abraham, but Hagar, an Egyptian, chose an Egyptian woman for Ishmael to marry. This means that Ishmael married a woman who was outside the covenant family and line of Shem. This was a tragic mistake that would create the conflict between the Arabs and the Hebrews/Jews. Ishmael's wife bore him twelve sons. Ishmael and his family moved to the geographic region that was populated by the descendants of Joktan. This is modern day Jordan and Saudi Arabia.

> So God was with the lad [Ishmael]; and he grew and dwelt in the wilderness, and became an archer. He dwelt in the Wilderness of Paran; and his mother took a wife for him from the land of Egypt (Genesis 21:20-21).

> (They dwelt from Havilah as far as Shur, which is east of Egypt as you go toward Assyria.) He [Ishmael] died in the presence of his brethren (Genesis 25:18).

Jacob's twin brother, Esau, had a number of wives, one of which was the daughter of his uncle, Ishmael. Later, Esau took his family and settled near Ishmael and his family.

> So Esau went to Ishmael and took Mahalath the daughter of Ishmael, Abraham's son, the sister of Nebajoth, to be his wife in addition to the wives he had (Genesis 28:9).

> Then Esau took his wives, his sons, his daughters, and all the persons of his household, his cattle and all his animals, and all his goods which he had gained in the land of Canaan, and went to a country away from the presence of his brother Jacob. ... So Esau dwelt in Mount Seir. Esau is Edom. And

> this is the genealogy of Esau the father of the Edomites in Mount Seir (Genesis 36:6, 8-9).

Isaac spoke a blessing over his son Esau. However, he also prophesied that there would be envy, jealous, and fighting between the descendants of Esau (Arabs) and Jacob (Jews) throughout history: "By your sword you shall live, and you shall serve your brother" (Genesis 27:40). This prophecy has certainly been fulfilled in the past, and we see how it is being fulfilled in our world today.

Abraham's nephew, Lot, was the man God rescued from the destruction of Sodom. He was a man of weak character. You recall the story of God delivering him from Sodom. Because his daughters believed their father was the only man left alive, they got him drunk and had intercourse with him in order to conceive and have children. In their mind, this was the only way the human race would survive. Lot had sons by his own daughters. Their children settled in land east of the Jordan River, as well as other parts of the modern Arab world.

Lot's firstborn son was called Moab. He was the father of the Moabites. The second son was named Ben-Ammi. He was the father of the Ammonites (Genesis 19). The Moabites and Ammonites became bitter enemies of the descendants of the children of Israel. Ancient Moab and Ammon are located in the geographic area known today as Jordan. Ironically, two female descendants of Lot married into the covenant family line and were ancestors of the Messiah.

We all know the story of Ruth, the Moabitess, marrying Boaz. Through their union, Ruth became the great-grandmother of King David, and eventually the Messiah came from her bloodline. Another descendant of Lot was a woman named Naamah. She was an Ammonite who was one of many wives of King Solomon. Through their union, Naamah gave birth to a son, Rehoboam who is listed as an ancestor of the Messiah (1 Kings 14:21, 31; Matthew 1:7).

Abraham took another wife after Sarah died. Her name was Keturah. She bore Abraham six sons. Not wanting to make family matters worse, Abraham gave gifts to these sons and sent them away to live near Esau.

> But Abraham gave gifts to the sons of the concubines which Abraham had; and while he was still living he sent them eastward, away from Isaac his son, to the country of the east (Genesis 25:6).

Origins of the Arab People

The purpose of learning this information is to understand the difference between Abraham's descendants through Isaac and his descendants through Ishmael. Isaac and his descendants married within the covenant family bloodline, stayed in the covenant land, and worshipped the covenant God. The descendants of Abraham through Ishmael, Esau, Lot, and Keturah, married outside the covenant family bloodline, moved outside of the covenant land, and worshipped deities other than the covenant God. They mixed with the descendants of Joktan and became the fathers of the modern Arab people.

These forefathers of the Arab people rejected the covenant of God and covenant blessings. They despised their spiritual inheritance. This was epitomized when Esau traded his priestly birthright to Jacob. That attitude was passed down to his descendants. One family line stayed true to the covenant God while the other did not. The Ishmael family line worshipped false gods, which is why the hatred between the Jews and the Arab Muslims is theological in nature. This is why the God of the Bible is not the same as the god of the Koran. The God of Abraham, Isaac, and Jacob is not the same as the god of Ishmael, Esau, and Lot. The God of Moses and Jesus is not the god of Mohammed.

An Ancient Hatred

We learn from the Hebrew Bible and from secular history that animosity has continued between the two groups of family members from generation to generation. We learn also that because of their thirst for blood, God would judge the Arabs by giving them a history of violence and bloodshed, which finds its religious expression in Islam.

The prophecy is found in Ezekiel and reads as follows:

> "Because you have had an ancient hatred, and have shed the blood of the children of Israel by the power of the sword

> at the time of their calamity, when their iniquity came to an end, therefore, as I live," says the Lord God, "I will prepare you for blood, and blood shall pursue you; since you have not hated blood, therefore blood shall pursue you" (Ezekiel 35:5-6).

Because of their hatred of God's chosen people, the LORD pronounces curses on the descendants of Ammon, Moab, and Edom, as well as other nations in the Middle East that seek to destroy the people of God. (See Ezekiel 25-30).

Psalm 83 clearly reveals the attitudes and purposes of the descendants of Ishmael and Esau (the Arab countries of our time) regarding their cousins, the present day descendants of Isaac and Jacob, who now make up the modern nation of Israel.

This alarming Scripture sounds strangely familiar to the covenant made by Muslim terrorists groups and the Arab nations concerning Israel. It is a prophecy of the end times regarding the Arabs. It reads as follows:

> Come, and let us cut them [Israel] off from being a nation, that the name of Israel may be remembered no more. For they have consulted together with one consent; they form a confederacy against You [God] (Psalm 83:4-5)
>
> They have said, "Let us take for ourselves the pastures of God for a possession" (Psalm 83:12).

House of Peace—House of War

The Arab-Israeli conflict is more than a family feud. It is a religious or spiritual battle. Islam cannot accept Israel as a neighbor because of the Islamic concept of relations between neighbors.

According to Islam, all nations controlled by Muslims are part of the "House of Peace." All others make up the "House of War." Once Islam controls a territory, Muslims consider it to be a permanent part of the Islamic world. If the territory is lost to Islam, Allah has been diminished and the territory must be retaken.

Because the land of Israel was, at various times, ruled by Islam, Muslims feel that it must be recovered for the glory of Allah. This is the heart of the Arab-Israeli-Palestinian conflict.

In Islamic tradition, Allah's kingdom will not be established until the Muslims kill all the Jews and/or subject them to Muslim rule. The same attitude exists towards Christianity. This is why Muslim religious leaders incite mobs to murder in the name of Allah. When a Muslim kills a Jew, he shouts, "Allah Akbhar," meaning, "Allah is Great."

The Islamic "holy war" is aimed at Christians as well as Jews. They also shout, "Today we kill the Saturday people (Jews), and tomorrow we kill the Sunday people (Christians)." This means that they first intend to destroy Israel and then establish Islamic rule over all that nations that have a Judeo-Christian history.

Western Naiveté

Failing to understand the nature of this conflict, the Western media paints Israel as unreasonable and stubborn. If only Israel would relinquish the West Bank to the PLO for the purpose of establishing a Palestinian state, there would be peace. It is terrible naïve for leaders of the West to think that such a concession would ever enable Israel and the Arab Islamic nations to settle their differences. The Arab nations will never agree to a real peace as long as one inch of territory is in Israeli hands and out of the control of Allah.

The PLO, Hamas, and the other terrorist organizations have stated that the establishment of a Palestinian state is just the first stage of its plan to destroy Israel and recapture the territory for the glory of Allah. In fact, a Palestinian state has already been established. It is called Jordan.

When the newly formed League of Nations agreed to the establishment of the State of Israel, they divided the land into two states. The land west of the Jordan River was allocated to Jews and called Israel. The land east of the Jordan River was allocated to Arabs and called Transjordan, meaning, across the Jordan River. In April 1949 the name of this Palestinian Arab country was changed to Jordan.

Westerners, unaware of the religious and political history of these nations, are easily confused. However, Israel and the Arab Islamic countries understand perfectly what is at stake.

Who are the Palestinians?

According to the PLO (and the Western media), the Palestinian Arabs have lived in Palestine from time immemorial. They were forced to flee by the Jewish Zionists when the modern State of Israel was created. The facts, however, tell a different story.

Although the Jews were scattered among the nations by the Romans in AD 70, there has always been a Jewish presence in the land. The dream of the Jews in exile since their dispersion has been, "Next year in Jerusalem."

It was the Romans who renamed the land of Israel after the Jews' ancient enemy, the Philistines. They called it Palestine.

Islamic rulers did dominate the Middle East for centuries. For the most part, however, these rulers were non-Arabs. During Arab domination of Palestine, the land was a neglected wasteland. It was sparsely populated by Jews and Arab peasants.

Jerusalem was never considered a sacred city to Islam and is not even mentioned in the Koran. There has never been a sovereign, independent, Palestinian or Arab state in the holy land from the time the Jews were dispersed until they declared their statehood in 1948. God has kept the land in trust all these centuries for the Jews.

The revival of modern Jewish life began in the late 1800's with the arrival of refugees from Russia and Eastern Europe. Later waves of immigration brought more Jews to their ancient land.

When the Jews arrived, they were greeted by a harsh land that had been neglected for centuries by its non-Arab Islamic rulers. Yet, these zealous Jewish immigrants were determined to redeem the soil.

As the Jews worked the land, it slowly began to prosper. The result was that thousands of Arab and non-Arab peasants from the neighboring countries came to Palestine as migrant farm workers. These migrant farm workers are the Palestinians. They have not been in the land from time immemorial. They are late arrivals who came to the land after it began to prosper as a result of Jewish blood and toil.

When Israel became a nation, 800,000 Jewish refugees fled from the Arab states to Israel. They were all assimilated in the new state and became citizens of Israel.

The growing Arab Palestinian population was not as fortunate. Arab leaders from the neighboring countries declared war against Israel. They then instructed the Arab Palestinians to flee the Jewish state until the Jews were annihilated. They could then return and possess the land. The Jews encouraged the Arabs to stay.

The hated Jewish Zionists did not force the Arab Palestinians to leave. Their own leaders forced them to leave the land. This created the Palestinian refugee problem. The Arab countries have refused to assimilate the Palestinians and care for their needs. Instead, they continue to use them as political pawns in their struggle against Israel.

Promising them glory, money, and paradise with seventy-two beautiful virgins, the PLO and other terrorist organizations have no problem recruiting young Palestinians to fight the Zionists enemy. These terrorist organizations are well financed by the moderate Saudi Arabian rulers, as well and Syria, Iran, and Iraq. They have all the money they need for weapons, and are very skillful at manipulating the Western media to brainwash the American public to believe their propaganda.

The United Nations Relief and Works Agency, (UNRWA) was given the responsibility of administering the refugee problem. The money given by the UNRWA to assist the refugees comes primarily from the American taxpayer. This is a big business with thousands profiting from it. No one connected with it has any interest in ending the plight of the displaced Palestinians. The real legitimate right of the Palestinians is to be assimilated by the Arab countries from which they initially came. It's a tragic situation for those in the refugee camps.

Judgments and Blessings

God loves the Arab people, but He has a different plan for them than He does for the Jews. God will bless the Arabs if they will submit to His plans and purposes. He will judge them if they do not. Edom, another name for Esau, is a symbolic term representing the Arab people as a whole, much like the word Israel represents the Jewish people as whole.

Joel 3:19-20 reads:

> Egypt shall be a desolation, and Edom a desolate wilderness, because of violence against the people of Judah, for they have shed innocent blood in their land. But Judah shall abide forever, and Jerusalem from generation to generation.

Isaiah 17:1 says, "The burden against Damascus. 'Behold Damascus will cease from being a city, and it will become a ruinous heap.'"

There are many of prophecies in the Bible where God pronounces judgments on the Arabs for their hatred of the Jewish people and the God of Israel.

In His own time, God will end this conflict by giving Israel a great victory over her Arab neighbors. This will show the nations of the world and the Arab people that the God of Abraham, Isaac, and Jacob, and not the god of Allah, is the one true God.

> In that day the LORD will defend the inhabitants of Jerusalem; the one who is feeble among them in that day shall be like David, and the house of David shall be like God, like the Angel of the LORD before them. It shall be in that day that I will seek to destroy all the nations that come against Jerusalem (Zechariah 12:8-9).

Micah 4:11-12 adds:

> Now also many nations have gathered against you, who say, "Let her be defiled, and let our eye look upon Zion." But they do not know the thoughts of the LORD, nor do they understand His counsel; for He will gather them like sheaves to the threshing floor.

Ezekiel 39 lists Arab countries as part of the end-time Russian confederation attacking Israel. God will destroy these armies and give Israel a great victory. Israel's victory will cause a great spiritual awakening within the Arab nations as they realize the terrible deception of Islam. Many will turn to the one true God of Israel as the prophet Isaiah predicted.

> In that day Israel will be one of three with Egypt and Assyria—a blessing in the midst of the land, whom the LORD

> of hosts shall bless, saying, "Blessed is Egypt My people, and Assyria the work of My hand, and Israel My inheritance" (Isaiah 19:24-25).

This is an incredible prophecy of hope for Egypt and Assyria. But even then, God warns the Egyptians that if they do not go to Jerusalem to celebrate the Feast of Tabernacles, God will withhold rain as judgment (Zechariah 14).

Israel's victory will also cause many Jewish people to return to their biblical heritage and seek the God of their ancestors as Joel states:

> So you shall know that I am the LORD your God, dwelling in Zion My holy mountain. Then Jerusalem shall be holy, and no aliens shall ever pass through her again (Joel 3:17).

> I will set My glory among the nations; all the nations shall see My judgment which I have executed, and My hand which I have laid on them. So the house of Israel shall know that I am the LORD their God from that day forward.... And I will not hide My face from them anymore; for I shall have poured out My Spirit on the house of Israel, says the Lord GOD (Ezekiel 39:21-22, 29).

Furthermore, the nations of the world will realize there is a God in heaven who is active in world affairs and is moving forward the course of human history according to His own plans and purposes for mankind.

> Thus I will magnify Myself and sanctify Myself, and I will be known in the eyes of many nations. Then they shall know that I am the LORD (Ezekiel 38:23).

CHAPTER 8

Gog and Magog in Prophecy

In the Hebrew Bible, we learn about the tragic fall of Jerusalem and the destruction of the first Temple by Nebuchadnezzar and the Babylonians. One of the people exiled to Babylon at that time was the prophet Ezekiel.

Ezekiel was born around the year 627 BC. He was from a priestly family, had a wife who died, and was called by God as a prophet to his people when they were in exile as judgment for their sins. He was deported along with King Jehoiachin in the second siege of Jerusalem about 597 BC. He lived in Babylon at the River Chebar near Nippur, which was an important shipping canal between the Euphrates and Tigris Rivers. This area was a major settlement of his fellow Jews taken into captivity. Ezekiel was not the only prophet in Babylon at this time. Daniel had been deported about nine years earlier, and Ezekiel mentions him three times.

While in captivity, Ezekiel received visions from God beginning around the year 593 BC. God required Ezekiel to act out his visions as a sign to his people. God instructed Ezekiel to do strange things, such as shutting himself up in his home, binding himself, laying on his right and left sides for 430 days, disgracing himself by shaving his head and beard, and other things. By acting out his prophecies, Ezekiel was a human prophetic word-picture to the people. Ezekiel spoke to the people about their own judgment for sin (Chapters 4-24), God's judgment on the nations (Chapters 25-32), and prophesied about God's future blessings for His covenant people (Chapters 33-48).

Through his prophetic visions, Ezekiel tells us some very important information about end-time events. Among his prophecies, he tells about the ingathering of the Jewish people, at which time God will not only restore them to their land but also pour out His Spirit upon them.

In chapter 36, Ezekiel gives a wonderful prophecy where he foretells the time when the Jewish people would multiply on the mountains of Israel and the mountains of Israel will once again be fruitful and its ruins be rebuilt and its cities inhabited. It is interesting that the mountains of Israel comprise the area today that the world calls the "West Bank." In the Bible, this land area is called Judea and Samaria.

Ezekiel's most famous prophecy is his vision about the "Valley of Dry Bones," which we find in chapter 37. Most Bible scholars and historians understand Ezekiel 37 as a prophecy of the Jews surviving the Holocaust and coming alive in the land of Israel. The context of chapters 36-37 is clearly the ingathering of the Jewish people to their land at the end of our era, prior to the coming of Messiah as David's Greater Son..

In chapters 40-48, Ezekiel gives the details for a rebuilt Temple in Jerusalem. Most Bible scholars believe this to be the Temple that will be in place during the Messianic age known as the Millennium. This is the golden age the prophets spoke of when Messiah would rule the nations from Jerusalem and peace would finally come to the world. As a priest, Ezekiel was certainly qualified to describe this Temple.

Between the ingathering of the Jews described in chapters 36-37 and the rebuilding of the Temple described in chapter 40-48, Ezekiel prophesies about a war that will take place. He says that Israel will be attacked by a confederation of nations led by a powerful leader whom he calls Gog and Magog.

In Jewish thinking, Gog and Magog are generic names referring to Gentile powers that represent the enemies of Israel. It is most interesting that when President Bush went to Israel in 2008 religious leaders in Israel gave him a letter in which they greeted him with the words, "President Bush, Chief Prince of Gog and Magog." Now since Ezekiel's prophesies recorded in chapters 36-37 have literally happened, at least in part, during our times, doesn't it seem logical to believe that the prophecy that follows in chapters 38-39 would also literally happen? I believe the answer is yes! As we study this prophecy and relate it to current world events, it seems that we may be the generation to see it happen. We mentioned this subject in chapter two as one of the prophetic signs. Russia is once against flexing her military muscle. She has rearmed and resumed bomber flights to England and America. I believe it very important that we renew our concerns about Russia and learn about "Gog and Magog" in prophecy. It seems that a great conflict is certain in the near future.

Why We Believe This is Russia (Ezekiel 38:1-9)

Let's begin our study by reading Ezekiel 38:1-9.

Now the word of the LORD came to me saying, "Son of Man, set your face against Gog, of the land of Magog, the prince of Rosh, Meshech and Tubal, and prophecy against him, and say, 'Thus says the Lord GOD: "Behold, I am against you, O Gog, the prince of Rosh, Meshech and Tubal. I will turn you around, put hooks into your jaws, and lead you out, with all your army, horses and horsemen, all splendidly clothed, a great company with bucklers and shields, all of them handling swords. Persia, Ethiopia, and Libya are with them, all of them with shield and helmet; Gomer and all its troops; the house of Togarmah from the far north and all its troops—many people are with you."

"""Prepare yourself and be ready, you and all your companies that are gathered about you; and be a guard for them. After many days you will be visited. In the latter years you will come into the land of those brought back from the sword and gathered from many people on the mountains of Israel, which had long been desolate; they were brought out of the nations, and now all of them dwell safely. You will ascend, coming like a storm, covering the land like a cloud, you and all your troops and many peoples with you."""

Ezekiel refers to this invader as "Gog, of the land of Magog, the prince of Rosh, Meshech, and Tubal" (Ezekiel 38:2). Modern western scholars identify Gog and Magog as modern day Russia. There are four reasons that would lead us to believe that Gog and Magog represent a Russian/Turkey/Iranian led confederation.

1. The Names

The first reason has to do with the names that Ezekiel mentions. The word "Gog" is not considered to be the name of a country or a person, but more of a title, such as Pharaoh or Caesar or Czar or Emperor. So Gog is the leader of this confederacy comprised of Rosh, Meshech, and Tubal. Ezekiel says that Gog dwells in the land of Magog. So our first challenge is to try to identify who Ezekiel is talking about.

In Genesis 10 we find a list of the ancient nations of the world as they descended from Noah's sons. The key names in Ezekiel's prophecy are mentioned in Genesis 10:2-3 which reads, "The sons of Japheth were Gomer, Magog, Madai, Javan, Tubal, Meshech, and Tiras. The sons of Gomer were Ashkenaz, Riphath, and Togarmah."

Historians and Bible scholars have traced the migration of Gomer, Magog, Tubal, Meshech, and Togarmah and discovered that they and their descendants settled in the geographic area of the Caucasus Mountains north of the Caspian and Black Sea. In ancient times these people were called Scythians. This is modern day Russia. Their names have changed over the centuries, but the geographic location is the same.

Ezekiel gives further details and says that Gog, in the land of Magog, is the "prince [or leader] of Rosh." In the study of how ancient words came into modern language, Rosh is understood to be an early form of the word from which we get the word "Russia." We understand Ezekiel to be prophesying that Gog will be the leader of a Russian confederation that will invade Israel.

2. The Time of the Invasion

The second reason we are led to believe this is a Russian-led invasion is the time when Ezekiel says these nations will be in power. Ezekiel says that God will make this confederation powerful and pull her into the Middle East in the "latter years" (Ezekiel 38:8). He further emphasizes the timing of this event by saying it will be in the "latter days" (Ezekiel 38:16).

These are key phrases in the Bible that refer to the end-times when Israel has been reborn as a nation prior to the Second Coming of Messiah Jesus. Thus this confederation would have to be in power at this point in time and history. Russia, as we know her today, did not even exist before the twentieth century. Even though Russia is weak at this point, she still has nuclear weapons, and supplies weapons to her client states in the Middle East, primarily Iran and Syria. Furthermore, with its vast oil and gas reserves, Russia is prospering and positioning itself to challenge America in a return to the "Cold War." Only this time, the war is going to go from cold to hot.

Also as we study the many wars of ancient Israel, none of them seem to fit the description of Ezekiel 38-39. It is a prophecy for the last days of the Times of the Gentiles. While it is clear this battle will take place in the end-times, Bible scholars are not certain as to the precise timing of this invasion in relationship to the seven-year tribulation period and the Battle of Armageddon.

3. Relationship to the State of Israel

The third reason we believe this is a Russian-led Coalition is in regard to its relationship to the state of Israel. Ezekiel says this will not take place until the Jews are back in their own land.

The first Jewish revolt against the Romans was in AD 70. Titus destroyed Jerusalem, burned down the Temple, put the Jews on merchant ships, and sold them as slaves throughout the Roman Empire. In the second Jewish revolt in AD 132-135, the Emperor Hadrian did the same thing. He banished the Jews from Jerusalem, renamed Jerusalem Aelia Capitolina, and renamed Israel Palestine. He also put the Jews on merchant ships and sold them as slaves throughout the Roman Empire. For the next 2000 years the Jews lived in exile but prayed each Passover, "Next Year in Jerusalem."

The State of Israel did not come into existence until 1948. The people were brought back from all the nations and the sword of Nazi Germany. The Israelis liberated the mountains of Israel and their ancient capital in 1967. Therefore Ezekiel's prophecy could not have been fulfilled before the modern rebirth of the State of Israel.

Ironically, Russia's development of nuclear weapons at the end of WWII has coincided with the establishment and growth of the state of Israel. In certainly seems that God is preparing them to make a military venture into the Middle East to fulfill this ancient prophecy.

4. Geographic Location of the Invaders

The fourth reason we are led to believe this is a Russian-led coalition is its geographic location. Three times Ezekiel identifies this invading coalition as being to the north of Israel (Ezekiel 38:6, 15; 39:2). Furthermore, the phrase Ezekiel uses pointing to the north means the extreme north. Russia is the only power to the extreme north of Israel. And when we look on a map, we see that Moscow is perfectly due north of Jerusalem.

Russia's Allies (38:5-6)

Ezekiel identifies a number of allies that will be a part of the Russian confederation. These are Persia, Ethiopia, Libya, Gomer, and Togarmah. Persia is the easiest to identify. Bible students remember that Persia was one of the great empires of the Bible. Cyrus the Great was the Persian king who allowed the Jews in his empire to return to Israel during the days of Ezra. We believe the Persians were descendants of Shem through his son Elam. The modern state of Persia was created by the British out of the Ottoman Turkish Empire. In 1935 Persia changed its name to Iran.

Iran is a non-Arab Shiite Muslim country. The leader of Iran is a devout believer in the coming of the Mahdi, the twelfth Imam, who is like the Muslim messiah. Followers of the Mahdi believe he will appear in the latter days during times of great chaos. The teachings are similar to beliefs in Judaism and Christian about the coming of Messiah. This is because Mohammed incorporated (stole) some of the teachings of Judaism and Christianity into his new religion of Islam. He got some of his facts confused, however, which is why the Koran often contradicts the Bible.

While Jews and Christians try to make the world a better place, the followers of the Mahdi believe it is their responsibility to cause chaos in the world so that the Mahdi will appear. When the Mahdi appears, the Arab countries will submit to his authority and become part of his army that will destroy Israel, kill or convert the Christians, and establish Islam as the world religion. In their theology, Jesus will also return as a great Shiite Moslem prophet who will assist the Mahdi in destroying the infidels—Jews and Christians.

Iraq also has a Shiite majority, which is why Iran is sponsoring their terrorism against the American presence in Iraq. Iran wants to take control of Iraq so they can cause even more chaos. We have all heard the Iranian leader call for the destruction of Israel. Iran also wants to take control of the oil of Saudi Arabia, which is Sunni Muslim.

Russia has been providing nuclear scientist and weapons technology and weapons to Iran for years. There are hundreds of Russian technical advisors in Iran. This is why Russia is against any kind of sanctions towards Iran. While Ezekiel was looking about 2600 years into the future, we don't have to be a prophet to see Russia leading a confederation to destroy Israel that includes Iran. The whole world is watching as Iran continues to develop its nuclear capabilities. Surely the stage is set for Gog to fulfill its end-time destiny with Persia.

Other allies Ezekiel mentions are Cush, translated as Ethiopia and Sudan, and Put, translated as Libya, and Gomer and Togarmah. Of all of these names, Cush and Put are the most difficult to identify, but they most surely represent Muslim dominated countries. It is estimated that by the year 2015, more than half of the soldiers in the Russian army will be Moslem.

Gomer and Togarmah would be located in modern day Turkey. Turkey is presently a secular non-Arab, pro-western, Islamic country. The radical Islamists, however, are fighting for control of Turkey so they can turn it away from the west and turn it into an Islamic ruled nation. The longer that NATO rejects Turkey as a member nation, the more likelihood Turkey will shift toward Islam. This would be a huge prophetic sign regarding the soon fulfillment of the prophecy of Ezekiel

Psalm 83 adds a whole list of Arab countries that will also form a confederacy against Israel. There are 22 countries in the Arab League of Nations. They could also be included in this Russian-led confederacy. There is no question that Syria and Lebanon, and possibly Jordan, will be part of this confederacy. Russian has been supplying Syria with technical support and is building a shipyard with Syria to facilitate Russian naval vessels in the area. Israel will use her nuclear weapons and destroy Damascus as Isaiah prophesied in Isaiah 17:1, which says that Damascus will "cease from being a city, and it will be a ruinous heap."

While we can only speculate on the exact time and details, the overall prophetic word is clear—Russia will lead a confederacy of nations to attack Israel in the latter days. Since there is no record of this in history, and it can only happen after Israel is reborn, it seems we are seeing the events rapidly unfolding that could bring about this war in our time, perhaps in the next few years.

Reason for the Invasion (38:10-12)

Now what is the reason for this invasion? Why would Russia invade Israel and risk American retaliation and WW III? First of all, Ezekiel tells us that it is God who actually puts these ideas in Russia's thinking (verse 4). God causes Russia to have this thought because He is going to use this invasion to destroy Russia, which will cause Israel and the nations to glorify His name.

Now have we read any other place in the Bible where God stirred up heathen leaders and nations to do His will? There are many examples of this in the Bible. One that comes to mind is the story of the Exodus. That account says that God hardened Pharaoh's heart in order to judge him and the gods of Egypt, so that they would know that the God of the Hebrews was the one true God. It is the situation here with Gog of the land of Magog.

In Revelation 17:17, we are told that God Almighty puts it in the hearts of the national leaders to give their allegiance to the false Messiah to fulfill Bible prophecy. God is sovereign and controls the flow of world history to bring His word to pass.

There is only one true God. He is not the generic god of the world. He is not the same as Allah or any other god. Nor is He the Greco-Roman god of Western Christianity. He is the God of Israel, the God of Abraham, Isaac, and Jacob. And He has a name. The Jewish people so revere God's name they won't even pronounce it.

So they call Him Hashem, which means, "the Name." Hashem will glorify Himself as the one true God. So when we see this Russian-led invasion, we should not be fearful, but rejoice knowing that our God is fulfilling His word, and His name will be sanctified in Israel and among the nations.

Russia and her allies do not know, of course, that it is the Almighty who is stirring them up to invade Israel. They think they have planned this invasion themselves out of their own brilliance.

Ezekiel 38:10-12 explains their reasoning:

> Thus says the Lord GOD: "On that day it shall come to pass that thoughts will arise in your mind, and you will make an evil plan: You will say, 'I will go up against a land of unwalled villages; I will go to a peaceful people, who dwell safely, all of the dwelling without walls, and having neither bars nor gates'—to take plunder and to take booty, to stretch out your hand against the waste places that are again inhabited, and against a people gathered from the nations, who have acquired livestock and goods, who dwell in the midst of the land."

The Russian leaders and their confederacy make a plan to invade Israel in order to take plunder and booty or spoil. There is no question that Russia desires to invade to control the Middle East. And defeating Israel will be the main pretense for the invasion.

Ezekiel adds that this is a time when Israel has unwalled villages and is living in peace. So it is a time when Israel is enjoying peace and prosperity. This is certainly not the situation in Israel today. Sometime in the future, there will be a false peace treaty, which the Israeli government will accept. But it is a trap set by the Almighty to bring Russia and her allies into this war against Israel.

Even though Israelis are suffering economically because of the wars and a stifling bureaucracy, compared to the rest of the Middle East Israel is prospering in every area of society, including medical research, agricultural, business, and scientific and hi-tech computer technology. Because it is the time to favor Zion, Israel will continue to prosper in spite of more war, trouble, and tribulation coming their way.

For example, the average per capita income in Israel is $25,000 compared to the average income in the Arab League of $5,000. Israel spends $110 per person each year on scientific research as opposed to the Arab world spending $2 per person each year on scientific research. Israel's productivity per worker is growing at a rate of 5.2 per cent compared to a negative growth rate in Arab countries. The state of Israel has six universities ranked among the best in the world. The entire Arab League does not have a single university ranked in the top four hundred. Only one out of two Arab women can read or write.

Israel has more engineers and scientists per capita than any other country with 145 engineers or scientists for every 10,000 Israelis. Israel ranks among the top seven countries worldwide for patents per capita. Six million Israelis buy 12 million books every year, making Israel one of the highest consumers of books in the world. In contrast, Spain, for example, translates more books in a year than the entire Arab world has in the past thousand years. Israel has the highest number of university degrees per capita in the world, while the Arab world has the lowest.

How the West Responds

Now let's see how the West responds to this attack upon Israel. Ezekiel explains in 38:13, "Sheba, Dedan, the merchants of Tarshish, and all their young lions will say to you, 'Have you come to take plunder? Have you gathered your army to take booty, to carry away silver and gold, to take away livestock and goods, to take great plunder?'"

We have a problem identifying Sheba and Dedan because there are two sets of them listed in the Bible. In Genesis 10:7 there is Sheba and Dedan listed as the grandsons of Ham and the sons of Cush, who settled in the Northeast African countries of Sudan, Ethiopia, and Somalia. It is interesting that Ethiopia and Somalia are fighting each other because of a radical Islamic threat in Somalia. This area is the horn of Africa, which is a strategic location for the control of the sea lanes.

In Genesis 25:3, there is a Sheba and Dedan listed at the grandsons of Abraham and Keturah. These descendants settled in Southwest

Arabia, which today would be in Saudi Arabia. While the Saudis hate Israel and the Jews, they also have a great fear of Iran. Even if they were part of this confederation, they would certainly protest an Iranian attempt to take over their oil fields, and they would certainly appeal to the U.S. for help.

Ezekiel also mentions the merchants of Tarshish and all their young lions. Tarshish was a Phoenician city located to the far west of Israel, perhaps in Spain. We cannot specifically identify it today but it seems to represent the Western nations. Perhaps the West will make a diplomatic protest but not confront the Russians militarily in the Middle East. The reason for this could very well be due to the fact that Iran could have nuclear weapons that it will use to keep America from attacking them. This is why Iran is working so hard to develop their nuclear weapons. Furthermore, Ezekiel says that God, not America, will defeat the Russians.

Unless Israel and America destroy Iran's nuclear facilities, Iran will soon have a nuclear weapon. This will be a disaster for the world because Egypt and Saudi Arabia will also want nuclear weapons to defend themselves against Iran. A nuclear Middle East will certainly pave the way for Armageddon.

In the next few verses (38:14-17), Ezekiel gives specific information regarding the geographic location of the invading force, the timing of this invasion, and the reason for the invasion. Ezekiel says that in the latter days the invading army will come from the far north when Israel is said to "dwell safely," so that the God of Israel will be acknowledged and feared when He destroys the invading force.

> Therefore, son of man, prophecy and say to Gog, "Thus says the LORD God: 'On that day when My people Israel dwell safely, will you not know it? Then you will come from your place out of the far north, you and many peoples with you, all of them riding on horses, a great company and a mighty army. You will come up against My people Israel like a cloud, to cover the land. It will be in the latter days that I will bring you against My land, so that the nations may know Me, when I am hallowed in you, O Gog, before their eyes.' Thus says the Lord GOD: 'Are you he of whom I have spoken in former days by My servants the prophets of Israel,

> who prophesied for years in those days that I would bring you against them?'"

The Outcome of the Invasion (Ezekiel 38:18;39:20)

Now what is the outcome of the invasion? Ezekiel says that God himself will destroy this invading force. Ezekiel predicts that God will fight against the invaders with great earthquakes, plagues, torrential rains, hailstorms, fire, and brimstone. As in biblical accounts, God will also confuse the enemy and cause them to fight among themselves, as we see Hamas and the Palestinian Authority doing today in Gaza.

Ezekiel 38:18-23 reads:

> "And it will come to pass at the same time, when Gog comes against the land of Israel," says the Lord GOD, "that My fury will show in My face. For in My jealousy and in the fire of My wrath I have spoken: 'Surely in that day there shall be a great earthquake in the land of Israel, so that the fish of the sea, the birds of the heavens, the beasts of the field, all creeping things that creep on the earth, and all men who are on the face of the earth shall shake at My presence. The mountains shall be thrown down, the steep places shall fall, and every wall shall fall to the ground.' I will call for a sword against Gog throughout all My mountains," says the Lord God, "Every man's sword will be against his brother. And I will bring him to judgment with pestilence and bloodshed; I will rain down on him, on his troops, and on many peoples who are with him, flooding rain, great hailstones, fire, and brimstone. Thus I will magnify Myself and sanctify Myself, and I will be known in the eyes of many nations. Then they shall know that I am the LORD."

Ezekiel informs us that God himself will destroy Russia and her coalition army. They will fall in the Mountains of Israel and in the plains, which may mean they will never reach Jerusalem. The destruction will be so bad that it will take seven years to burn all the destroyed weapons. Ezekiel 39:1-10 states:

> And you, son of man, prophecy against Gog, and say, "Thus says the LORD God: "Behold, I am against you, O

> Gog, the Prince of Rosh, Meshech, and Tubal; and I will turn you around and lead you on, bringing you up from the far north, and bring you against the mountains of Israel. Then I will knock the bow out of your left hand, and cause the arrows to fall out of your right hand. You shall fall upon the mountains of Israel, you and all your troops and all the peoples who are with you; I will give you to birds of prey of every sort and to the beasts of the field to be devoured. You shall fall on the open field; for I have spoken," says the LORD God. "And I will send fire on Magog and on those who live in security in the coastlands. Then they shall know that I am the LORD. So I will make My holy name known in the midst of My people Israel, and I will not let them profane My holy name anymore. Then the nations shall know that I am the LORD, the Holy One in Israel. Surely it is coming, and it shall be done," says the LORD God. "This is the day of which I have spoken.
>
> "Then those who dwell in the cities of Israel will go out and set on fire and burn the weapons, both the shields and bucklers, the bows and arrows, the javelins and spears; and they will make fires with them for seven years. They will not take wood from the field nor cut down any from the forests, because they will make fires with the weapons; and they will plunder those who plundered them, and pillaged those who pillaged them," says the LORD God.

Ezekiel says in 39:6, that God will send fire on Magog and on those who live in security in the coastlands. Then they shall know that I am the LORD. This could very well be a nuclear exchange between America and Russia on their respective homelands as opposed to the Middle East, because neither wants to destroy the oil fields. Or it could be God bringing the devastation himself thorough the forces of nature. We don't know. But this is a warning that the Western nations are not going to sit around watching television and avoid God's judgment, however He may choose to administer it.

The destruction of Gog and his armies will be so great that it will take seven months just to bury the dead. The Israeli government will actually need to employ people for seven months to clean up the mess. Ezekiel says in 39:11-16:

> "It will come to pass in that day that I will give Gog a burial place there in Israel, the valley of those who pass by east of the sea; and it will obstruct travelers, because there they will bury Gog and all his multitude. Therefore they will call it the Valley of Hamon Gog [The Multitude of Gog]. For seven months the house of Israel will be burying them, in order to cleanse the land. Indeed all the people of the land will be burying, and they will gain renown for it on the day that I am glorified," says the LORD God.
>
> "They will set apart men regularly employed, with the help of a search party, to pass through the land and bury those bodies remaining on the ground, in order to cleanse it. At the end of seven months they will make a search. The search party will pass through the land; and when anyone sees a man's bone, he shall set up a marker by it, till the buriers have buried it in the Valley of Hamon Gog. The name of the city will also be Hamonah. Thus they shall cleanse the land."

To assist the human cleanup crew, the vultures and wild animals will feast on the dead bodies in their important role of cleansing the land, as we learn in 39:17-20:

> And as for you, son of man, thus says the Lord GOD, "Speak to every sort of bird and to every beast of the field: 'Assemble yourselves and come; gather together from all sides to My sacrificial meal which I am sacrificing for you, a great sacrificial meal on the mountains of Israel, that you may eat flesh and drink blood. You shall eat the flesh of the mighty, drink the blood of the princes of the earth, of rams and lambs, of goats and bulls, all of them fatlings of Bashan. You shall eat fat till you are full, and drink blood till you are drunk, at My sacrificial meal which I am sacrificing for you. You shall be filled at My table with horses and riders, with mighty men and with all the men of war,' says the LORD God."

The Result of the War (Ezekiel 39:21-29)

The result of this war is that God will glorify His name and the people of Israel will once again turn their hearts towards God. The nations also will recognize that the God of the Bible is the one true God. Israel will experience a great spiritual awakening and repentance. Profession Christians who are lukewarm will finally become serious in their commitment to the Lord. The nations will fear God, and those who worship false gods will acknowledge the God of Israel. While God will be acknowledged, not all will actually turn to Him in repentance until Messiah comes in power and glory to establish the Kingdom of God on the earth.

Ezekiel 21:30 says it plainly:

> "I will set My glory among the nations; all the nations shall see My judgment which I have executed, and My hand which I have laid on them. So the house of Israel shall know that I am the LORD their God from that day forward. The Gentiles shall know that the house of Israel went into captivity for their iniquity; because they were unfaithful to Me, therefore I hid My face from them. I gave them into the hands of their enemies, and they all fell by the sword. According to their uncleanness and according to their transgressions I have dealt with them, and hidden My face from them."
>
> Therefore thus says the LORD God: "Now I will bring back the captives of Jacob, and have mercy on the whole house of Israel, and I will be jealous for My holy name—after they have borne their shame, and all their unfaithfulness in which they were unfaithful to Me, when they dwelt safely in their own land and no one made them afraid. When I have brought them back from the peoples and gathered them out of their enemies' lands, and I am hallowed in them in the sight of many nations, then they shall know that I am the LORD their God, who sent them into captivity among the nations, but also brought them back to their land, and left none of them captive any longer. And I will not hide My face from them anymore; for I shall have poured out My Spirit on the house of Israel," says the LORD God.

With Russia defeated, there will be a power vacuum in Europe that could prepare the way for the rise of the false Messiah, who will establish himself as the world's savior. At that time, the nations will pledge their allegiance to the one known as the Anti-Christ. After a brief period of a false peace, the Antichrist and his false prophet will reveal their true demonic nature. He will persecute God's people and lead the world into a period of great tribulation. The Jews speak of this time as the "birth pangs of the Messiah."

The Lord revealed these times to the prophet Daniel who wrote these words of victory:

> At that time Michael shall stand up, the great prince who stands watch over the sons of your people; and there shall be a time of trouble, such as never was since there was a nation, even to that time. And at that time your people shall be delivered, every one who is found written in the book.
>
> And many of those who sleep in the dust of the earth shall awake, some to everlasting life, some to shame and everlasting contempt. Those who are wise shall shine like the brightness of the firmament, and those who turn many to righteousness like the stars forever and ever. But you, Daniel, shut up the words, and seal the book until the time of the end; many shall run to and fro, and knowledge shall increase (Daniel 12:1-4).

The Jewish apostle Paul confirmed this wonderful word of encouragement to believers:

> For God did not appoint us to wrath, but to obtain salvation through our Lord Jesus Christ, who died for us, that whether we wake or sleep, we should live together with Him. Therefore comfort each other and edify one another, just as you also are doing (1 Thessalonians 5:9-11).

CHAPTER 9

America in Prophecy

Since the title of this chapter is "America in Bible Prophecy," it might be appropriate for me to begin with these familiar words, "my fellow Americans." Most Bible-believing Christians believe that we are living in what the Bible calls the end times. If this is a correct understanding of the times in which we live, we would think that America would have a very significant role in Bible prophecy.

America has been the greatest nation in the history of nations. Our military, economy, form of government, wealth and prosperity, with all its faults, has far exceeded all the other nations in our world today. With our freedom and prosperity, America has been the envy of every nation. Will the U.S. continue to be a great nation or is America in the twilight of its destiny? Since America has turned away from its Judeo-Christian heritage, can we truly expect the Almighty to continue to bless us with His favor? While politicians continue to speak soothing words many believe the U.S. has lost its way and has already entered into its period of decline. Will the U.S. go the way of Britain or will a financial collapse and military attack lead to anarchy and a dictatorship?

When we read the prophecies in the Bible about the end times, we don't find any mention of America. There is not even the vaguest reference to America in the Bible. As American people who love our country and enjoy the good life of living here, thinking that it will go on forever, we should ponder why America is not mentioned in all the great end-time events. What could this mean? The question that should concern all of is: "Where is America in Bible prophecy."

It is a sobering question. Before trying to answer that question, it is important to point out what is not America in Bible prophecy.

What is Not America

Merchants of Tarshish

Probably the most popular verse in the Bible that people try to identify with America is found in Ezekiel 38. This chapter, along with chapter 39, describes the invasion of Israel by Gog and Magog. This invader is said to be "from the far north country" (Ezekiel 39:2). It invades Israel in the latter years after the Jewish people have been gathered back to their ancient land. From the description Ezekiel gives of this invader, and the timing in history, it certainly seems like he is talking about Russia.

Now the interesting verse in question is Ezekiel 38:13 which reads:

> Sheba, Dedan, the merchants of Tarshish, and all their young lions will say to you, "Have you come to take plunder? Have you gathered your army to take booty, to carry away silver and gold, to take away livestock and goods, to take great plunder?"

When Russia invades Israel, some group of people named Sheba, Dedan, and the merchants of Tarshish and all their young lions protest. Sheba and Dedan were located in modern Saudi Arabia. While we are not sure about the location of Tarshish, Bible scholars believe it to have been located in the Western Mediterranean, possibly in Spain. Regardless of the exact location, to the Hebrews, Tarshish was as far West as one could go. When God called Jonah to go East to Nineveh, he went as far West in the opposite direction he could go. He went to Tarshish. Over time, the ships of Tarshish became a way the Hebrews referred to any large merchant ships from the West that were built like the ships of Tarshish.

It is unwise to associate biblical names and places with modern countries when we are not certain as to the identity of the original names. Because Great Britain once ruled the seas, some interpreters have identified the ships of Tarshish with Great Britain. Furthermore, they have identified the young lions as the English speaking nations like the U.S. that were founded by British immigrants. So the teaching goes that the young lions in Ezekiel 38:13 is speaking about nations like the U.S., Australia, and New Zealand. I think we can all agree that is quite a stretch in biblical interpretation.

The Great Eagle

A second Bible reference that people try to identify with the U.S. is in the 12th chapter of the book of Revelation. The context of the story is during the period of tribulation when God provides a way for the Jews to escape into the desert, where He protects them from Satan during the last 3-1/2 years of tribulation. Revelation 12:14 reads, "But the woman was given two wings of a great eagle, that she might fly into the wilderness to her place, where she is nourished for a time and times and half a time, from the presence on the serpent."

Over the years, people have told me that because the eagle is the national symbol of America, this Scripture refers to a U.S. airlift of Jews to safety. Once again, this is a nice thought, and I wish it was true. But this Scripture really has nothing to do with America. The Bible is its own best commentary. If you want to know what this means, you see if you can find a similar statement elsewhere in the Bible. And we can.

The book of Exodus tells about God delivering the Hebrews from Egypt. In Exodus 19:4, the LORD says, "You have seen what I did to the Egyptians, and how I bore you on eagles' wings and brought you to Myself."

Of course there was no America during the time of the Exodus. But God was there, and it was God, and God alone, who brought the Hebrews out of Egypt. So it will be during the tribulation period. The record is clear in the book of Revelation that God will supernaturally provide for and protect the Jewish people from Satan and the Antichrist, the false Messiah.

Babylon

A third reference in the Bible that people identify with America is also in the book of Revelation. Revelation 18 talks about the fall of

"Babylon the great." Now when you read the description of Babylon, it certainly sounds a lot like America, particularly our economic prosperity. While the American dollar is no longer considered "the unrivaled currency of choice," the economies of the world still depend on a prosperous American middle class buying foreign made products. Even as the U.S. financial power continues to decline, the nations of the world are interconnected in a globalist economic union. We can certainly understand that when God judges America and our economy crumbles, the world will go down with us. The economies of all the nations will collapse.

Once again, we have to read what the Bible actually says before we can interpret what we think it means. In Revelation 18, Babylon the great is called a city, not a country. In Revelation 17:9, 18 we are told that this city sits on seven hills. In the first century context of the book of Revelation, the only city this could possibly be is Rome, which was known as the city of seven hills. Because of the persecution by Rome, the apostle John, writing from Patmos, could not actually identify Rome. So he used the code word early believers had for Rome, which was Babylon. Peter also called Rome by the name Babylon in 1 Peter 5:13. So we have a confirmation from Peter as well as history that Babylon was the code word for Rome. It seems that Revelation 18 is referring to a last great, Gentile, world empire, probably a United States of Europe that is greatly influenced by Rome.

General Prophecies

So if these references are not speaking about America, where is America in Bible prophecy? Why is it that our nation, the greatest of all nations in all of history, and the last Gentile superpower is not mentioned specifically in Bible prophecy?

There are two types of prophecies in the Bible regarding nations. One is general prophecies and the other is specific prophecies. America is included in the general prophecies about the nations.

For example, Jesus said in Luke 21:24b, "And Jerusalem will be trampled by Gentiles until the times of the Gentiles are fulfilled." While America is home to about 6 million Jews, America is a Gentile nation. All Gentile nations, including America, have a life-cycle. They have a beginning, a time of development, and an end to their prominence. While only the Almighty knows the details, when Israel liberated Jerusalem in 1967, many believe this signaled the end of the times of the Gentiles. America, it seems, is the last sovereign, superpower, Gentile nation. Those of us who live in America love our country and are grateful to be Americans. But we must understand that as a Gentile nation, our days of glory and prominence will, in God's time, come to an end.

There are numerous Scriptures that speak of the end of the nations. When the Bible says that God will destroy the nations, He doesn't mean that all the people will die but that the empire will die. But at the end of days, the former empires of the nations will worship the one true God and His kingdom will rule over the earth. Here are a few Scriptures.

Zephaniah 3:8-9, "My determination is to gather the nations to My assembly of kingdoms, to pour on them My indignation, all My fierce anger; all the earth shall be devoured with the fire of My jealousy. For then I will restore to the peoples a pure language, that they all may call on the name of the LORD, to serve Him with one accord."

Haggai 2:21b-22a, "I will shake heaven and earth. I will overthrow the throne of kingdoms; I will destroy the strength of the Gentile kingdoms."

Zechariah 12:2-3, 9, "Behold, I will make Jerusalem a cup of drunkenness [trembling or threshold] to all the surrounding peoples, when they lay siege against Judah and Jerusalem. And it shall happen in that day that I will make Jerusalem a very heavy stone for all peoples; all who would heave it away will surely be cut in pieces, though all nations of the earth are gathered against it. … It shall be in that day that I will seek to destroy all the nations that come against Jerusalem."

Isaiah 34:1-2, "Come near, you nations, to hear; and heed, you people! Let the earth hear, and all that is in it. The world and all things that come forth from it. For the indignation of the LORD is against all nations."

Joel 3:1-2, "For behold, in those days and at that time, when I bring back the captives of Judah and Jerusalem, I will also gather all nations, and bring them down to the Valley of Jehoshaphat; and I will enter into judgment with them there on account of My people, My heritage Israel, whom they have scattered among the nations; they have also divided up My land."

Zechariah 8:22, "Yes, many peoples and strong nations shall come to seek the LORD of hosts in Jerusalem, and to pray before the LORD."

Isaiah 2:1-4, "Now it shall come to pass in the latter days that the mountain of the LORD's house shall be established on the top of the mountains, and shall be exalted above the hills; and all nations shall flow to it. Many people shall come and say, 'Come, and let us go up to the mountain of the LORD, to the house of the God of Jacob; He will teach us His ways, and we shall walk in His paths.' For out of Zion shall go forth the law, and the word of the LORD from Jerusalem. He shall judge between the nations, and rebuke many people; they shall beat their swords into plowshares, and their spears into pruning hooks; nation shall not lift up sword against nation, neither shall they learn war anymore."

Now with all these wonderful promises in the Bible, we can rejoice knowing that God's people have a glorious future and all the nations, including America, will one day acknowledge the rule of God.

Even though America and the empires of all the Gentile nations will come to an end, there is one country that has a promise from God that it will last forever. That everlasting nation is Israel.

Jeremiah 46:28 reads, "Do not fear, O Jacob My servant, says the LORD, for I am with you; for I will make a complete end of all the nations to which I have driven you, but I will not make a complete end of you. I will rightly correct you, for I will not leave you wholly unpunished." (Jeremiah 30:11 says essentially the same thing.)

Specific Prophecies—Why Not?

After all of this encouragement, we are still left with the question, "Why is America not specifically mentioned in Bible prophecy?" The best our human minds can understand is because America will not be the superpower that it is today. What are some reasons that could cause the demise of America as the leading superpower of the world? I want to briefly mention six possibilities.

1. Economic Collapse

The first is economic collapse. When God judges a nation, He does so by judging the gods of the nations. This is what He did in Egypt with the 10 plagues. The plagues were against the gods of Egypt. So, if want to know how God would judge America, all we have to do is list the gods of America. And at the very top of the list is money.

Greed will destroy America. With all of our great wealth as a nation, America has become a debtor nation. That means we owe more than we have. Every individual household understands this. If you keep spending more than you are earning, eventually you go bankrupt. Our government debt is in the trillions of dollars. The rate of our debt increases in billions of dollars every day. Regardless of our government's fiscal and monetary policies, we will never be able to balance the books. And sooner or later, probably sooner, the economy will collapse under the weight of our debt. Without our economic power, America will no longer be a superpower. This could happen overnight as we have seen in the weakening of the dollar and the panic on Wall Street.

American believers must learn to put their trust in God and not His blessings, as we learn in Proverbs:

> Trust in the LORD with all your heart, and lean not on you own understanding; in all your ways acknowledge Him, and He shall direct your paths. Do not be wise in your own eyes; fear the LORD and depart from evil. It will be health to your flesh, and strength to your bones. Honor the LORD with your possessions, and with the firstfruits of all your increase; so your barns will be filled with plenty, and your vats will overflow with new wine (Proverbs 3:5-10).

In 1787, about the time America established its independence from Britain, a Scottish history professor at the University of Edinburgh named Alexander Tyler made the following comment about the fall of Athens.

> A democracy is always temporary in nature; it simply cannot exist as a permanent form of government. A democracy will continue to exist up until the time that voters di[illegible] they can vote themselves generous gifts from th[illegible]

treasury. From that moment on, the majority always vote for the candidates who promise the most benefits from the public treasury, with the result that every democracy will finally collapse due to loose fiscal policy, which is always followed by a dictatorship.

The average age of the world's greatest civilizations from the beginning of history, has been about 200 years. During those 200 years, those nations always progressed through the following sequence:

1. From bondage to spiritual faith
2. From spiritual faith to great courage
3. From courage to liberty
4. From liberty to abundance
5. From abundance to complacency
6. From complacency to apathy
7. From apathy to dependence
8. From dependence back into bondage

2. Moral Collapse

We can learn from the above list that economic collapse usually follows moral collapse. The great empires of history collapsed because of moral failures as much as they did from military defeats. America is the only nation in the history of nations that was birthed out of religious persecution and with a Judeo-Christian worldview and vision. It is this Judeo-Christian heritage that has made America great. The Pilgrims and Puritans came to America because of religious persecution by the State Church of England. They were godly people who saw themselves establishing a colony in the new world that would be a shining light of God's redemption to the nations.

William Bradford, who was appointed governor of the new colony wrote:

> Thus out of small beginnings, greater things have grown by His hand who made all things out of nothing, and gives being to all things that are; and as one small candle may light a thousand, so the light enkindled here has shown to many, yes,

> in a sense our whole nation; let the glorious name of Jehovah have all the praise.

Cotton Mather wrote that William Bradford, was a person of study as well as action. He had mastered Latin and Greek but he studied Hebrew most of all. Because it was said:

> He would see with his own eyes the ancient oracles of God in their native beauty. He was also well skilled in history, antiquity, philosophy, and theology. But the crown of all was his holy, prayerful, watchful, and fruitful walk with God.

There were 102 passengers aboard the Mayflower who survived the 65 days at sea. They arrived at Plymouth, Massachusetts. on December 26, 1620. Of this number, more than half died in the first winter due to sickness and inadequate provisions. Less than 50 pilgrims were left, and of that number, some were too old to have children. Only a small handful of godly women gave birth to America. Miraculously, thirty years later, in 1650, thirty of the original colonists were still alive and they had 160 living descendants.

Before they landed, the pilgrims wrote the Mayflower Compact, which was the covenant they would live by as a colony. It was modeled on the covenant of their separatist congregation in England. It reads in part:

> In the name of God, Amen. We, whose names are underwritten, the Loyal Subjects of our dread Sovereign Lord, King James, by the Grace of God, of England, France and Ireland, King, defender of the faith, etc. Having undertaken for the Glory of God, and Advancement of the Christian Faith, and the Honour of our King and Country, a voyage to plant the first colony in the northern parts of Virginia; do by these presents, solemnly and mutually in the Presence of God and one of another, covenant and combine ourselves together into a civil Body Politick, for our better Ordering and Preservation, and Furtherance of the Ends aforesaid; And by Virtue hereof to enact, constitute, and frame, such just and equal Laws, Ordinances, Acts, Constitutions, and Offices, from time to time, as shall be thought most meet and convenient for the

> General good of the Colony; unto which we promise all due submission and obedience.

Whether one likes or not, the record is clear that the Pilgrims intended to establish America as a Christian democratic republic. Unfortunately, America has lost its vision.

[I urge you to get a copy of the book entitled, *Of Plymouth Plantation* published by Vision Forum, San Antonio, TX. It is the journal of William Bradford on the history of the Plymouth Settlement from 1608-1650. When you read this book you will understand clearly that America was founded for the purpose of religious freedom, to spread the Judeo-Christian message to the world, and that only the hand of God enabled the pilgrims to survive.]

Ivy League Colleges

Most Americans are unaware that our earliest Ivy League Colleges and Universities were established for the primary purpose of educating Christian ministers, and many of its earliest graduates were ministers In 1636, Harvard was the first college established in the new colonies. It was named for its benefactor John Harvard. A brochure published in 1643 stated the purpose of Harvard, "To advance learning and perpetuate it to posterity; dreading to leave an illiterate ministry to the churches."

Other Ivy League colleges were founded for the same purpose—to educate the Christian ministers. Because of their love for the Bible and their connection to their Jewish roots, Hebrew was a required course at the colleges.

Our founding fathers stated that the American democracy was designed for a moral people and would not survive unless there was a moral consensus of the citizens. While America has been a great light to the nations, our light has gone out because we have abandoned our Judeo-Christian heritage. Born as a self-governing people under the moral laws of God, America now despises the laws of God and flaunts its immorality in the face of God, as if it dares Him to judge it.

God is already judging America. One of the ways God judges a people or a nation is by giving them up to their own lusts. As we see America becoming more and more depraved, mocking all that is holy and good, this is a sign that God has given America up to its own lusts.

The Apostle Paul wrote of our times in 2 Timothy 3:1-5:

> But know this, that in the last days perilous times will come: for men will be lovers of themselves, lovers of money, boasters, proud, blasphemers, disobedient to parents, unthankful, unholy, unloving, unforgiving, slanderers, without self-control, brutal, despisers of good, traitors, headstrong, haughty, lovers of pleasure rather than lovers of God, having a form of godliness but denying its power. And from such people turn away!

3. Natural Disasters

A third danger that could weaken America is natural disasters. Is it just the fact that we have the Weather Channel telling us more than we used to know, or is America experiencing more natural disasters than anytime in its history?

It seems that nature itself is attacking America. There are so many natural disasters in America that one of the most popular TV programs is called, "Storm Stories." We see the devastation caused by fires in the West, tornadoes in the Midwest and hurricanes and flooding in the East. And we are all wondering when the "Big One" is going to hit California.

The whole world witnessed the destruction of New Orleans, which was caused by Katrina. Regardless of the positive spin from the politicians, New Orleans will never fully recover from Katrina. It was a disaster on a scale of biblical proportions.

Shortly after Katrina, hurricane Rita headed towards Houston. Once again, the whole world saw a million people from the Houston area desperately trying to get out of town, only to be stuck on Interstate 45 with no gas, food, or water, overheated cars, crying babies, etc. Rita was a huge hurricane heading directly to Houston. For a while, it looked as if Interstate 45, which was supposed to be the escape route, was going to be coffin as it was right in the path of Rita.

It was only the mercy of God that Rita, ever so slowly, had landfall just to the East of Houston. Houston was only a prayer away from untold destruction and the loss of thousands of lives. Houston is the fourth largest city in America. Could our country have survived if Houston had experienced the same destruction as New Orleans?

Someone from New Orleans asked a well-known Christian leader the question, "Where was God? Why did He allow this to happen?" The person gave a very wise answer and said, "We expelled God from school. We voted Him out of our political system. We dismissed Him from our judicial system. We told Him we didn't want Him involved in our lives. And we wonder why He allowed this? God doesn't go where He is not wanted."

God is a God of mercy but He doesn't go where He is not wanted. When God is not wanted, He lifts His cloud of protection over a country or a people and leaves them to themselves. When disasters happen, we blame Him rather than ourselves.

4. Internal Enemies

The fourth possible reason for America being weakened is attacks within our borders from our enemies. It was said in the past that America had two great friends, the Atlantic and the Pacific. The point of the comment was that America was protected from the wars in Europe by the oceans. That was before jet planes and suicide bombers.

The call of jihad from the radical Muslim terrorists is, "Today we fight the Saturday people, tomorrow the Sunday people." Israel is the Saturday people who, for over 50 years, has experienced the front-line wrath of jihad because Israel lives in the neighborhood of the jihadists. On 9/11, the Sunday people (Christian America) was awakened to what Israel experiences everyday. The events of 9/11 changed the world and changed our way of life as Americans.

No matter how much we try, it is impossible to secure our borders. There is no way we can keep out terrorists that are coming into our country. And once in our country, it is relatively easy for determined terrorists to weaken America through more bombings. America is a big, easy, target. It is not a matter of *if* we will have another 9/11, but *when*.

There are many terrorist sleeper cells already in America. They are not sleeping but are waiting for the right moment for them to activate their cell and cause great destruction. Included in this vast Islamic terrorist network are groups that are becoming household names, such as Hamas, Al-Qaeda, Islamic Jihad, Hezbollah, Muslim Brotherhood, and others. They all have the same goal, which is the destruction of the Great Satan, America. Some of these groups probably already have nuclear suitcase bombs that have been smuggled into the country. They only need to detonate one of these to bring America as we know it to an end.

In addition to this violent threat, there is also the internal threat of radical Muslims who have infiltrated every aspect of our society: military, political organizations, prison systems, homeland security, universities, business, etc. They operate under the cover of our political correctness, freedom of speech, generous laws of charitable giving, etc., to use their influence at the highest levels of American society. For more information on this subject, you can order my book online, entitled, *Radical Islam's War Against Israel, Christianity and the West.*

5. External Enemies

A fifth event that could dramatically weaken America is an external attack from our enemies. Whenever possible, nations at war attack their enemies when they are perceived to be weak internally. If America has an economic collapse as well as a continued moral collapse, our enemies will see this as an opportunity to attack us. But who would dare attack America—seeing that were are far superior militarily to any nation?

Of course the answer is Russia. When the Soviet Union collapsed, Russia had thousands of nuclear weapons. While they have been weak economically and militarily, they are recovering, and their nuclear weapons make them a threat to our survival. Neither Russian nor Vladimir Putin are our friends. Russia is actively working to arm Syria and Iran with nuclear weapons because they want to reassert their influence in the Middle-East. Russian nuclear scientist and technicians are in Iran and Syria, assisting them in developing weapons of mass destruction, with Israel as the target. Russia is building a modern naval base in Syria to be operated by Russians. They have attack submarines deployed off our East and West coasts, armed with enough fire power to destroy America.

Most Bible scholars believe Ezekiel 38-39 is talking about Russia as the nation that will lead an end-time confederation against Israel. At the time of that invasion, Ezekiel 39:6, says that fire will fall on those dwelling safely in the coastlands. When Russia attacks Israel, it is certain they will also attack America. The Ezekiel 39:6 Scripture could be referring to America.

6. The *Aliyah* of Jews from America

The last happening in America that would certainly weaken us is the *aliyah* of Jews from America. *Aliyah* is the Hebrew word for "going up." In the biblical context, it means "going up to the Land."

Ezekiel spoke about the latter years of history when God would bring the Jews back to their land and pour out His Spirit on them. It will be the last great move of God prior to the coming of Messiah. Ezekiel 39:28-29 reads:

> "Then they shall know that I am the LORD their God, who sent them into captivity among the nations, but also brought them back to their land, and left none of them captive any longer. And I will not hide My face from them anymore; for I shall have poured out My spirit on the house of Israel," says the LORD God.

God says He will leave none of them behind. His plan is to gather all the Jews back to their ancient land. Because of violent anti-Semitism in Europe, Jews in France, and soon Great Britain, will make *aliyah* for Israel. America will soon be the last nation with a large population of Jews. God is now calling them back to their land. Even though it is only a small number of several thousand, it is growing every year. The number will get larger and larger until it becomes a massive exodus of the Jewish people from America. This will certainly cause America to lose its place as the economic power of the world. It is not a matter of if this will happen, but when. It is already happening.

Somewhere in the process, Israel will fulfill her destiny as the head of nations. It is at this time that Zechariah 8:22-23 will be fulfilled:

> Yes, many peoples and strong nations shall come to seek the LORD of hosts in Jerusalem, and to pray before the LORD. Thus says the LORD of hosts: "In those days ten men from every language of the nations shall grasp the sleeve [tzitzit] of a Jewish man, saying, 'Let us go with you, for we have heard that God is with you.'"

In Conclusion

What can American believers do to bless our country? A Scripture we all know well:

> If My people who are called by My name will humble themselves, and pray and seek My face, and turn from their wicked ways, then I will hear from heaven, and will forgive their sin and heal their land (2 Chronicles 7:14).

If God-fearing Americans will renew themselves, America will be renewed. While America has been the greatest nation in the history of nations, it cannot compare to the kingdom of God. The kingdom of God is at hand. It is ready to be revealed. For the people of God, our best days are the latter days. We are living in the latter days. We can expect to soon see and experience the greatest outpouring of the Spirit of God the world has ever seen. This is not a time for believers to live in fear; it is a time to live in faith.

We turn again to the words of the Jewish apostle Paul:

> But thanks be to God, who gives us the victory through our Lord Jesus Christ. Therefore, my beloved brethren, be steadfast, immovable, always abounding in the work of the Lord, knowing that your labor is not in vain in the Lord (1 Corinthians 15:57-58).

George Washington—Bulletproof Warrior

I want to conclude this chapter on America in Prophecy with two accounts from the life of George Washington. George Washington was truly a remarkable man that God clearly raised up and used to give birth to the new nation and lead America in its early days. George

Washington reverenced God and often prayed for divine guidance and strength. Any honest historian must acknowledge that the Almighty really did guide, strengthen, and protect him. For without God's intervention, the new nation would have never been born.

The following first-hand report of God's providential protection of George Washington was included in many school textbooks until the 1930s. Few Americans know this story that Washington often told. He said it helped shape his character and made him realize his divine destiny. The story is the account of an event that took place on July 9, 1755 in the French and Indian War.

> The American Indian chief looked scornfully at the soldiers on the field before him. How foolish it was to fight as they did, forming their perfect battle lines out in the open, standing shoulder to shoulder in their bright red uniforms. The British soldiers—trained for European warfare—did not break rank, even when braves fired at them from under the safe cover of the forest. The slaughter at the Monongahela River continued for two hours. By then 1,000 of the 1,459 British soldiers were killed or wounded, while only 30 of the French and Indian warriors firing at them were injured. Not only were the soldiers foolish, but their officers were just as bad. Riding on horseback, fully exposed above the men on the ground, they made perfect targets. One by one, the chief's marksmen shot the mounted British officers until only one remained.
>
> "Quick, let your aim be certain and he dies," the chief commanded. The warriors—a mix of Ottawa, Huron, and Chippewa tribesmen—level their rifles at the last officer on horseback. Round after round was aimed at this one man. Twice the officer's horse was shot out from under him. Twice he grabbed a horse left idle when a fellow officer had been shot down. Ten, twelve, thirteen rounds were fired by the sharpshooters. Still, the officer remained unhurt.
>
> The native warriors stared at him in disbelief. Their rifles seldom missed their mark. The chief suddenly realized that a mighty power must be shielding this man. "Stop firing!" he commanded. "This one is under the special protection of the

Great Spirit." A brave standing nearby added, "I had seventeen clear shots at him and still could not bring him to the ground. This man was not born to be killed by a bullet."

As the firing slowed, the lieutenant colonel gathered the remaining troops and led the retreat to safety. That evening, as the last of the wounded were being cared for, the officer noticed an odd tear in his coat. It was a bullet hole! He rolled up his sleeve and looked at his arm directly under the hole. There was no mark on his skin. Amazed, he took off his coat and found three more holes where bullets had passed through his coat but stopped before they reached his body.

Nine days after the battle, having heard a rumor of his own death, the young lieutenant colonel wrote his brother to confirm that he was still very much alive:

"As I have heard since my arrival at this place, a circumstantial account of my death and dying speech, I take this early opportunity of contradicting the first and assuring you that I have not as yet composed the latter. But by the all-powerful dispensations of Providence I have been protected beyond all human probability or expectation; for I had four bullets through my coat, and two horses shot under me yet escaped unhurt, although death was leveling my companions on every side of me!"

The battle on the Monongahela, part of the French and Indian War, was fought on July 9, 1755, near Fort Duquesne, now the city of Pittsburg. The twenty-three year old officer went on to become the commander-in-chief of the Continental Army and the first president of the United States. In all the years that followed in his long career, this man, George Washington, was never once wounded in battle.

Fifteen years later, in 1770, George Washington returned to the same Pennsylvania woods. A respected Indian chief, having heard that Washington was in the area, traveled a long way to meet with him. He sat down with Washington, and face-to-face over a council fire, the chief told Washington the following:

I am a chief and ruler over my tribes. My influence extends to the waters of the great lakes and to the far blue mountains.

> I have traveled a long and weary path that I might see the young warrior of the great battle. It was on the day when the white man's blood mixed with the streams of our forests that I first beheld this chief (Washington).
>
> I called to my young men and said, "Mark that tall and daring warrior? He is not of the red-coat tribe—he has an Indian's wisdom and his warriors fight as we do—he alone is exposed. Quick, let your aim be certain, and he dies."
>
> Our rifles were leveled, rifles which, but for you, knew not how to miss—it was all in vain, a power mightier far than we shielded you.
>
> Seeing you were under the special guardianship of the Great Spirit, we immediately ceased to fire at you. I am old and shall soon be gathered to the great council fire of my fathers in the land of the shades, but before I go, there is something bids me speak in the voice of prophecy:
>
> "Listen! The Great Spirit protects that man (pointing at Washington), and guides his destinies. He will become the chief of nations, and a people yet unborn will hail him as the founder of a mighty empire. I am come to pay homage to the man who is the particular favorite of Heaven, and who can never die in battle."

George Washington's Prophetic Vision of America

While all Americans know George Washington as the "Father of our Country," not many know that he received a prophetic vision regarding the future of America. It was in the winter of 1777 at Valley Forge that George Washington received his vision while preparing a dispatch and beseeching God for divine assistance.

Anthony Sherman was a soldier who served with George Washington. On July 4, 1859, when he was 99 years old, Sherman gave the following account of Washington's vision to Wesley Bradshaw, who published the account in the *National Review*, Vol. 4, No. 12, December 1880. The *National Review* was later renamed *The Stars and Stripes* and the article was reprinted in that publication. Sherman explained that he was repeating the vision as Washington told it to him. The following is readily available on internet sites about George Washington.

> I do not know whether it is owing to anxiety of my mind, or what, but this afternoon, as I was sitting at this table engaged in preparing a dispatch, something seemed to disturb me. Looking up, I beheld standing opposite me a singularly beautiful female. So astonished was I, for I had given strict orders not to be disturbed, that it was some moments before I found language to inquire the cause of her presence. A second, a third, and even forth time did I repeat my question, but received no answer from my mysterious visitor except a slight raising of her eyes.
>
> Presently I heard a voice saying, "Son of the Republic, look and learn," while at the same time my visitor extended her arm eastward. I now beheld a heavy white vapor at some distance rising fold upon fold. This gradually dissipated, and I looked upon a strange scene. Before me lay spread out in one vast plain all the countries of the world—Europe, Asia, Africa, and America. I saw rolling and tossing, between Europe and America, the billows of the Atlantic, and between Asia and America lay the Pacific.
>
> "Son of the Republic," said the same mysterious voice as before, "look and learn." At that moment I beheld a dark, shadowy being, like an angel, standing, or rather floating, in the hollow air, between Europe and America. Dipping water out of the ocean in the hollow of each hand, he sprinkled some upon America with his right hand while with his left hand he cast some on Europe. Immediately a cloud raised from these countries and joined in mid-ocean. For a while it remained stationary, and then moved slowly westward, until it enveloped America in its murky folds. Sharp flashes of lightening gleamed through it at intervals, and I heard the smothered groans and cries of the American people.
>
> A second time the angel dipped water from the ocean, and sprinkled it out as before. The dark cloud was then drawn back to the ocean, in whose heavy billows it sank from view. A third time I heard the mysterious voice saying, "Son of the

Republic, look and learn." I cast my eyes upon America and beheld villages and town and cities springing up one after another until the whole land, from the Atlantic to the Pacific, was dotted with them. Again I heard the mysterious voice say, "Son of the Republic, the end of the century cometh, look and learn."

At this the dark shadowy angel turned his face southward, and from Africa I saw an ill-omened specter approach our land. It flitted slowly over every town and city of the latter. The inhabitants presently set themselves in battle array against each other. As I continued looking, I saw a bright angel, on whose brow rested a crown of light, on which was traced the word "Union," bearing the American flag which he placed between the divided nation, and said, "Remember ye are brethren." Instantly, the inhabitants casting from them their weapons became friends once more, and united around the National Standard.

And again I heard the mysterious voice saying, "Son of the Republic, look and learn." At this, the dark shadowy angel placed a trumpet to his mouth and blew three distinct blasts; and taking water from the ocean, he sprinkled it upon Europe, Asia, and Africa. Then my eyes beheld a fearful scene. From each of these countries rose thick, black clouds that were joined into one. And throughout this mass, there gleamed a dark red light by which I saw hordes of armed men, who, moving with the cloud, marched by land and sailed by sea to America, which country was enveloped in the volume of the cloud. And I dimly saw these vast armies devastate the whole country, and burn the villages, towns, and cities that I beheld springing up.

As my ears listened to the thundering of the cannon, clashing of swords, and the shouts and cries of millions in mortal combat, I again heard the mysterious voice saying, "Son of the Republic, look and learn." When the voice had ceased, the dark shadowy angel place his trumpet once more to his mouth, and blew a long and fearful blast.

Instantly a light as of a thousand suns shone down from above me, and pierced and broke into fragments the dark cloud which enveloped America. At the same moment the angel upon whose head still shone the word "Union," and who bore our national flag in one hand and a sword in the other, descended from the heavens attended by legions of white spirits. These immediately joined the inhabitants of America, who I perceived were well-nigh overcome, but who immediately taking courage again closed up their broken ranks and renewed the battle. Again, amid the fearful noise of the conflict, I heard the mysterious voice saying, "Son of the Republic, look and learn."

As the voice ceased, the shadowy angel for the last time dipped water from the ocean and sprinkled it upon America. Instantly the dark cloud rolled back, together with the armies it had brought, leaving the inhabitants of the land victorious.

Then once more I beheld the villages, towns and cities, springing up where I had seen them before, while the bright angel, plating the azure standard he had brought in the midst of them, cried with a loud voice: "While the stars remain, and the heavens send down dew upon the earth, so long shall the Union last." And taking from his brow the crown on which was blazoned the word "Union," he placed it upon the Standard, while the people, kneeling down, said, "Amen."

The scene instantly began to fade and dissolve, and I at last saw nothing but the rising curling vapor I at first beheld. This also disappearing, I found myself once more gazing upon he mysterious visitor, who in the same voice I heard before, said, "Son of the Republic, what you have seen is thus interpreted. Three great perils will come upon the Republic. The most fearful is the third."

[The comment on his word *third* is: the help against the THIRD peril comes in the shape of Divine assistance; passing which, the whole world united shall not prevail against her. Let every child of the Republic learn to live for his God, his land and Union.]

> With these words the vision vanished, and I started from my seat and felt that I had seen a vision wherein has been shown me the birth, progress, and destiny of the UNITED STATES.

Sherman concluded his report to Bradshaw with these words, "Such, my friend were the words I heard from Washington's own lips, and America would do well to profit from them."

CHAPTER 10

The Kingdom of God in Prophecy

One of the most important subjects in the Bible is that of the kingdom of God. The clear and consistent message from Genesis to Revelation is that God reigns over the earth. While God allows evil to have its way up to a point, He overrides evil and uses it to further His kingdom purposes on the earth. Psalm 47:2, 8, reads, "For the LORD Most High is awesome; He is the great King over all the earth ... God reigns over the nations; God sits on His holy throne."

The Bible claims and emphasizes that God is King and Lord, and all nations are accountable to Him for the way their run their affairs, and all people are accountable to Him for the way they live their lives. He is the Master of the universe and owner of all that He created. We do not own what God gives to us. We are only stewards, and He will hold us accountable for how, when, where, and why we administer the resources He places in our hands.

As Americans we are greatly blessed to live in a democracy. But this blessing can also hinder our understanding of God as King. We have not lived under the rule of a monarch. Our founding fathers left England because they did not want to live under the tyranny of bad kings. They put in place a Constitution so that we could live under the rule of law—not under the rule of a sovereign king. So it is difficult for us to relate to God as King.

This is not only true for those of us who are Americans; it is also true for us as believers. We clearly see this evident in the way we present the Gospel. Our biblical presentation is not of God as King but God as Savior.

For example, instead of proclaiming the Gospel of the kingdom, we preach the Gospel of salvation. Now the Gospel of salvation is a wonderful gospel. It has blessed the lives of millions of people and we honor those who faithfully proclaim it. But I want you to understand that our gospel or message is about to radically change. God is beginning to awaken people to a greater awareness of the Gospel of the kingdom. It is the Gospel of the kingdom that is proclaimed in the Bible. As we draw nearer to the coming of the King, God is beginning to restore to us the principle, the proclamation, and the priority of the Gospel of the kingdom.

False Teachings Regarding the Gospel of the Kingdom

So what is the Gospel of the kingdom? What do we mean when we talk about the kingdom of God? Let's see first what it is not. The kingdom of God does not relate to time. This is very important. It is not a question of when; like, "When will Jesus come and establish His kingdom?" I want to share with you three teachings that are not biblical regarding the Gospel of the Kingdom then we will see what is the biblical view.

1. Dispensationalism

First is Dispensationalism. Many of us who have been believers for a long time had the Scofield Bible as our primary study Bible. C.I. Scofield was an outstanding scholar and a great man of God. We owe him a tremendous debt for helping us better understand the Bible.

Scofield first produced his study Bible in 1909. It is still one of the best-selling study Bibles in the world. It is a great edition of the Bible. In his study Bible, Scofield gave some wonderful explanations and interpretations in the footnotes. The challenge in reading his explanations is that people often think his comments are actually part of the Bible itself. While we honor him for his work, Scofield was not connected to his biblical Hebraic roots. He was a western scholar who accepted the writings of J. N. Darby that God governs the world through seven different dispensations or administrations of time.

The last of these dispensations is the 1,000 year rule of Jesus on the earth, which is commonly called the Millennium. The problem with this view is that it puts the kingdom of God on the earth in the future when Jesus comes. It is a view that relegates God's kingdom to time—in this view, a future time.

As a side note, Dispensational teaching also says that God stopped doing miracles when the Bible was completed, and that miraculous healings and the gifts of the Spirit ceased. Now that makes perfect theological sense to a dispensationalist because God does miracles as a manifestation of His kingdom on the earth. But if you believe His kingdom is in the future, and not in the present, then your theology has no place for God to do signs and wonders in our midst today. That is all for the future. Furthermore, since God is not supposed to do this anymore, whenever there is a manifestation of the gifts of the Spirit, the manifestation would be considered a work of the devil because God doesn't do that anymore. Contributing a work of the Holy Spirit to the devil is a frightening theological teaching.

We appreciate that Dispensationalism teaching does recognize that God has an everlasting covenant with Israel and the Jewish people. It has had a tremendous influence for good regarding God's love and faithfulness to the Jewish people. It has been a strong defense against replacement theology. But regarding the kingdom of God, which is always in the present, it is not a correct view of the kingdom because it is based on time.

2. Kingdom Now

Another teaching about the Kingdom of God is just the opposite of Dispensationalism. In fact it is a reaction to the ultra Dispensationalism that puts God's kingdom in the future. This teaching is called "Kingdom Now." It sounds good when compared to Dispensationalism.

Kingdom Now teaching says that the Church will establish God's kingdom on the earth before Jesus comes. Once this happens, the church will invite Jesus to come and rule over His kingdom. I don't think anyone who understands the perilous times in which we are living would agree with this teaching.

The Kingdom Now proclamation grew out of an extreme teaching in the 80s by some of the leading hyper-faith preachers and teachers. I certainly do not fault spiritual leaders who want to encourage people to walk in the fullness of God's Kingdom. Personally, I would rather have wildfire than no fire. But the Kingdom Now teaching is wildfire out of control. It is based on a fundamental misunderstanding of Scripture that teaches that believers are little gods who can confess God's kingdom into existence by speaking the word of faith. We simply use our God-like powers to confess it into being.

Kingdom Now teaching reached its peak in the 1980s at the height of the Charismatic Renewal and Word of Faith movement. Compared to the lifeless teaching of Dispensationalism, the Kingdom Now message was very exciting and embraced by many. It was refreshing but out of balance. The problem is, it didn't work. The world has gotten worse, not better.

3. Dominion Theology

A third false teaching regarding the kingdom of God is called "Dominion Theology." Like the Kingdom Now teaching, Dominion Theology also teaches that the Church will establish God's kingdom on the earth. This view was also popular in the 1980s. Whereas Kingdom Now theology is a hyper-faith charismatic teaching, Dominion Now theology is non-charismatic and teaches that the church will establish God's kingdom on the earth through worldwide missionary efforts and political activism.

We should certainly support missionary efforts around the world. I believe we should be involved in the political process. I believe we should do everything we can to put godly people in public office and address the moral and social issues of our day.

I definitely believe we should be activist. I believe we should demonstrate in Washington on behalf of Israel. I have done this myself personally. I have stood in the rain with fellow Christian Zionist across the street from the White House. I had one of my colleagues distribute my book on Christians Supporting Israel to the office of every congressman in Washington.

I believe we should operate in the supernatural and proclaim God's word over the nations. I am an activist. I encourage others to take their convictions outside the four walls of the church building. I believe the kingdom of God should flow out of us into the lives of others. I believe we should live as salt and light to our community. We should partner with God to bring His kingdom to the earth. Jesus instructed us to pray that God's kingdom come to the earth. I don't believe we have to wait for the coming of Messiah to operate in His kingdom, which is always present. But I don't believe we are going to speak it into being with the right charismatic confession, nor do I believe we are going to convert the world to Jesus before He comes.

Both Kingdom Now and Dominion Theology are anti-Semitic, replacement theology, teachings, which by their nature tell us they are not biblically sound.

What and Where is the Kingdom of God?

These teachings err because they relate the kingdom of God to time. They ask the question, "When?" But in the Bible, the kingdom of God is not related to time. It is related to space. It is not a question of when, but where? What is the kingdom of God and where is it?

The kingdom of God is the rule of God over His creation. His kingdom is everywhere present. It is expressed through the lives of His people who have chosen to live under His rule and obey His royal decrees and commandments. By so doing, they manifest His kingship on the earth. In biblical times this was called taking on the yoke of the kingdom. When Jesus said, "Take My yoke upon you" (Matthew 11:29), He meant we should acknowledge the kingdom of God in our lives.

God has always had a people living under His rule. In this sense, the kingdom of God is past, present, and future. But since God is outside of time, His kingdom is always present. It always was, always is, and always will be. All people can experience God's kingdom when they obey God's commandments and live under His rule.

Since many western Christians generally believe that grace means no commandments, few experience kingdom life. While all true believers live in God's kingdom, they don't experience God's kingdom blessings because they don't keep His commandments.

Jesus said in John 14:15, 21, "If you love Me, keep My commandments.... He who has My commandments and keeps them, it is he who loves Me. And he who loves Me will be loved by My Father, and I will love him and manifest Myself to him."

God's commandments are His instructions for living in His kingdom. They are not the legalism of man-made rules.

God's Kingdom Past

Adam and Eve

In the past, God's kingdom rule was delegated to Adam who was given dominion over all of God's creation. He was only given one commandment, which he didn't keep. When Adam and Eve sinned, they no longer enjoyed God's kingdom blessings. While God's kingdom fills heaven and earth, we can only operate in it when we obey Him. With the exception of Noah, Adam and Eve's descendants chose not to live in God's kingdom.

Abraham

Around 4,000 years ago, God created a new company of people through whom He would express His kingdom to the world. Jewish tradition teaches that Abraham was the first person to address God as Master or Adonai (Lord), thus declaring His kingdom over the world.

God declared that the descendants of Abraham, Isaac, and Jacob would be a unique people who would be a kingdom of priests to the nations. As they lived under His kingship and obeyed His commandments, they would manifest His kingdom to the nations (Exodus 19:6).

At Sinai

At Sinai, God's chosen people said, "All that the LORD has said we will do, and be obedient" (Exodus 24:7). History teaches otherwise. As a company of people, the Jewish people have not lived up to their high calling. Even so, they do acknowledge God as King, even when they are not operating in His kingdom.

Many of us have learned the first part of the Jewish blessing which says, "Baruch ata Adonai Eloheinu Melech Ha Olam," meaning, "Blessed are You O Lord our God, King of the universe." God is king of the universe even though we may not personally acknowledge Him as King in our lives.

Jewish people do not ask the question, "Are you saved?" They ask, "What have you done to make the world a better place?" Jews are often at the forefront in social movements, good ones as well as bad ones. While often misguided, they are motivated to establish God's kingdom on earth, even though they may be very confused about what that means.

A central theme in Judaism is "Tikkun Olam," which means repairing the world. It is the vision of the prophets in the Bible to make the world a better place where justice, righteous, and peace—that is, kingdom conditions—prevail over evil. We are not put on this earth as mere spectators to live a certain number of days on the earth and accumulate things. We are to actively partner with God in establishing His kingdom on the earth, knowing that it will not fully come to earth until Messiah comes as King and Lord of the nations.

King David

The kingdom of God manifested on the earth is the focus and plan of the Bible. When God appointed David as king, David prayed to the Lord:

> Blessed are You, LORD God of Israel, our Father, forever and ever. Yours, O LORD, is the greatness, the power and the glory, the victory and the majesty; for all that is in heaven and in earth is Yours; Yours is the kingdom, O LORD, and You are exalted as head over all (1 Chronicles 29:10-11).

Psalms

The kingdom of God was a frequent acknowledgment in the Psalms. For example:

Psalm 72:11, "Yes, all kings shall fall down before Him; all nations shall serve Him."

Psalm 22:27-28, "All the ends of the world shall remember and turn to the LORD, and all the families of the nations shall worship before You. For the kingdom is the LORD's, and He rules over the nations."

Prophets

The prophets also spoke about a golden age when God's kingdom would be manifested on the earth. For example:

Daniel 2:44, "And in the days of these kings the God of heaven will set up a kingdom which shall never be destroyed; and the kingdom shall not be left to other people; it shall break in pieces and consume all these kingdoms, and it shall stand forever."

Daniel 7:27, "Then the kingdom and dominion, and the greatness of the kingdoms under the whole heaven, shall be given to the people, the saints of the Most High. His kingdom is an everlasting kingdom, and all dominions shall serve and obey Him."

Zechariah 14:9, "And the LORD shall be King over all the earth. It that day it shall be–the LORD is one and His name one."

Intertestamental Period

The Kingdom of God was also a major emphasis during the intertestamental period between Malachi and Matthew. This was the period of time between the closing of the writings of the Hebrew Bible (Old Testament) and the opening of the New Testament. Somewhere during that time, the Jewish people, out of reverence to God, were afraid they would misuse God's name. A simple solution to their concern was simply not to say His name. So instead of saying God's name, the Jews substituted other words that they considered to be synonyms for God's name.

For example, instead of saying the kingdom of God, or God, they would say the kingdom of Heaven, or heaven, as a substitute. Western scholars not connected to their biblical Hebraic roots have written volumes of pages and books trying to explain the difference between the kingdom of God and the kingdom of Heaven not knowing they are the same thing. This is like children, out of respect, don't call their parents by their first names. They call their parents Father and Mother or Dad and Mom rather than using their parents names.

We do the same thing today. We sometimes say, "Thank Heaven," when we really mean, "Thank God." Or we say, "Only Heaven knows," when we really mean, "Only God knows."

Some examples in the book of Maccabees that was written in the period between the Testaments are:

> It is easy for many to be hemmed in by few, for in the sight of Heaven, there is no difference between saving by many or by few. It is not on the size of the army that victory in battle depends, but strength comes from Heaven (1 Maccabees 3:18-19).
>
> And now let us cry to Heaven, to see whether He will favor us and remember His covenant with our ancestors and crush this army before us today (1 Maccabees 4:10)

God's Kingdom Present

John the Baptist and Jesus

While Christianity in America has not emphasized the Gospel of the kingdom, it is the emphasis in the New Testament as the New Testament is just a continuation of what was proclaimed in the Hebrew Bible. In between the writings of the two sections of the Bible, the people often substituted the word "heaven" for God.

I want to make it clear that we have the greatest respect and gratitude for our western scholars, theologians, and seminary professors. God bless them for all of their years of dedication and study. I have learned much from them. But they are part of the same Greco-Roman Christianity that we are part of as Western believers. It is a Christianity cut off from its root. With their best intentions, they tell us that us that we are living in the age of grace, as if people didn't have grace prior to the time of Jesus.

We are told that the God of the Hebrews in the Old Testament was an angry Law God but somehow He transformed himself into sweet graceful Jesus in the New Testament. But all the writers of the New Testament were Jews who received their concepts and understandings of grace and faith from the writers of the Hebrew Bible. We have always, from the time of Adam and Eve, lived in the age of grace operating in the kingdom of God. The kingdom of God is not only a past reality, it is a present reality extended to Gentiles who acknowledge Jesus as their King and live, by God's mercy and grace, under God's rule.

The New Testament opens with John the Baptist proclaiming, "Repent, for the kingdom of heaven is at hand!" (Matthew 3:2). Jesus had the same message in Matthew 4:17,"Repent, for the kingdom of heaven is at hand."

The phrase "at hand" means immanent, bursting forth, ready to be revealed. Whenever Jesus did a miracle, it was a manifestation of the kingdom of God in their midst. Jesus preached the kingdom of God, and then He demonstrated it by healing people and delivering them from demons.

Matthew 4:23 reads:

> And Jesus went about all Galilee, teaching in their synagogues, preaching the gospel of the kingdom, and healing all kinds of sicknesses and all kinds of disease among the people.

The most famous Christian prayer is really a Jewish prayer that we have called the Lord's Prayer. It is a basic prayer that was similar to what Jewish people, including Jesus, prayed. In this prayer, Jesus taught His disciples to pray to the Father in heaven, "Your kingdom come, Your will be done on earth as it is in heaven" (Matthew 6:9-13). God's kingdom is manifested on the earth when God's people do God's will.

In His greatest recorded teaching in the Bible, what is called the Sermon on the Mount, Jesus explained how to live as kingdom people. And in Matthew 6:33, He said to "Seek first the kingdom of God and His righteousness and all these other things shall be added to you."

After this teaching, Jesus sent His talmid (disciples) to preach the very same gospel of the kingdom. Matthew 10:7 reads, "And as you go, preach, saying, 'The kingdom of heaven is a hand.' Heal the sick, cleanse the lepers, raise the dead, cast out demons."

Luke 10:9, "And heal the sick there, and say to them, 'The kingdom of God has come near to you.'"

In a similar statement in Luke 17:21, Jesus said that the kingdom of God is within your midst. Most English translations say "within you." The exception is the NASB, which says "within your midst," which is correct.

In Matthew 24:14, Jesus said, "This gospel of the kingdom will be preached in all the world as a witness to the nations, and then the end will come."

Paul and the Kingdom of God

Paul also focused his preaching on the kingdom of God. Because we put so much emphasis on his message of faith and grace, we don't realize that his message of faith and grace was within the context of his central message of the kingdom of God. Let's read Paul's own words as well as those of Luke, James, and Peter.

In Acts 14: 22, Paul said, "We must through many tribulations enter the kingdom of God."

Acts 19:8 tells us, "And he (Paul) went into the synagogue and spoke boldly for three months, reasoning and persuading concerning the things of the kingdom of God."

Acts 20:25, Paul gives his farewell to the believers at Ephesus and reminds them that he preached to them the message of the kingdom of God. "And indeed, now I know that you all, among whom I have gone preaching the kingdom of God, will see my face no more."

In Acts 28:23, when the Jews in Rome came to see Paul in prison, it says that Paul "explained and solemnly testified of the kingdom of God, persuading them concerning Jesus from both the Law of Moses and the Prophets, from morning till evening."

In this story, we discover an incredible truth: the gospel of Jesus is the gospel of the kingdom of God and this message is found in the Law of Moses and from the lips of the prophets.

Acts 28:30-31 reads, "Then Paul dwelt two whole years in his own rented house, and received all who came to him, preaching the kingdom of God and teaching the things which concern the Lord Jesus Christ [Messiah] with all confidence, no one forbidding him."

In Acts 8:12, Phillip "preached the things concerning the kingdom of God."

In James 2:5 we are told that God has promised that those who love Him would be heirs of the kingdom.

2 Peter 1:11 tells us we can enter the everlasting kingdom of our Lord.

God's Kingdom Future

Finally, we learn in the Bible that God's kingdom is not only past and present, it is also future as the Scriptures declare.

In Matthew 25:34, Jesus said that those who help His brethren in time of need will inherit God's kingdom. It reads:

> Then the King will say to those on His right hand, "Come, you blessed of My Father, inherit the kingdom prepared for you from the foundation of the world."

Revelation 11:15 is a most interesting verse. From it we learn that it will actually be angels that preach the final message of the Gospel of the kingdom. It reads, "Then the seventh angel sounded: And there were loud voices in heaven, saying, 'The kingdoms of this world have become the kingdoms of our Lord and of His Christ [Messiah], and He shall reign forever and ever!'"

Revelation 20:1-6 tells us that God's covenant kingdom people will reign with the Lord for a thousand years on this earth.

Finally, we learn in Revelation 21:1that God will create a new heaven and a new earth in which God will make all things new (verse 5). Unlike the kingdoms of men which rise and fall, God's Kingdom is everlasting. It is from vanishing point to vanishing point, before the beginning of time and after time is no more. The Lord God will reign into eternity over His creation as sovereign King and Master.

As we awaken to this shift of emphasis from the Gospel of salvation to the Gospel of the kingdom, from "Churchianity" to kingdom life, we will soon see biblical kinds of miracles as common place for ordinary believers who are willing to submit themselves to the yoke of the kingdom of God. The greatest outpouring of God's supernatural manifestations is at hand. While evil will increase, the glory of God's Spirit will anoint His people with His presence and His power as in the days of the first coming of Messiah.

We will soon see the time when the kingdom of God in Heaven will so fill the earth that God's people will be ready for the coming of the Lord. God's kingdom is past, present, and future. It was, it is, and it is to come. May His kingdom come, may His will be done on earth as it is in heaven. May we all embrace the yoke of His Kingdom.

> Blessed are You, LORD God of Israel, our Father, forever and ever. Yours, O LORD, is the greatness, the power and the glory, the victory and the majesty; for all that is in heaven and in earth is Yours; Yours is the kingdom, O LORD, and You are exalted as head over all. Both riches and honor come from You, and you reign over all. In Your hand is power and might; in your hand it is to make great and to give strength to all. Now therefore, our God, we thank You and praise Your glorious name (1 Chronicles 29:10-13).

CHAPTER 11

The Messianic Kingdom in Prophecy

The most important event in ancient history was when the one true God revealed himself to Abraham and called Abraham to leave Babylon for the Promised Land. There God made a covenant with Abraham. It was a sacred blood covenant. It was a literal, unconditional, everlasting covenant that absolutely cannot be broken. And although any one generation of Hebrews could dishonor the covenant, the covenant itself remained in force throughout all of history.

The pivotal Scripture is Genesis 12:1-3 which reads:

> Now the LORD had said to Abram: "Get out of your country, from your family and from your father's house, to a land that I will show you. I will make you a great nation; I will bless you and make your name great; and you shall be a blessing. I will bless those who bless you, and I will curse him who curses you; and in you all the families of the earth shall be blessed."

The three particular covenant blessings God promised Abraham and his descendants were a land, a nation, and spiritual blessings through the Messiah. These blessings were conditional based on the Hebrews' obedience to God. Tragically, the Hebrews were not obedient. They worshipped other gods in spite of God's continuous warnings from the prophets. As a result, the people were driven from their land, banished as a nation, and missed the blessings offered to them by Messiah Jesus.

Yet God has not forgotten His covenant people. He is a covenant-keeping God. He has preserved a remnant throughout history and brought them back to the land, where He is going to make them a great nation and turn their hearts back to Him. Jesus will come and rule, not only as King of the Jews, but as King of kings and Lord of lords. It is at this time that the fullness of God's promises to Abraham will take place.

When Messiah returns, He will rule over the nations from Jerusalem.

Isaiah 2:2-4 reads:

> Now it shall come to pass in the latter days that the mountain of the LORD's house shall be established on the top of the mountains, and shall be exalted about the hills; and all nations shall flow to it. Many people shall come and say, "Come and let us go up to the mountain of the LORD, to the house of the God of Jacob; He will teach us His ways, and we shall walk in His paths." For out of Zion shall go forth the law, and the word of the LORD from Jerusalem.
>
> He shall judge between the nations, and rebuke many people; they shall beat their swords into plowshares, and their spears into pruning hooks; nation shall not lift up sword against nation, neither shall they learn war anymore.

Because Jesus will be ruling from Jerusalem, Israel will be the head nation of the world:

> The LORD will open to you His good treasure, the heavens, to give the rain to your land in its season, and to bless all the work of your hand. You shall lend to many nations, but you shall not borrow. And the LORD will make you the head and not the tail; you shall be above only, and not beneath (Deuteronomy 28:12-13). (See also Zechariah 8:23.)

They will live in peace among their neighbors in the land God promised them (Isaiah 2:4). The blessings of Messiah Jesus will be enjoyed by all. It is at this time that God's three covenant promises to

Abraham will find their complete fulfillment. Let's now take a closer look at this golden age that lies ahead for the Jewish people and all who await the coming of Jesus.

The Messianic Kingdom

This golden age is called the Messianic kingdom because it is the period of time when God will rule the nations through Messiah Jesus.

We learn in the Hebrew Scriptures that it was God's desire to rule Israel as their king (1 Samuel 8:9). But the Jews wanted a human king like the nations among them. They said, "Now make us a king to judge us like all the nations" (1 Samuel 8:5).

Naturally, Samuel was upset with the people. But the Lord comforted him with these words:

> Heed the voice of the people in all that they say to you; for they have not rejected you, but they have rejected Me, that I should not reign over them (1 Samuel 8:7).

The people insisted and said to Samuel:

> No, but we will have a king over us, that we also may be like all the nations, and that our king may judge us and go out before us and fight our battles (1 Samuel 8:19-20).

God granted their request and gave them human kings. But none of these kings could rule with the perfect moral character of God. They certainly could not judge them with righteousness nor fight their battles for them with victory. Being only human, they failed in many ways. In view of this, God determined that He would rule them himself through a human King—the person of Messiah Jesus. He would be their perfect King, ruling with perfect righteousness, backed by the full authority and power of heaven.

The Bible says this Messianic kingdom will last for 1,000 years (Revelation 20:1-7). Revelations 20:4-6 reads:

> And I saw thrones, and they sat on them, and judgment was committed to them. Then I saw the souls of those who had been beheaded for their witness to Jesus and for the word of God, who had not worshiped the beast or his image,

> and had not received his mark on their foreheads or on their hands. And they lived and reigned with Christ [Messiah] for a thousand years.
>
> But the rest of the dead did not live again until the thousand years were finished. This is the first resurrection. Blessed and holy is he who has part in the first resurrection. Over such the second death has no power, but they shall be priests of God and of Christ [Messiah], and shall reign with Him a thousand years.

This period of time is known as the Millennium, from the Latin words milli (one thousand) and annum (year). It's the utopia for which man has so desperately strived, but never achieved. Man has never achieved it because he's tried to achieve it without God.

When Jesus returns, there will be certain divine judgments on those who have survived the tribulation period (Ezekiel. 20:34-38, Matthew 25:31-46). This is to determine who will be able to enter into the Messianic kingdom in their earthly bodies. The result of this judgment is that only believing Jews and Gentiles will enter the kingdom. The rest will be cut off and banished from His presence.

The Messianic Government

The type of government during the Messianic kingdom will be a theocracy. This means that God himself will rule as King over all the earth through Messiah Jesus. This theocracy will unite in Messiah Jesus both the kingdom of God and the kingdom of David.

Jesus, as the divine Son of God, will administer the kingdom of God through the resurrected believers of all ages. Jesus, as the human Son of David, will administer the kingdom of David through the remnant of believing Jews who are alive at His coming, and who will enter into the Messianic kingdom.

Thus all believers shall rule with Jesus. Resurrected believers will have a part in the administration of the kingdom of God. The Jewish believers will have their part in the administration of the kingdom of David. The blessings of the kingdom of God will come to the Gentiles through the nation of Israel as they live under the righteous rule of Messiah Jesus, who will sit on the throne of David (Isaiah 49:6, 62:2,

11:10; Jeremiah 3:17, 16:19-21). There are many Scriptures that speak of this time.

The writer of Psalm 2 gives us a clear statement concerning the rule of Jesus in the Messianic kingdom. He writes:

> Yet I have set My King on My holy hill of Zion. I will declare the decree: The Lord has said to Me, "You are My Son, today I have begotten You. Ask of Me, and I will give You the nations for Your inheritance, And the ends of the earth for Your possession. You shall break them with a rod of iron; You shall dash them to pieces like a potter's vessel" (Psalm 2:6-9).

Daniel was privileged to have a vision of the coming of Messiah Jesus in all of His glory and power to rule as king. Daniel wrote:

> And in the days of these kings the God of heaven will set up a kingdom which shall never be destroyed; and the kingdom shall not be left to other people; it shall break in pieces and consume all these kingdoms, and it shall stand forever (Daniel 2:44).

> I was watching in the night visions, and behold, One like the Son of Man, coming with the clouds of heaven! He came to the Ancient of Days, and they brought Him near before Him. Then to Him was given dominion and glory and a kingdom, that all peoples, nations, and languages should serve Him. His dominion is an everlasting dominion, which shall not pass away, and His kingdom the one which shall not be destroyed (Daniel 7:13-14).

The prophet Isaiah often spoke about the kingdom of God. One of his more well-known statements reads like this:

> For unto us a Child is born, unto us a Son is given; and the government will be upon His shoulder. And His name will be called Wonderful, Counselor, Mighty God, Everlasting Father, Prince of Peace. Of the increase of His government and peace there will be no end, upon the throne of David and over His kingdom, to order it and establish it with judgment

and justice from that time forward, even forever. The zeal of the Lord of hosts will perform this (Isaiah 9:6-7).

These and many other prophecies about the kingdom of God fully manifested on the earth are fulfilled at the coming of Jesus when He rules over the nations as a descendant of Abraham and the greater Son of David.

Jerusalem—the World Capital

Jesus will rule from Jerusalem, which will be the capital of the world. The news media and wire services will dateline their stories from Jerusalem, not Washington, Moscow, Paris, or London. The nations of the world will submit to the policies that the Messiah decrees from the holy city of God. The ancient prophets spoke of this time when Jerusalem would be the center of the world government.

Repeating the statement from Isaiah:

> Now it shall come to pass in the latter days that the mountain of the LORD's house shall be established on the top of the mountains, and shall be exalted above the hills; and all nations shall flow to it. Many people shall come and say, 'Come and let us go up to the mountain of the LORD, to the house of the God of Jacob; He will teach us His ways, and we shall walk in His paths.' For out of Zion shall go forth the law, and the word of the LORD from Jerusalem (Isaiah 2:2-3).

Isaiah also declared:

> And in that day there shall be a Root of Jesse, who shall stand as a banner to the people; for the Gentiles shall seek Him, and His resting place shall be glorious (Isaiah 11:10).

Micah confirmed Isaiah's prophecy and wrote the same thing:

> Now it shall come to pass in the latter days that the mountain of the LORD's house shall be established on the top of the mountains, and shall be exalted above the hills; and peoples shall flow to it, many nations shall come and say, "Come, and let us go up to the mountain of the LORD, to the house of the God of Jacob; He will teach us His ways, and we

shall walk in His paths. For out of Zion the law shall go forth, and the word of the LORD from Jerusalem" (Micah 4:1-2).

Micah added these words:

"In that day," says the LORD, "I will assemble the lame, I will gather the outcasts, and those who I have afflicted; I will make the lame a remnant, and the outcast a strong nation; so the LORD will reign over them in Mount Zion from now on, even forever" (Micah 4:6-7).

Jesus warned people not to swear "by Jerusalem, for it is the city of the great King" (Matthew 5:35).

A Unified Government

The Messianic kingdom will be the true and lasting one-world government that the nations are now trying to establish, but without God. There will be no need for a United Nations. Jesus will rule with absolute authority and power. All nations will submit to Him, and no open rebellion will be tolerated. In addition to the Scriptures just noted, the following references give us further insight:

"Ask of Me, and I will give You the nations for Your inheritance, and the ends of the earth for Your possession. You shall break them with a rod of iron; You shall dash them to pieces like a potter's vessel" (Psalm 2:8-9).

"The LORD said to my Lord, 'Sit at My right hand, till I make Your enemies Your footstool.' The LORD shall send the rod of Your strength out of Zion. Rule in the midst of Your enemies!" (Psalm 110:1-2).

"He shall strike the earth with the rod of His mouth, and with the breath of His lips He shall slay the wicked" (Isaiah 11:4b).

"And the LORD shall be King over all the earth. In that day it shall be—The LORD is one, and His name one" (Zechariah 14:9).

"Now out of His mouth goes a sharp sword, that with it He should strike the nations. And He Himself will rule them with a rod of iron. He Himself treads the winepress of the fierceness and wrath of Almighty God. And He has on His robe and on His thigh a name written: KING OF KINGS AND LORD OF LORDS" (Revelation 19:15-16).

"The kingdoms of this world have become the kingdoms of our Lord and of His Christ [Messiah], and He shall reign forever and ever!" (Revelation 11:15b).

A Righteous Rule

Jesus will rule with righteousness and justice for all. All social problems will be solved. No one will be oppressed, taken advantage of, or cheated in any way. There will be no need for social workers because discrimination, inequities, or inequalities of any kind will no longer exist. The Scriptures declare:

> But the LORD shall endure forever; He has prepared His throne for judgment. He shall judge the world in righteousness, and He shall administer judgment for the peoples in uprightness. The LORD also will be a refuge for the oppressed, a refuge in times of trouble (Psalm 9:7-9).
>
> His delight is in the fear of the LORD, and He shall not judge by the sight of His eyes, nor decide by the hearing of His ears; but with righteousness He shall judge the poor, and decide with equity for the meek of the earth; He shall strike the earth with the rod of His mouth, and with the breath of His lips He shall slay the wicked. Righteousness shall be the belt of His loins, and faithfulness the belt of His waist (Isaiah 11:3-5).
>
> The throne will be established; and One will sit on it in truth, in the tabernacle of David, judging and seeking justice and hastening righteousness (Isaiah 16:5).

> "Behold, the days are coming," says the Lord, "that I will raise to David a Branch of righteousness; a King shall reign and prosper, and execute judgment and righteousness in the earth. In His days Judah will be saved, and Israel will dwell safely; now this is His name by which He will be called: THE LORD OUR RIGHTEOUSNESS" (Jeremiah 23:5-6).

Peace At Last

Because Jesus will be able to rule absolutely with perfect justice and righteousness, peace will finally come to the earth. There will no longer be border disputes between neighboring countries. Nations will not seek to dominate others. The military academies will be closed and the war machines dismantled. Repeating the words of the prophets:

> He shall judge between the nations, and rebuke many people; they shall beat their swords into plowshares, and their spears into pruning hooks; nation shall not lift up sword against nation, neither shall they learn war anymore (Isaiah 2:4).

> He shall judge between many peoples, and rebuke strong nations afar off; they shall beat their swords into plowshares, and their spears into pruning hooks; nation shall not lift up sword against nation, neither shall they learn war anymore (Micah 4:3).

The Messianic Religion

The Messianic kingdom will also have a one-world religion. But it won't be man's One World Religious system. Instead, both the political and spiritual aspects of the Messianic kingdom will center in the Messiah. Jesus will rule as the King-Priest uniting both functions in himself.

Zechariah wrote:

> Yes, He shall build the temple of the LORD. He shall bear the glory, and shall sit and rule on His throne; so He shall be a priest on His throne, and the counsel of peace shall be between them both (Zechariah 6:13).

Because of man's sinful nature, it is not wise for the political and religious affairs of a nation to be under one authority. An ungodly leader who controlled both of these could become a ruthless dictator destroying and corrupting lives in the worse kind of way. This is exactly what the false messiah will do in the great tribulation.

But Jesus will be able to function in both capacities because He is the perfect God-man. He will exercise His political authority with perfect righteousness, while keeping the spiritual worship pure and free from perversion.

Jerusalem will not only be the world's capital, it will also be the religious center of the world. Jeremiah wrote:

> At that time Jerusalem shall be called The Throne of the LORD, and all the nations shall be gathered to it, to the name of the LORD, to Jerusalem. No more shall they follow the dictates of their evil hearts (Jeremiah 3:17).

At this time, the One True God, the God of Israel, the God of Abraham, Isaac and Jacob, the God and Father of our Lord Jesus (Yeshua) will be worshipped by all the nations. There will be no false deities or many different paths to God. God alone will be worshipped. Zephaniah 2:11 reads:

> He will reduce to nothing all the gods of the earth; people shall worship Him, each one from his own place, indeed all the shores of the nations.

Psalm 22:27-28 says, "All the ends of the earth shall remember and turn to the LORD, and all the families of the nations shall worship before You. For the kingdom is the LORD's, and He rules over the nations."

Because Jesus (Yeshua) is a Jewish Lord and King, the worship expressions during this time will be Jewish, not Greco-Roman. This is why the prophets describe worship in Jewish terms. Western Greco-Roman Christianity, as we know it today, is not in the Bible. It was established by Constantine in the fourth century of our era. All the prophets in the Bible are Jewish. Jesus and His followers in the New Testament were all Jewish. They spoke of a Jewish King and High Priest who would rule and minister in a Jewish way. They would not have had a concept of Western Greco-Roman Christianity. It is not in the Bible and it is not in the Messianic Kingdom of God.

When Jesus was here the first time, He came as a Jew. When He returns He is coming as a Jew, not a Christian. The Bible is very clear on this. In Revelation 5:5 Jesus is called the "Lion of the Tribe of Judah—the Root of David." In Revelation 22:16, Jesus calls Himself "The Root and the Offspring of David."

One of my primary goals is to awaken Christians to the Biblical Hebraic roots of our faith. Non-Jewish Christian believers need to be prepared for worship when Messiah comes. Those who are not prepared will be shocked when they realize Jesus is not going to have *church*. He will be a Jewish King ruling over His kingdom, which will be led by a Jewish state of Israel, and have Biblical Jewish worship expressions. Those who are prepared will be ready to enter fully into the expressions and experiences of worshipping the Lord in a biblical way. Furthermore, believing Jews will be shocked when they discover that Jesus is not going to preside over modern rabbinic services. This is why it is important to learn the Biblical Hebraic roots of our faith as they point to Jesus.

Let me make it very clear. There will be no anti-Semitic replacement theology Christians living in the Messianic Kingdom of God. If you are anti-Israel, there will be no place for you in the Messianic Kingdom of God. And if you are resisting God's sovereign work of restoring Christianity to its Biblical Hebraic roots, you will be miserable in the Messianic Kingdom of God.

With a Jewish King and Messiah, Isaiah tells us that the world will function on the Biblical Jewish calendar not the Greco-Roman calendar. The Biblical Jewish calendar is a lunar calendar for keeping the Feast. The Greco-Roman calendar is a solar calendar based on sun worship. Furthermore, Shabbat will be universally recognized as the special Day of the Lord for worship and rest.

Isaiah explains:

> And it shall come to pass that from one New Moon to another, and from one Sabbath to another, all flesh shall come to worship before Me, says the LORD (Isaiah 66:23).

We also learn that people will celebrate the Feast of the Lord not the Feast of Constantine. We will regulate our worship on the sacred Biblical calendar and celebrate God's holy days not Greco-Roman holidays. Zechariah explains:

> And it shall come to pass that everyone who is left of all the nations which came against Jerusalem shall go up from year to year to worship the King, the LORD of hosts, and to keep the Feast of Tabernacles (Zechariah 14:16).

The prophet Ezekiel provides information concerning worship activities during the Messianic kingdom (Ezekiel 40-48). In these chapters, Ezekiel describes a religious system that includes a temple, priesthood, and sacrifices. None of this is in any way meant to diminish the completed work of Jesus as the perfect human temple of God, as the perfect High Priest of God, or as the once and for all perfect sacrifice for our sins. The sacrifices at the temple are not for sin but offerings of praise and worship to the Lord.

Although the Messiah will be the center of worship, He will use the religious expressions as physical object teaching lessons to show in a tangible way who He is and what He has done. The religious teachers will use these object lessons to point people who are born during the millennium to the Messiah and their need for Him as personal Lord and Savior.

Isaiah tells us that God's house (temple) will be called a house of prayer for all nations (Isaiah 56:7).

Zechariah tells us:

> People shall yet come, inhabitants of many cities; the inhabitants of one city shall go to another, saying, "Let us continue to go and pray before the LORD, and seek the LORD of hosts. I myself will go also." Yes, many peoples and strong nations shall come to seek the LORD of hosts in Jerusalem, and to pray before the LORD. Thus says the LORD of hosts: "In those days ten men from every language of the nations shall grasp the sleeve (tzitzit) of a Jewish man say, 'Let us go with you, for we have heard that God is with you'" (Zechariah 8:20-23).

Because Israel will be the head nation, Hebrew, not English, will be the universal language. Zephaniah 3: 9 reads, "For then I will restore to the peoples a pure language that they all may call on the name of the LORD."

Jeremiah 31: 23 reads, "Thus says the LORD of hosts, the God of Israel: They shall again use this speech in the land of Judah and in its cities, when I bring back their captivity."

The presence of the Messiah will insure great spiritual blessings for everyone. All citizens will be able to have full knowledge of God through the Messiah and will enjoy the new covenant blessings to the fullest (Isaiah11:9-10).

Messianic Living Conditions

Living conditions in the Messianic kingdom will be blessed beyond our present abilities to imagine. As just noted, there will be no more wars (Isaiah 2:4; Micah 4:1-4). In view of this, we won't need to dispatch peace-keeping forces to different trouble spots on the globe. There will be no iron curtain, bamboo curtain, Berlin wall, demilitarized zones, revolutions, or terrorist groups. The vast sums of money which are now spent on the arms race will be used for the benefit of mankind.

Because Jesus will rule with perfect justice and righteousness, social problems will no longer burden society. Everyone will have an equal opportunity to work and provide for their family with dignity and honor. There will be a fair day's wage for a fair day's work. The rich will not be allowed to exploit the poor. There will be no special interest groups in Jerusalem seeking to gain favor at the expense of others. Messianic justice will be administered to all citizens without partiality.

There will be great economic prosperity and full employment (Isaiah 65:21-23; Joel 2:24-26). Government housing, welfare and ghettos will be a thing of the past. There will be no need for food relief programs. Everyone will have plenty to eat for the earth will be greatly productive (Amos 9:13-14).

Management and labor will work together for the common good. There will be no need for collective bargaining or crippling strikes that cut off needed services and goods. Plants will operate at full capacity. The world's economy will stabilize without the ups and downs of inflation and depression. Goods and services will be freely exchanged for the benefit of all.

Moral conditions will conform to the biblical standard (Isaiah 2:3). We won't need the Moral Majority to raise our moral consciousness, nor the Coalition for Better Television to rate the networks. There will be no smut peddlers, drug pushers, drunk drivers, pimps, prostitutes, gambling halls, crime or violence of any kind allowed.

The curse of sin will be partially removed (Romans 8:19-23). The result is that life expectancy will be lengthened so that a 100-year-old person will be considered a child (Isaiah 65:20). There will be no use for hospitals as there will be little or no sickness and death (Isaiah 33:24; Jeremiah 30:17). The world will experience a great population explosion to replenish the earth (Jeremiah 30:19-20). As I mentioned, everyone will speak the same language—Hebrew (Zephaniah. 3:9), so we will be able to communicate easily with everyone.

Light will be increased seven-fold so that more can be accomplished (Zechariah 14:6-7). The land will be fruitful (Isaiah 35:1-2; Zechariah 8:12). Even the animals will live together in peace (Isaiah 11:6-9; 65:25).

In every way, life will be better than we can possibly imagine because God himself will rule the nations through a perfect human King who is also divine—Jesus/Yeshua—the Son of David who is also the only begotten, uniquely born, Son of God.

Revelation 11:15 says:

> Then the seventh angel sounded: and there were loud voices in heaven, saying, "The kingdoms of the world have become the kingdoms of our Lord and of His Christ [Messiah], and He shall reign forever and ever."

The Lord is coming to establish the physical manifestation of His kingdom on the earth through Messiah Jesus. The "times of the Gentiles" are coming to an end. Now the reality is that kings don't normally give up their kingdoms without a fight. The leaders of the Gentile nations are not going to meekly surrender their kingdoms to a Jewish King. So the Bible says that when the Lord comes He is going to judge and make war against the kingdoms or nations of the world (Revelation 19:11).

As we get closer to this glorious event, we will see the judgment of God on the nations, including our own. A spiritual tsunami is about to take place in our world. The waves of the glory of God are about to overtake the nations. The glory of God will soon cover the earth as the waters cover the sea.

Revelation 19:11-16:

> Now I saw heaven opened, and behold, a white horse. And He who sat on him was called Faithful and True, and in righteousness He judges and makes war. His eyes were like a flame of fire, and on His head were many crowns. He had a name written that no one knew except Himself. He was clothed with a robe dipped in blood, and His name is called The Word of God. And the armies in heaven, clothed in fine linen, white and clean, followed Him on white horses. Now out of His mouth goes a sharp sword, that with it He should strike the nations. And He Himself will rule them with a rod of iron. He Himself treads the winepress of the fierceness and wrath of Almighty God. And He has on His robe and on His thigh a name written: KING OF KINGS AND LORD OF LORDS.

Our King is coming to establish His righteous kingdom on the earth. The prophet Habakkuk tells us, "For the earth will be filled with the knowledge of the glory of the LORD, as the waters cover the sea" (Habakkuk 2:14). This is the time on the earth believers have been anticipating and yearning for their whole lives. This is the future hope and expectation of God's people throughout the ages.

As we draw near to the Lord's return, He must judge the nations. This means that the world system as we know it will dramatically change. We must know in our heart of hearts that things have to change before the Lord comes.

But this is not a time to be fearful. It is a time to have faith and hope. It is a time to rejoice. It is time to sing the Song of Redemption. When Habakkuk learned of the coming destruction from Babylon, he praised the Lord with these words:

> Though the fig tree may not blossom, nor fruit be on the vines; though the labor of the olive may fail, and the fields yield no food; though the flock may be cut off from the fold, and there be no heard in the stalls—Yet I will rejoice in the LORD, I will joy in the God of my salvation (Habakkuk 3:17-18)

No matter what was happening around him, Habakkuk found joy in the God of his salvation. The God of Habakkuk is also the God of our salvation. He promises that if we will seek first His kingdom and His righteousness, He will give us everything we need to live and serve Him during this kingdom transition (Matthew 6:33). He has not given us a spirit of fear, but of power, love and a sound mind (2 Timothy 1:7). His word to his people is, "Do not fear, little flock, for it is the Father's good pleasure to give you the kingdom" (Luke 12:32).

CHAPTER 12

The Church in Prophecy

Most of us who are Bible believers look to the prophetic signs of our times and believe we are living in the last days of the latter days. It seems to us that Bible prophecies are being fulfilled before our very eyes.

We have witnessed the rebirth of the State of Israel in 1948. We have seen Israel liberate Jerusalem in 1967. Some of us have assisted in helping over a million Jews make aliyah from the former Soviet Union. Since Israel is God's prophetic clock, most of our attention and teaching on Bible prophecy focuses on Israel and the Jews.

The Church in Prophecy

But what about the Church? What is the role of the Church in Bible prophecy? Does God have a separate plan for Israel and the Church or do we share the same destiny? Has the Church replaced Israel in God's prophetic plan? Does God have an earthly people—Israel and a heavenly people—the Church?

Almost all books and seminars about the church in Bible prophecy are about the rapture or "catching up" of the Church to heaven. While all scholars agree there is a rapture, there is much disagreement about the timing of this event. Some read the Bible and see the rapture of the Church before the tribulation. Others read the same Bible and see the rapture in the middle of the tribulation. While still, others, reading the same Bible, believe the rapture will be at the end of the tribulation.

Over the centuries, dedicated men and women of God have read the same Scriptures but come to different conclusions on this subject. This can only mean that the Bible is not clear enough on this subject for us to be dogmatic about our beliefs regarding the rapture. Furthermore, there is very little said about the subject. Since it is not that clear, and there is little said about the subject, scholars have to interpret what they think the Bible means when it talks about this subject. While we can bet our life on what the Bible says, it is not wise to bet our life on what others tell us the Bible means, since all human interpretation of the Scriptures is subject to error. When we teach our interpretation of what we think the Bible means, rather than what it actually says, we need to do so with humility and openness to other views.

Regardless of your views on this subject, the Bible **is** very clear that trials and tribulation are a normal part of Christian living. In fact, Paul writes to his young disciple Timothy that "all who desire to live godly in Christ Jesus will suffer persecution" (2 Timothy 3:12). Furthermore, Jesus said, "In the world you will have tribulation; but be of good cheer, I have overcome the world" (John 16:33). We need to clearly understand that all of God's people, be they Jew or Christian, are going to have plenty of tribulation before "the tribulation" begins. It would be to our advantage to make sure we know how to overcome the world rather than arguing about theology and doctrine.

The Church on the Earth

Having said that, the biblical emphasis on the Church is not the Church in heaven but the Church on the earth. It seems to me that we would please the Lord by emphasizing what the Bible emphasizes. Bible prophecy emphasizes the Church ruling on the earth with our Lord, not floating on clouds in heaven. So how did we get off focus, emphasizing the Church in heaven rather than on the earth? It comes from Greek philosophy, which has influenced Church doctrines and thinking much more than most Christians realize. Let me explain.

In the Bible, when God created, He said that His creation was very good. Genesis 1:31 reads, "Then God saw everything that He had made, and indeed it was very good." God does not distinguish the physical-material world from His spiritual world. He does not consider the physical-material world to be inherently evil and unholy as opposed to His spiritual world which is good and holy.

In God's view, everything He created is good and is to be enjoyed within the boundaries of His teachings in the Bible. Whatever we do, the Bible says, we do it as unto the Lord. In other words, God does not distinguish between the sacred and the secular. As believers, everything we do is sacred unto the Lord. In God's view, cleaning the floor is just as sacred as preaching a sermon because all of life is sacred to God.

The Lord considers the way we live our lives, how we spend our time, how and where we spend our money, how we perform our job, and how we use the gifts He has given us, a sacred trust. We are stewards of the life He has given us—that includes our life in the physical-material world as well as our spiritual life.

Abraham Joshua Heschel was a very important Jewish scholar and spiritual man. He said what every Christian should understand, "Every home can be a temple, every table an altar, and all of life a song to God."

It is Greek philosophy that teaches that the Creator made a distinction between the physical-material world and the world of the spirit. This worldview is called "dualism." Greek philosophy teaches that the physical-material world is inherently evil as opposed to the spirit world of God which is good. Greek philosophy teaches that in order to be spiritual, we must separate ourselves from the inherently evil physical-material world. The only way for people to be spiritual is for us to live in a heaven that is free from the earth.

This teaching was embraced by the Greco-Roman church of the fourth century and enforced with the sword of Constantine. It was passed on to later generations through the pen of Augustine and became official church doctrine through the ages. In this view, the only way for people to live in the good world of the spirit is to be removed from the physical-material earth to heaven.

What is the Church?

Before we talk about the Church in Bible prophecy, we must first understand what we mean by the word "Church." When we talk about the Church in prophecy, what are we talking about? What is the Church? Before clarifying what the Church is it is important to understand what the Church is not.

What the Church is Not

What comes to your mind when you hear the word Church? For most of the world, even Christians, the word Church is the name of a religious institution of Christianity. For example, the world speaks of the Roman Catholic Church, or the Protestant Church, the Baptist Church, Methodist Church. Lutheran Church, Presbyterian Church, Pentecostal Church, charismatic Church, Bible Church, Church of Scotland, Anglican Church, Episcopal Church, Russian Orthodox Church, Egyptian Coptic Church, Church of God, Church of Christ, the local Church, etc.

There are thousands of denominational groups called "the Church." No wonder people are confused. These are organized representations of the Christian religion. But they in themselves are not the Church. The true Church can be found in these institutions but the institutions are not the Church. When I talk about the Church in prophecy, I am not talking about the religious institutions of Christianity. So what am I talking about? What is the Church?

The *Kahal* and *Edah*

Of course the Bible is the book we must consult to answer this question. In the *Tanakh* (commonly called the Old Testament); there are two Hebrew words that were eventually translated into English as "church." These words are *"edah"* and *"kahal."*

Proverbs 5:14 reads, "I was on the verge of total ruin, in the midst of the assembly [*kahal*] and congregation [*edah*]."

These words both mean the same thing. They both mean, "a community of people, a congregation, a gathering, or an assembly." They in no way refer to a building or a religious institution.

In the period between the Testaments, Alexander the Great conquered most of the known world and established Greek as the universal language. During this time, the Jews who lived outside the land of Israel under Alexander's rule spoke Greek as their primary language. Now this presented a problem because the *Tanakh* is written in Hebrew with a little in Aramaic. The younger generation of Jews growing up in a Greek speaking world, were losing their ability to understand their own Bible written in Hebrew. This would be like people today coming to America from another country and learning English as their primary language. Their children, born in America, would learn English from their parents. Over time, they would lose their knowledge of their native tongue.

The *Septuagint*

So around 250 BC, the *Tanakh* was translated from Hebrew to Greek. This Greek translation of the Tanakh was called the "*Septuagint*." We need to understand how important the *Septuagint* is to us. The *Septuagint* was the Greek translation of the Hebrew Bible that was used by the writers of the New Testament.

In other words, Paul and Luke did not sit down with the Hebrew language *Tanakh* in one hand and write what became part of the New Testament with the other hand. Because they were writing to Greek speakers, they used the *Septuagint* as their Hebrew Bible text. A large percentage of the New Testament was written using the Greek language *Septuagint*, not the Hebrew language *Tanakh*.

Kahal/Edah/Ekklesia/Sunagoge

So why is this important? When the Hebrew words "*kahal*" and "*edah*" were translated into Greek in the *Septuagint*, they were translated by two Greek words that have the same meaning. These two Greek words are "*ekklesia*" and "*sunagoge*." *Edah* was translated as *sunagoge* while *kahal* was translated as *sunagoge* and *ekklesia*. So *edah* and *kahal* equal *sunagoge* and *ekklesia*. *Sunagoge* and *ekklesia* mean the same as *edah* and *kahal*. They mean a community of people, a congregation, an assembly, a gathering.

These were common generic neutral words that referred to any group of people, of any number, meeting for any reason, anywhere and at any time. There was no religious meaning to the terms. The terms were not connected to any specific group or cause. They just described a community of people congregating for any purpose. They were not used to reference any organization or institution but a company of people, any people. As they were not religious words, they did not specifically refer to Jews and Christians or any specific group.

In the New Testament writing, the word *sunagoge* is used about 50 times and *ekklesia* is used about 100 times. The Greek word *sunagoge* was translated into English by Western scholars as "synagogue" which makes us thing they are writing about a Jewish house of worship. Today, the word "synagogue" specifically refers to a religious meeting place of Jews. So when we read the word "synagogue" in the New Testament, we think the writer is talking about Jews meeting in a building for religious purposes. The word had nothing to do with Jews but referred to any group meeting for any purpose.

It is the same with "*ekklesia*." The word "*ekklesia*" was translated in our English Bible as "church," which makes us think they were writing about a Christian house of worship. This plants in our minds the idea that there were two different religious groups—the Jews and the Christians. The Jews, we have believed, met at the synagogue and the Christians met at the church.

Over time, synagogue and church became two separate religious institutions called Judaism and Christianity. We have been told that the Jews and Christians have a different destiny. The church, we are told, replaced the Jews and the synagogue as the people of God. Christianity replaced Israel and the church, that is the religious institution, became the kingdom of God. The Jews are to suffer on the earth while the Christians are to live forever in heaven. This entire theology of a separate people with a separate destiny came about because of a mistranslation and misunderstanding of these words.

Again, the word *sunagoge* does not specifically refer to Jews and *ekklesia* does not refer specifically to the church. Because they are neutral words, they could be used interchangeably. When Jews today meet for their worship services, biblically speaking, they are the *kahal/sunagogue/ekklesia/*church gathering. When Christians meet for their worship services, biblically speaking, they are the *kahal/sunagogue/ekklesia/*church gathering. In the Bible, there is no distinction. Those meeting at the *sunagoge* could be Christians and those meeting at the *ekklesia* could be Jews. Or it could be neither group. It could be the Republicans and the Democrats.

The English word "church," in its biblical meaning, could be a meeting of the high school band to practice for the big game. It could be the Rotary club, the Lions club, the office party, the political conventions, the high school football team practice, friends meeting in a home for dinner, the garden club, Jews, Christians, Buddhist, Muslims, Hindus meeting for worship, a Nazi rally, an Islamic terrorist group meeting, an ice cream social, or any group, of any number, meeting anywhere, anytime, and for any purpose.

In Acts 7:38, the English translation has Steven referring to Israel as the "church in the wilderness," although some translations do use the word assembly in the wilderness. Steven did not speak English. He most likely spoke Hebrew and would have said the "*kahal* in the wilderness." Israel was the *kahal* of God.

How the English Word "Church" Got Into the New Testament

Now let's flash forward 1500 years. When William Tyndall translated the Bible into English in 1525, he translated the word *ekklesia* into English as "community." There is a major difference in what we think when we hear the word community versus the word church. For most of the world the word church means the religious institutions of Christianity with all its accompanying buildings, ecclesiastical hierarchy, doctrines, etc. The word community doesn't mean that at all.

When King James wanted to issue a formal English translation of the Bible, He instructed his translators to use the Tyndall Bible as the primary English source. In other words, most of the King James Bible was taken from the Tyndall translation. This is good. Now at that time there was no separation between the government of England and the Church of England. Both functioned under the rule of King James.

Since King James was the head of the "Church of England" and wanted to keep it under his authority, he set the rules the translators had to follow. The third rule was that the translators were not to translate *ekklesia* as "community" as Tyndall had correctly done but to translate ekklesia into the English word "church."

Since King James was the head of the "Church," he needed the word Church in his translation. Now think how different we would understand who we are as the people of God if King James would have used the word community, congregation, assembly, gathering, covenant people, etc. rather than the word "Church" and all it means today. He couldn't do that because he would have lost control of the people.

What is the Church?

Now with all that background, what is the church and what is its role in Bible prophecy? Matthew 16:13-18 reads, "When Jesus came into the region of Caesarea Philippi, He asked His disciples, saying, 'Who do men say that I, the Son of Man, am?' So they said, 'Some say John the Baptist, some say Elijah, and others Jeremiah or one of the prophets.' He said to them, "But who do you say that I am?' Simon Peter answered, 'You are the Christ [Messiah], the Son of the living God.' Jesus answered and said to him, 'Blessed are you, Simon Bar-Jonah, for flesh and blood has not revealed this to you, but My Father who is in heaven. And I also say to you that you are Peter, and on this rock I will build My church *[kahal/ekklesia]*, and the gates of hell shall not prevail against it."

The English has Jesus saying, "Upon this rock I will build my church." When we read that we think about Christianity and the church as we know it today. But Jesus didn't speak English. He didn't speak Greek. He spoke Hebrew. (See Acts 26:14.) He would have said, "Upon this rock I will build My *kahal*." He meant His community, His congregation, His assembly of people, His gathering, His followers. It is the same as what Steven was referring to when he spoke of Israel as the assembly in the wilderness.

The idea of the word "church," as we think of it today, being the religious institutions of Christianity, is not found in the Bible. The biblical *kahal/sunagoge/ekklesia*, as it relates to believers, means a company of people who are in covenant with God through Yeshua, the Jewish Messiah be they Jew or Gentile. We have had a revelation from the God of Abraham, Isaac, and Jacob, the God of Israel, that Jesus [Yeshua in Hebrew] is the anointed One of God. He is the Prophet greater than Moses, the Priest greater than Aaron and the King greater than David. As such, He is the faithful and true witness, the first born from the dead and the ruler of the kings of the earth.

Wherever and whenever this company of people meets, they themselves are the *kahlal/ekklesia*/community of God. This company of people meets in buildings dedicated for religious gatherings, they meet in homes, they meet at retreat centers, they meet at lunch for Bible study at work, they meet for prayer meetings, they meet in hotels for conferences, they meet at a Christian school, they meet as a family to home school their children, they meet for coffee, and whatever other venue is necessary. One month I conducted Christian meetings in a fire station, a hotel, and an ex-pornographic movie house.

Wherever and whenever God's people are gathered, even if it is just two or three, they are the *kahal/ekklesia*, covenant community of God. When a husband and wife have Bible study at home with their children, they are the *kahal/ekklesia*/community of the Lord. Biblically speaking, we don't go to church, we are the church. It's the people.

This is what and who we are talking about when we use the word "Church." We are talking about people in covenant with God. Whenever and wherever a single group of believers assemble, for whatever purposes, they are considered to be the full expression of the community of people, and not just a part of the larger expression.

We have not replaced Israel and the Jews. We are connected to them. Not through a Greco-Roman Christ but a Jewish Lord and King who is returning as the Lion from the Tribe of Judah, the Root and the Offspring of David. We are grafted in to the Jewish people and are part of the common wealth of Israel. As such, we are not separate from them. They are not the earthly people and us the heavenly people.

We are one with them and share a common destiny in Bible prophecy. This common destiny is not in heaven but on the earth where we will rule and reign with our Lord. Jesus said "the meek shall inherit the earth" (Matthew 5:5). We have a glorious prophetic future with God. But it is not in heaven, it is on the earth.

What is the role of the Church in Bible Prophecy?

So what is the role of the Church in Bible prophecy? What are we going to be doing on the earth? We are going to be a kingdom of priests administering the kingdom of God on the earth. This has always been God's destiny for mankind and is why He created us in the first place.

Made for Dominion and Rule

The Bible says when God made Adam and Eve He gave them dominion or rule on the earth. Genesis 1:27-28 says: "So God created man in His own image; in the image of God He created him; male and female He created them. Then God blessed them, and God said to them, 'Be fruitful and multiply; fill the earth and subdue it; have dominion over the fish of the sea, over the birds of the air, and over every living thing that moves on the earth."

God made mankind in His image and empowered us to function as His co-regents on the earth. We were to rule over His creation as His royal priests. We were to administer His kingdom over the earth.

When Adam and Eve failed to live up to their high calling, this did not put an end to God's plan for mankind. As the descendants of Adam and Eve grew in number, they too rebelled against God and missed their destiny. But God always has a remnant of His people who want to please Him and serve Him. So the Bible says that Noah was a just man who walked with the Lord and found grace in the eyes of the Lord (Genesis 6:8-9). Even though it was necessary for God to destroy evil with the great flood, He confirmed His covenant with Noah and declared Noah to be righteous (Genesis 6:18; 7:1).

After the flood, the descendants of Noah served God. But over time the flood became a story passed down to later generations who did not fear God. But this did not change God's plans, purposes, and destiny for mankind.

God called a man named Abraham and told Abraham that God would renew His covenant with him and his descendants. Abraham's descendants would be an entire nation of royal priests, demonstrating and administrating the kingdom of God on the earth.

When God delivered the Hebrews from Egypt, He said to them:

> Now therefore, if you will indeed obey My voice and keep my covenant, then you shall be a special treasure to Me above all people; for all the earth is Mine. And you shall be to me a kingdom of priests and a holy nation (Exodus 19:5-6).

Under the influence of Joshua, and later Samuel and David, the people feared God. But once again the chosen people failed to live up to their high calling and destiny. Most of their kings were evil, they had a civil war that split the nation, and in spite of constant warnings from the prophets, the people turned their back on God and the covenant. They preferred to be like the other nations. They didn't want to be God's kingdom of priests. They didn't want to be a holy nation.

While the people turned their back on God, He never turns His back on us. He promised David that he would forever have a descendant who would sit on his throne and unite the kingdom of David and the kingdom of God in a righteous rule over the earth, "And your house and your kingdom shall be established forever before you. Your throne shall be established forever" (2 Samuel 7:16).

The Lord's plans, purposes, and destiny for us never change. It is the same today as in times of old. We read in Isaiah:

> Remember the former things of old, For I am God, and there is no other; I am God, and there is none like Me, declaring the end from the beginning, and from ancient times things that are not yet done, saying, "My counsel shall stand, and I will do all My pleasure" (Isaiah 46:9-10).

The Lord's counsel and pleasure was for mankind to administer His kingdom on the earth. Knowing that we would fail Him, the Lord planned from eternity past to come to the earth Himself to show us how it is done. Through the man God would become, the Lord would fulfill His own heart's desire to have a man ruling in His place on the earth

The prophets spoke of this Man with these words:

> For unto us a Child is born, unto us a Son is given; and the government will be upon His shoulder. And His name will be called Wonderful, Counselor, Mighty God, Everlasting Father, Prince of Peace. Of the increase of His government and peace there will be no end, upon the throne of David and over His kingdom (Isaiah 9:6-7).

The Psalmists speaks of the time when the divine ruler will administer God's kingdom on the earth. Psalm 22:27-28 says:

> All the ends of the world shall remember and turn to the LORD, and all the families of the nations shall worship

before You. For the kingdom is the LORD'S. And He rules over the nations.

Daniel says it this way:

I was watching in the night visions, and behold, One like the Son of Man, coming with the clouds of heaven! He came to the Ancient of Days, and they brought Him near before Him. Then to Him was given dominion and glory and a kingdom, that all peoples, nations, and languages should serve Him. His dominion is an everlasting dominion, which shall not pass away, and His kingdom the one which shall not be destroyed (Daniel 7:13-14).

Daniel adds:

Then the kingdom and dominion, and the greatness of the kingdoms of under the whole heaven, shall be given to the people, the saints of the Most High. His kingdom is an everlasting kingdom, and all dominions shall serve and obey Him (Daniel 7:27).

The writings in the New Testament identify Jesus of Nazareth as this man who will be God's chosen divine ruler, establishing His kingdom on the earth. Luke 1:31-33 reads:

And behold, you will conceive in your womb and bring forth a Son, and shall call His name JESUS [Yeshua]. He will be great, and will be called the Son of the Highest; and the Lord God will give Him the throne of His father David. And He will reign over the house of Jacob forever, and of His kingdom there will be no end.

According to the sovereign plan of God, His people are destined to live under the righteous rule of the Messiah on the earth. While the Messiah is the one who fulfills God's plan to have a man ruling for Him on the earth, everyone in covenant with the Messiah will rule with Him as administrators of His kingdom.

John explains in the book of Revelation:

> And they sang a new song saying, "You are worthy to take the scroll, and to open its seals; for Your were slain, and have redeemed us to God by Your blood out of every tribe and tongue and people and nation, and have made us kings and priest to our God; and we shall reign on the earth"(Revelation 5:9-10).

When Messiah comes a second time to the earth, He is coming as King of Kings and Lord of Lords. Revelation 19:11-16 reads:

> Now I saw heaven opened, and behold, a white horse. And He who sat on him was called Faithful and True, and in righteousness He judges and makes war. His eyes were like a flame of fire, and on His head were many crowns. He had a name written that no one knew except Himself. He was clothed with a robe dipped in blood, and His name is called The Word of God. And the armies in heaven, clothed in fine linen white and clean, followed Him on white horses. Now out of His mouth goes a sharp sword, that with it He should strike the nations. And He Himself will rule them with a rod of iron. He Himself treads the winepress of the fierceness and wrath of Almighty God. And He has on His robe and on His thigh a name written: KING OF KINGS AND LORD OF LORDS.

Jesus is not coming as a Greco-Roman Christian. He is coming as the Lion from the Tribe of Judah—the Root and Offspring of David (Revelation 5:5). The Lord is not coming to a religious institution. He is coming for a people. Everyone who embraces the Messiah is part of a covenant community of people that live in the Kingdom of God on the earth. This is a kingdom of people living under the rule of the greater Son of David who is also King of Kings and Lord of Lords. Those of us who are non-Jews are grafted into the Jewish people and share their destiny in the Commonwealth of Israel.

The New Jerusalem

Revelation 20:1-5 says that we will rule on the earth with the Lord for 1,000 years. After this time, the New Jerusalem, which is our eternal home, will come from heaven to earth (Revelation 21-22). The New Jerusalem is the place Jesus went to prepare for us. We will live forever on the earth with God dwelling in our midst in the New Jerusalem.

As described in a previous chapter, the Lord has prepared an amazing place for us. Our home town on the earth is 1,500 miles high. The wall around the city has 12 gates, with each attended by an angel. The wall is made of jasper and each gate is made of a single pearl. The gates are named after the 12 tribes of Israel, representing the Jewish people.

The wall of the city has 12 foundations made of precious stones. Each foundation is named after one of the 12 apostles of Jesus who ultimately brought the gospel of the kingdom to the Gentiles. The foundations are made of precious stones. The city itself is pure gold, like clear glass. The glory of God is the light of the city. The Lord's presence, which permeates through the city, is the Temple.

Because the glory of the Lord shines brighter than the sun at its brightest, there is no night time. Because all evil and sin is purged from the earth, the gates will always remain open. The nations shall walk in the light of God's brightness and bring their glory and honor to Him in our hometown on the earth. John says that we will see God face-to-face and reign forever with Him on the earth (Revelation 22:4-5).

While we are living in perilous times, the Lord has promised us a glorious future. We do not live in fear of God's judgments on the earth but in faith in our Father in heaven. He is a faithful, covenant-keeping, God who will bring to pass the clear and certain promises He has made to His own.

Jesus explains:

> And there will be signs in the sun, in the moon, and in the stars; and on the earth distress of nations, with perplexity, the sea and the waves roaring; men's hearts failing them from fear and the expectation of those things which are coming on the earth, for the powers of the heavens will be shaken. Then they will see the Son of Man coming in a cloud with power and great glory. Now when these things begin to happen, look up and lift up your heads, because your redemption draws near (Luke 21:25-28).

CHAPTER 13

Preparing for the End-Times

As we see the prophetic signs happening before our very eyes, many conclude that we are living in the end-times prior to the coming of Messiah. If this is true, how do we prepare for the challenging days ahead? Whether one believes in a pre-, mid-, or post-tribulation rapture, the world is beginning to change, and we need to be prepared. I have written six action steps that I believe are necessary for us to stand firm in faith and hope. These are action steps for walking with God in good times and bad times. God will show each of us how to apply these steps to our personal lives on an individual basis as world events unfold. As believers, we should be taking these steps everyday of our lives, but especially in preparation for the days ahead.

Step 1. Realize that God Sovereign

Step one is to realize that God is sovereign over the nations and has a wonderful plan for your life and for all who love Him. The one true God is outside of time and space but works in time and space to bring forth His redemptive plans and purposes for His creation. In a Bible verse we quoted earlier, God tells us in Isaiah 46:9-10, "Remember the former things of old, for I am God, and there is no other; I am God, and there is none like Me, declaring the end from the beginning, and from ancient times things that are not yet done, saying, 'My counsel shall stand, and I will do all My pleasure.'"

The Lord reminds us that He alone is God and there is no other. He is not the generic god of the world who goes by different names. He is not the Greco-Roman god of Constantine. He is the God of

Abraham, Isaac, and Jacob; the God of Israel. He is the same in the New Testament Scriptures as He is in the First Testament. He is the God who changes not. He is the one and only true God and all other pretend deities are deceiving spirits. This means that we do *not* all worship the same God by different names.

The one true God of the Bible has a plan or counsel that He has foreordained before He ever created. He has written this plan in the Scriptures so His people can know Him, what He has done in the past, what He is doing in the present, and what He will do in the future. We call His future plans "Bible prophecy." While we can and should partner with God through prayer and fasting to shape the destiny of nations, there are some things that are predetermined. No matter the personal plans and ambitions of world leaders, God will fulfill His prophetic words.

In Psalm 2, God says He laughs at the schemes of the leaders of the nations to overthrow Him. He shall break them with a rod of iron and dash them to pieces like a potter's vessel.

Psalm 33:10-12 says, "The LORD brings the counsel of the nations to nothing; He makes the plans of the people of no effect. The counsel of the LORD stands forever, the plans of His heart to all generations. Blessed is the nation whose God is the LORD, the people He has chosen as His own inheritance."

Psalm 22:27-28 reads, "All the ends of the world shall remember and turn to the LORD, and all the families of the nations shall worship before You. For the kingdom is the LORD's, and He rules over the nations."

The world only offers false hope, true hope for a glorious future comes from the Lord. Jeremiah explains, "For I know the thoughts that I think toward you, says the LORD, thoughts of peace and not of evil, to give you a future and a hope" (Jeremiah 29:11).

The Apostle Paul also encourages us with these words, "And we know that all things work together for good to those who love God, to those who are the called according to His purpose. For whom He foreknew, He also predestined to be conformed to the image of His son, that He might be the firstborn among many brethren. Moreover who He predestined, these He also called; whom He called, these He also justified; and who He justified, these He also glorified" (Romans 8:28-30).

While there are difficult days ahead, God will fulfill His prophetic purposes for the nations and in our individual lives. Peter adds these encouraging words:

> Blessed be the God and Father of our Lord Jesus Christ, who according to His abundant mercy has begotten us again to a living hope through the resurrection of Jesus Christ from the dead, to an inheritance incorruptible and undefiled and that does not fade away, reserved in heaven for you, who are kept by the power of God through faith for salvation ready to be revealed in the last time.
>
> In this you greatly rejoice, though now for a little while, if need be, you have been grieved by various trials, that the genuineness of your faith, being much more precious than gold that perishes, though it is tested by fire, may be found to praise, honor, and glory at the revelation of Jesus Christ, whom having not seen you love. Though now you do not see Him, yet believing, you rejoice with joy inexpressible and full of glory, receiving the end of your faith—the salvation of your souls (1 Peter 1:3-9).

We do not need to fear the negative things happening in our world. The Lord God rules over the nations and will use their evil intentions to further His purposes on the earth as He has done throughout history. As Franklin Roosevelt said, "The only thing we have to fear is fear itself." Paul reminds us that "God has not given us a spirit of fear, but of power and of love and of a sound mind" (2 Timothy 1:7).

In view of God's sovereign rule and the glorious future and hope He has for us, Psalm 47:1-3 says how we should view the end-times, "Oh, clap your hands, all you peoples! Shout to God with the voice of triumph! For the LORD Most High is awesome; He is a great King over all the earth. He will subdue the peoples under us, and the nations under our feet."

We can rejoice in difficult times knowing that our God has a plan, He is fulfilling His plan, we are part of that plan, and it is a plan for His glory and our good. He will establish His rule on the earth. All nations will acknowledge Him as the one true God. We will rule over the nations with Him. And we may just be alive to see all happen. Praise God!

As believers we need to make sure that we are worshipping the right God—the God as He has revealed Himself in the Bible, not through the eyes of Western culture. We need to make sure we are worshipping the God of Abraham, Isaac, and Jacob, not the Greco-Roman god of Constantine.

And not only that we worship Him, but we know Him intimately in His core essence and being. We can do this is by meditating on specific Scriptures that speak about His awesome majesty and His character of holiness, love, justice, and goodness. May I suggest you consider buying a copy of my book, *What Everyone Needs to Know About God*, which you can order from my Internet bookstore at www.rbooker.com.

Step 2. Accept the Yoke of the Kingdom of God

The second step is to accept the yoke of the King and the kingdom of God. In other words, acknowledge God as King of your life. In Bible times, nations were ruled by kings and emperors who were thought to be human representatives of the gods the people worshipped. Great empires did not have a Constitution or Bill of Rights giving people the freedoms we enjoy as Americans. There was no democratically elected representative government. When the king or emperor issued a decree, the people did not vote on it. They obeyed it.

God was also understood and reverenced as "King of the Universe." He was addressed as Master or Ruler of all. King David addressed God in this way:

> Blessed are You, LORD God of Israel, our Father, forever and ever. Yours O LORD is the greatness, the power and the glory, the victory and the majesty; for all that is in heaven and in earth is Yours; Yours in the kingdom, O LORD, and you are exalted as head above all. Both riches and honor come from You, and You reign over all. In Your hand is power and might; in Your hand it is to make great and to give strength to all. Now therefore, our God, we thank You and praise your glorious name (1 Chronicles 29:10-13).

In the New Testament, what became known as the Lord's Prayer began with this same recognition that God was both King and Father. Jesus said pray, "Our Father in heaven." Now surely Jesus knew that God lived in heaven. So He was not thinking in terms of location. He was acknowledging the sovereign rule of God and His awesome holiness, greatness, and majesty.

There is an ancient Jewish prayer called the *Avinu Malkeinu*, which means, "Our Father, Our King." Jewish people still pray a version of that prayer today. Each verse begins with the words, *Avinu Malkeinu* and is followed by an appeal to the Almighty to extend His mercy as a loving Father, while acknowledging the responsibility of the worshipper to serve and obey God our King.

Bible people focused on seeing the fullness of the kingdom of God manifested on the earth. They had a burning passion for the sovereign rule and kingship of God in heaven to be fully realized on the earth. Whereas Christian prayers and thinking most often express concern for individual salvation, people of the Bible sought God as King, Master, and Sovereign Ruler over the nations and their lives personally.

Formal Jewish prayers today express this understanding and begin with the phrase, "Baruch Atah Adonai Eloheynu Melech Ha Olam" meaning "Blessed are You O LORD our God, King of the Universe."

The American Constitution and form of government is by far the best human inspired national declarations in all of history. Those of us who are Americans owe a great debt to our founding fathers for their wisdom and willingness to establish a government that could represent the will of the people. Our founding documents are historic in this regard.

But in some ways, they are a hindrance to American believers understanding our relationship to God. For unlike our human government, the government of heaven is not a democracy. The government of heaven is a theocracy, which means that God reigns as sovereign King and Master of His universe and over His people. His decrees as recorded in the Bible are not there for us to vote on, nor are they there to represent the will of the people. They are His sovereign decrees representing His will to be obeyed as our loving Father and Sovereign King.

In Matthew 11:28-30 Jesus said:

> Come to Me, all you who labor and are heavy laden, and I will give you rest. Take My joke upon you and learn from Me, for I am gently and lowly in heart, and you will find rest for your souls. For My yoke is easy and My burden is light.

Now what does this mean? In the Bible, the Jewish people understood God as Lord and Master of the universe. They looked to God, not just as Savior, Deliverer, and Redeemer but as the sovereign King over His kingdom. To take on the yoke of the kingdom meant to submit to His Lordship and obey His commandments. Because He was Master and Lord, He was able to save, deliver, and redeem.

As stated previously, while Christianity in America has not emphasized the Gospel of the kingdom, it is the emphasis in the New Testament, as the New Testament is just a continuation of what was proclaimed in the Hebrew Bible. And it is definitely the emphasis in the end-times.

John the Baptist and Jesus and Paul all preached the Gospel of the kingdom. Jesus sent out His disciples to preach the Gospel of the kingdom. In Matthew 24:14, Jesus said, "This Gospel of the kingdom will be preached in all the world as a witness to the nations, and then the end will come."

We thank God for the Gospel of salvation. But in these end-times the emphasis is the Gospel of the kingdom. As believers, we must walk with God beyond the level of salvation and accept the kingship of God. We must come to understand that we are only stewards of the life, the resources, the money, the time, and the talents God has given to us. We must obey God and live to please Him in our words, our thoughts, and our deeds everyday of our lives. We must submit our will to God as King, Master, and Lord. We must do it now!

As we see the prophetic signs, we must understand that everything is about to change. We can rejoice in the knowledge that the coming of the Lord is at hand. And while there are perilous times, as Paul mentioned, our hope and trust is in the Lord, not in America and our materialism.

If you will accept the yoke of the kingdom of God, the Lord promised to meet all your needs. Jesus said in Matthew 6:33, "But seek first the kingdom of God and his righteousness, and all these things shall be added to you."

In Luke 12:32, Jesus said, "Do not fear, little flock, for it is your Father's good pleasure to give you the kingdom."

In Matthew 8:11 Jesus said, "And I say to you that many will come from east and west, and sit down with Abraham, Isaac, and Jacob in the kingdom of heaven."

Let us prepare for the days ahead by acknowledging God, not only as our loving Father, but as our sovereign King who rules over His creation, including His people. One thing we can do that will help us do this is to meditate on those Scriptures that speak of God in this way. One example is Psalm 47:6-8 which says, "Sing praises to God, sing praises! Sing praises to our King, sing praises! For God is the King of all the earth; sing praises with understanding. God reigns over the nations; God sits on His holy throne."

Step 3. Commit to Jesus as Lord and Not Just as Savior

Step three is to commit to Jesus as Lord and not just as Savior. We thank God for sending Jesus to save us, deliver us, and redeem us. But Jesus can do this for us because He is Lord.

In the New Testament, Jesus gave a rebuke to some who were following Him. He said, "But why do you call Me 'Lord, Lord,' and do not do the things which I say" (Luke 6:46).

He went on to say"

> Not everyone who says to Me, "Lord, Lord," shall enter the kingdom of heaven, but he who does the will of My Father who is in heaven. Many will say to Me in that day, "Lord, Lord, have we not prophesied in Your name, cast out demons in Your name, and done many wonders in Your name?" And then I will declare to them, "I never knew you; depart from Me, you who practice lawlessness" (Mathew 7:21-23).

Jesus then gave an example to illustrate His point. He said:

> Therefore whoever hears these sayings of Mine, and does them, I will liken him to a wise man who built his house on the rock: and the rain descended, the floods came, and the winds blew and beat on that house; and it did not fall, for it was founded on the rock. But everyone who hears these sayings of Mine, and does not do them, will be like a foolish man who built his house on the sand: and the rain descended, the floods came, and the winds blew and beat on that house; and it fell. And great was its fall! (Matthew 7:24-27).

We thank God for the basic message of salvation and for the servants of God who have faithfully proclaimed this message. We thank God that Jesus is our Savior. But the reason Jesus can be our Savior is because He is Lord. In the days ahead, professing Christians who only know Jesus as Savior, but not as Lord, will be like the house built on sand. They will not be able to stand strong against the powerful end-time spiritual rain, floods, and winds that God will send as judgments on the earth in preparation for His coming.

So let us examine ourselves and make a renewed commitment to Jesus as Lord of our lives. While God is certainly full of grace and mercy, He expects us to obey Him. As we obey, He will manifest Himself to us with His power, glory, peace, love, joy and comfort beyond measure. Let us seek His will and ask the Holy Spirit to empower us so that we can fully obey Him and serve Him as we prepare for His coming to redeem the world and establish His kingdom on the earth.

Step 4. Actively Partner with God in His Redemptive Work

Step four is to actively partner with God in His redemptive work. All of God's people have a calling from God to serve Him in the way He has uniquely equipped us. We are all ministers of the Most High God. We are all in full-time ministry. Some of us do our ministry as a livelihood, while most serve God while earning a living in their work life. In God's mind, there is no separation between the sacred and the secular. Whatever we do, we do it as unto the Lord.

God had made each of us unique. He has given each of us natural talents and abilities that He anoints for service by His Spirit. Instead of using those God-given talents and abilities for ourselves, He wants us to use them to serve Him and others for the purpose of partnering with Him in His redemptive work. In addition, God gives each of us spiritual gifts that are separate and different from our natural abilities.

God then puts a part of His vision or burden for the prophetic season in which we are living into our hearts. He then assigns us to congregations and ministries with that same vision. This is how we know where God wants us to serve Him. This is where we give our time, our talents, and our money. As we corporately serve Him with our unique anointed abilities and spiritual gifts, we partner with Him and others who share the same vision to bring His will from heaven to earth. There is no place in the end-times for spectator Christianity. We must become active participants with God in these last days.

Paul wrote in Romans 12:6-8:

> Having then gifts differing according to the grace that is given to us, let us use them: if prophecy, let us prophecy in proportion to our faith; or ministry [service], let us use it in our ministering [serving], he who teaches, in teaching; he who exhorts, in exhortation; he who gives, with liberality; he who leads, with diligence; he who shows mercy, with cheerfulness.

Peter wrote in 1 Peter 4:7-11:

> But the end of all things is at hand; therefore be serious and watchful in your prayers. And above all things have fervent love for one another, for love will cover a multitude of sins. Be hospitable to one another without grumbling. As each one has received a gift, minister it to one another, as good stewards of the manifold grace of God. In anyone speaks, let him speak as the oracles of God. If anyone ministers, let him do it as with the ability which God supplies, that in all things God may be

glorified through Jesus Christ [Messiah], to whom belong the glory and the dominion forever and ever. Amen.

As we actively partner with God, He will use us in ways beyond anything we could possible imagine. We will no longer just read about prophecy, we will actually be part of its fulfillment as God works in us, through us, and out of us to bring His will from heaven to earth. In the midst of great darkness, we will shine as bright lights of His majesty and mercy, He greatness and goodness, His charisma and character, His power and His purity to those without hope. May His name be praised forever in us.

Step 5. Live in Community

The fifth step is to live in community with fellow believers. The believers in the New Testament were not "isolated believers." They did not meet in large, impersonal, cathedrals. They were not spectators to a religious performance by a minister. They did not consider themselves to be individual believers apart from the community of believers. They lived in community with their fellow believers. Their blessings and their problems were shared by the community. When one rejoiced they all rejoiced, but when one suffered the community suffered.

They met primarily in homes where the family functioned as the basic church, with each member serving and loving one another through their God-given gifting and ministries. While the father functioned as the lead priest of the home, each member of the family was an active participant in worship, prayer, study, and fellowship. Individual families would join with other families for extended home gatherings around the covenant meal, study, and prayer.

While families joined with others for corporate gatherings to celebrate, the emphasis was the family as the sanctuary of the Lord. The families understood that they, not a building, were the basic unit of the church where the primary ministry to one another was to take place in a safe, loving, learning environment of caring, sharing, and bearing one another's burdens. The focus was community and relationships, not religious activity.

We read in the books of Acts:

> And they continued steadfastly in the apostles' doctrine and fellowship, in the breaking of bread, and in prayers. Then fear came upon every soul, and many wonders and signs were done through the apostles. Now all who believed were together, and had all things in common, and sold their possessions and goods, and divided them among all, as everyone had need. So continuing daily with one accord in the temple, and breaking bread from house to house, they ate their food with gladness and simplicity of heart, praising God and having favor with all the people. And the Lord added to the church daily those who were being saved (Acts 2:42-47).

In the fourth century, Constantine embraced Christianity and turned it into a Greco-Roman religion patterned after Greek philosophy and Roman pagan practices. The institutional church of Constantine appointed a special class of clergy who replaced the people as the priests of God. A few specially called priests performed the work of God while the people sat and watched in magnificent cathedrals which would replace the family, the home, and the community as the focus of Christian life and ministry.

The institutional church of Constantine changed Christianity from it vital community-family-focused life and ministry to a performance-based spectator form of religion. Religious buildings, programs, and activities replaced the community and the home, the Spirit, and relationships as the focus of church life and ministry.

Over time, the people were content to let the experts worship, study, and pray on their behalf. The institutional church with its professional clergy, where people go to a building to have church, remains the common understanding of the meaning of church.

This is all about to change. The Lord is awakening a godly remnant of believers with a holy dissatisfaction with the traditional performance-based, spectator form, of Christianity lacking community and relationships. A "Spiritual Tsunami" will soon shake the world and the church will change as dramatically as the change in the coastline of those countries hit by a recent Tsunamis.

For many, this will mean a return to a New Testament form of Christianity where believers meet primarily in their homes with an emphasis on community and covenantal relationships. For some, this will mean establishing a community of like-minded believers where people will live together and share in the common needs of the community much like a *Kibbutz* or *Moshav* in Israel. However God leads the end-time remnant of believers, they will recognize and live in community with one another in some form or fashion as we realize we need each other.

Step 6. Trust God for the Future

Step six is to trust God for the future. Proverbs 3:5-10 reads:

> Trust in the LORD with all your heart, and lean not on your own understanding; in all your ways acknowledge Him, and He shall direct your paths. Do not be wise in your own eyes; fear the LORD and depart from evil. It will be health to your flesh, and strength to your bones [divine health]. Honor the LORD with your possessions, and with the firstfruits of all your increase; so your barns will be filled with plenty, and your vats will overflow with new wine [prosperity].

I believe this is one of the hardest spiritual principles for American believers to understand and practice. The reason is because our culture and way of life emphasizes ownership. We believe that we own our possessions, our time, our talents, and our lives. So we live our lives and use our resources and our abilities for ourselves as if all that we are and all that we have belongs to us. We use our abilities; spend our time and our money as if it was ours.

The Bible does not emphasize ownership. It emphasizes stewardship. The Bible says that God owns everything including us and that we are only stewards of the life and possessions God gives us. Psalm 24:1 says, "The earth is the LORD'S, and all its fullness, the world and those who dwell therein."

God has a wonderful plan for your life in the end-times. Jeremiah 33:3 says, "Call to Me, and I will answer you, and show you great and mighty things, which you do not know."

The Lord wants to use us in His kingdom in ways our natural minds could never imagine. As we seek Him, God will reveal His plan for our lives. And His plan will always be beyond our natural abilities to accomplish. If you can explain your life at the natural level, you have not yet found God's full purpose for your life. His vision and purpose for your life will always involve doing things we could never make happen ourselves. So we must have God's favor to open doors we could not open ourselves.

When we find God's calling for our life and began to live it out, God takes responsibility for us. He becomes responsible to give us what we need to fulfill that plan. He gives us the resources and the favor. The burden of provision is on His shoulders not ours. So when He does bless us with the necessary resources, we realize they came from God, belong to God, and we are to use them for God, not for our own pleasure, nor by our own wisdom. Of course, when we do this, God is faithful to give us more than we need for His work so there is an abundance of extra for us to enjoy His blessings at a personal level.

In Deuteronomy, God warned the people not to get proud and arrogant and selfish regarding the prosperity He would give them. Deuteronomy 8:17-18 reads:

> Then you say in your heart, "My power and the might of my hand gave gained me this wealth." And you shall remember the LORD you God, for it is He who gives you power to get wealth, that He may establish His covenant which He swore to your fathers, as it is this day.

God gives us the resources we need, not to consume on ourselves or spend them as we think best, but to establish His covenant on the earth. King David understood this. When David offered the money and resources to the Lord to build the Temple, he said:

> Now therefore, our God, we thank You and praise You glorious name. But who am I, and who are my people, that we should be able to offer so willingly as this? For all things come from You, and of Your own we have give you. ... O LORD our God, all this abundance that we have prepared to build You a house for Your holy name is from Your hand, and is all your own (1 Chronicles 29:13-14,16).

While God becomes responsible to give us what we need to serve Him, we become accountable to God for the stewardship of our life. We belong to God and everything we are and everything we have is God's. The Bible gives two requirements of a steward. One is wisdom (Luke 16:1-13) and the other is faithfulness (1 Corinthians 4:1-2). As we meditate on God's word, we learn wisdom. As we walk with God, we become faithful to His plan for our life. So when we stand before our Creator at the end of our life, we will hear Him say, "Well done good and faithful servant."

Until then, we face the challenges ahead of us with faith and hope. No one has suffered for the faith more than the Apostle Paul. His words of assurance to us come from his own experiences with God. Writing to the believers in Rome, he says:

> Who shall separate us from the love of Christ? Shall tribulation, or distress, or persecution, or famine, or nakedness, or peril, or sword? As it is written, 'For Your sake we are killed all day long; we are accounted as sheep for the slaughter.' Yet in all these things we are more than conquerors through Him who loves us.
>
> For I am persuaded that neither death nor life, nor angels nor principalities nor powers, nor things present nor things to come, nor height nor depth, nor any other created thing, shall be able to separate us from the love of God which is in Christ [Messiah] Jesus our Lord (Romans 8:35-39).

CHAPTER 14

Serving God in the End Times

If we believe that we are living in the end times, then certainly everything we are comfortable with is about to change. When peoples' comfort zones are disturbed, they will react in one of two ways: they will either bless God or curse God. Either way, the greatest opportunity for ministry and service to God and people will happen in the end times. Does the Bible say anything to us about ministering in the end times? The answer is yes! Peter gives a wonderful teaching about serving God in the end times. Let's see what he has to say and how it applies to our lives.

> But the end of all things is at hand; therefore be serious and watchful in your prayers. And above all things have fervent love for one another, for "love will cover a multitude of sins." Be hospitable to one another without grumbling. As each has received a gift, minister it to one another, as good stewards of the manifold grace of God. If anyone speaks, let him speak as the oracles of God. If any one ministers, let him do it with the ability which God supplies, that in all things God may be glorified through Jesus Christ, to whom belong the glory and dominion forever and ever. Amen (1 Peter 4:7-11).

The End of All Things is at Hand

Peter most likely wrote this letter in the early 60's. He would write a second letter as well. He wrote both of them near the end of his life. The Roman leadership hated the Christians. Because the Christians did not worship the many Roman gods, the Romans considered them pagans. The carnal Roman mind misunderstood the early believer's love feasts to be meetings for incest rather than pure spiritual love. They thought that the communion service was some strange form of cannibalism.

When Rome burned in AD 64, Nero (who probably burned it himself) needed someone to blame. The Christians were a convenient scapegoat. For the next four years before his death in AD 68, Nero persecuted the Christians without mercy. It is believed that Hebrews 11:35-40 describes some of this torture. Peter, along with the apostle Paul, was probably martyred during this time. A few years later in AD 70, Titus destroyed Jerusalem, burned the Temple and scattered the Jews to the nations. To Peter and the early believers, the end of all things was clearly at hand. Everything was about to change.

I believe Peter's words are relevant for us today. In the next few years, we will see dramatic changes in our world. The end of the world system and our way of life as we know it is at hand. Everything that can be shaken is going to be shaken. The Lord is going to disturb the world's (and our) comfort zone. Peter wrote to believers who were about to experience times of dramatic change. He instructed them how to serve God during these times.

In this wonderful exhortation, Peter mentions five active aspects of serving God in the end times. These are: 1) endure (be sober and watchful), 2) pray, 3) love, 4) serve, and 5) minister. Let's explore these aspects of end-time ministry.

1. Enduring to the End

To endure means to be sober and watchful, as the end of all things is at hand. What did he mean by this? The phrase, "the end," means to finish, to bring to a close, or the limit at which a things ceases to be. Jesus said, "But he who endures to the end shall be saved. And this gospel of the kingdom will be preached in all the world as a witness to all the nations, and then the end will come" (Matthew 24:13-14).

Paul was no stranger to persecution, trials, and tribulation. He certainly knew first hand about enduring. He said, "I endure all things for the sake of the elect (2 Timothy 2:10). He also wrote to Timothy,

"But you be watchful in all things, endure afflictions, do the work of an evangelist, fulfill your ministry" (2 Timothy 4:5).

I believe that the glory of God is soon to fill the earth. I believe we are going to soon see the greatest outpouring of God's Spirit that the world has ever known. I am certain that the best for God's people is at hand. But there is an enduring until that happens. God is calling us to endure in a world system that is increasing hostile to Bible believers, be they Christian or Jew.

The Gospel of the Kingdom

This great outpouring of the glory of God will happen by the preaching of the "gospel of the kingdom." I have written much about the gospel of the kingdom because it is so important for us to understand this subject. To review, Jesus spoke about the gospel of the kingdom. The gospel of the kingdom is different from the gospel of salvation. Whereas the gospel of salvation preaches Jesus as Savior, the gospel of the kingdom preaches Jesus as Lord and King.

As I have said previously, we thank God for those who have faithfully preached the basic message of salvation from sin. But the gospel of salvation does not have the spiritual power to help us endure to the end. We must have the gospel of the kingdom that proclaims Jesus as Lord and King. We must have the spiritual power and anointing to boldly proclaim that Jesus is Lord over principles and powers (such as Islam, etc.). We must have the spiritual power and anointing to proclaim that Jesus is Lord over the nations, governments, government policies that are contrary to God's holy word, etc. We must have the spiritual power and anointing to proclaim that Jesus is Lord and King over His people.

Jesus said to His followers in Matthew 23:39, "For I say to you, you shall see Me no more till you say, "Baruch Haba b'Shem Adonai" (Blessed is He who comes in the name of the Lord).

The word blessed means to increase and overflow like a river overflows its banks. More recently we understand the image of a tsunami overflowing from the ocean. When this happens the coastline dramatically changes.

When we call Jesus blessed we are asking Him to come and establish His rule from Jerusalem so that the glory of God will cover the earth as the waters cover the sea. We want His kingdom to overflow to cover all the nations. We want the spiritual coastline of every nation to change as God's glorious kingdom fills the earth.

Revelation 11:15 speaks of this great spiritual tsunami with these words, "There were loud voices in heaven, saying, 'The kingdoms of this world have become the kingdoms of our Lord and of His Christ, and He shall reign forever and ever.'"

Revelation 14:6 tells us that an angel of heaven will preach this everlasting gospel to all the nations and people groups.

Isaiah tells us that the government will be upon His shoulder and of the increase of His government there will be no end (Isaiah 9:6-7).

Our basic Western cultural gospel of salvation is going to change to the gospel of the kingdom. When we proclaim the gospel of the kingdom, the power of God will produce a spiritual tsunami that will not only save, but heal and deliver millions of people around the world. God will perform miracles everywhere though ordinary believers in their everyday lives as they proclaim the gospel of the kingdom. Miracles of salvation, healing, and deliverance will be the norm, not the exception from special anointed ministers. We will all be anointed by Gods' Spirit for this ministry.

All Things

Peter says the end of "all things" is at hand. What did he mean by "all things?" Just as in his own time, he meant the present world order as we know it. When Rome destroyed Jerusalem, burned the Temple and scattered the Jews, Peter's world came to an end.

Likewise, the present world order is coming to an end. God is judging the nations, including America, as well as Israel and His own people. Peter also wrote in 1 Peter 4:17:

> For the time has come for judgment to begin at the house of God; and if it begins with us first, what will be the end of those who do not obey the gospel of God?

All things that are contrary to the will of God are coming to an end. All things that are evil and godless are coming to an end. Crooked politicians, evil government decrees, wars, pornography, abortion, child molesters, murders, rape, greedy corporations, injustice, false gods, propaganda and bias news, poverty and disease, divorce, heartache, sorrow, and despair, carnal lukewarm Christianity, secular Israel, etc. are all coming to an end. The only thing that will be left standing is the kingdom of God.

At Hand

Peter says the end of all things is "at hand." What did he mean by "at hand?" The phrase means, "near, close, imminent, approaching, ready to be revealed, bursting forth, breaking out."

Jesus said, "The kingdom of heaven (God) is at hand" (Matthew 3:2; 4:17). Every time Jesus did a miracle it was a manifestation of the kingdom of God bursting forth in their midst. We will soon see the kingdom of God bursting forth on the earth. This is not a time to be fearful. It is a time to rejoice. The kingdom of God is at hand. Hallelujah!

2. Therefore Pray

Peter mentions four things we need to do while we are enduring. First, he says to pray as a serious watchman. The Greek word translated as serious means to be "right minded." Have you ever done something out of character and someone asked you if you were in your "right mind?"

We find this same word and thought in Mark 5:15, describing a demon possessed man that Jesus encountered. The man had so many demons that he lived away from town among the tombs. The neighbors tried to shackle him but the demons in him were so strong they broke the chains. The man cried out in torment day and night, cutting himself with stones. The demons had driven the poor man insane. Jesus cast the legion of demons out of the man into two thousand pigs that went crazy and ran off the edge of the cliff and drowned in the Sea of Galilee. Then the town folk came to Jesus and saw the man sitting calmly, fully clothed and in his "right mind."

The full meaning of *serious* is to be of sound mind, sane, right minded, sober minded, self-controlled, disciplined, and able to reason with a sanctified mind. This describes our behavior and thinking as we approach the end of the age. If we are going to witness the end of all things as we know them, we have a greater responsibility than those who have gone before us in less perilous times.

Peter says we are to have watchful prayers. A watchman has to be sober, awake, and alert. A watchman must know what God is doing and what the enemy is doing. A watchman must know the prophetic season in which we are living. A watchman must warn, prepare, defend, and listen to what is happening.

This means we must pray with alertness to what God is saying and doing and what the enemy is saying and doing. We must ask the Lord to help us understand the prophetic times and seasons in which we are living. We must be alert to the spiritual tsunami that is coming. And we must make lifestyle changes to prepare for it.

3. Therefore Love Fervently

Second, Peter says that above everything else we are to "love fervently." In 1 Peter 1:22, Peter further wrote, "in sincere love of the brethren, love one another fervently with a pure heart."

Paul gave the following prayer:

> And this I pray, that your love may abound still more and more in knowledge and all discernment, that you may approve the things that are excellent, that you may be sincere and without offense till the day of Christ [Messiah] (Philippians 1:9-10).

The Greek word translated into English as fervent means sincere and pure. It means with pure motives without pretension and hypocrisy. It means genuine and real without an agenda or ulterior motives. It means true love that is selfless and unconditional without wanting something in return. In biblical times it meant "sun tested and found to be without wax." Now what does this mean?

Sometimes when a merchant would make pottery, the vessel would crack. Instead of throwing it away, a dishonest merchant would seal the crack with wax. He then would put the pottery on the shelf of his store in a dark area and sell it as "first merchandise" when he should have sold it at a discount as damaged goods. He should have sent it to an outlet mall where everything else was sold that was not first quality goods. It was a cracked pot.

Now before buying any item, a wise shopper would first take the item off the shelf, go outside, and hold the item up to the sun. The light of the sun would show if there was any wax. It would expose the item as being something it was not. This would let the buyer know that there was a crack in the item and it was not a first quality item.

When Peter and Paul say that our love should be fervent, sincere and pure, their readers would understand what they meant. Their love should be "sun tested and found to be without wax." Their love should be real, without pretense, without hypocrisy, without an agenda, without a selfish motive, without wanting to get something from the person we are pretending to love.

We can certainly tell if our love is without wax by the kind of relationships we have with people. If our love is conditioned on using the person for our own purposes, we will break off the relationship when we can no longer use that person for selfish reasons. So let the "S-O-N" test our love to see if is real or pretend. Let the Holy Spirit shine the light of God on our hearts to see if we are covering up cracks in our relationships. Let us have genuine love for people and not pretend to be something we are not. Let us examine ourselves to see if we are without wax or whether we are nothing but "cracked pots."

4. Practice Hospitality (Serving)

The next exhortation Peter gives us is to practice hospitality or serve, and he adds, without grumbling. It interesting that Peter makes this comment because he had his own dramatic experience with hospitality and serving.

You recall in the book of Acts, Chapter Ten, that Peter went to the rooftop of his house around noon to pray. Since it was lunch time, he got hungry. But before he could fix himself a good kosher sandwich, the Lord put Peter into a trance. And the Lord put non-kosher creatures in a *tallit* and lowered it from heaven to Peter and told him to eat that bad stuff. Now Peter had never eaten anything non-kosher so he argued with the Lord. He grumbled. Three times the Lord told him to eat and Peter grumbled. Then the Lord lifted the *tallit* back to heaven. We see that Peter did not eat the non-biblical creatures. The Lord never intended Him to do so. It was preparation for Peter to receive the three unclean Gentiles that were knocking at his door.

Now Cornelius had a visitation from the Lord who told him to send for Peter. So at the same time Peter was having his vision of the unclean creatures, three unclean Gentiles were knocking at his door. Peter did not socialize with Gentiles. The Jews considered them to be unclean. I'm sure he had never invited a Gentile into his house before. But there they were knocking at his door. God was asking Peter to overcome thousands of years of ethnic hostility towards Gentiles.

The Lord himself told Peter to go with the Gentiles to the house of Cornelius. The Lord added, "Doubting nothing for I have sent them." In other words, don't grumble and argue with Me like you did with the unclean creatures. Since it was late in the evening, Peter actually invited the Gentiles into his home to spend the night. That must have been a major trauma for Peter. The next day he went with them and entered Cornelius' home. This was another major test for Peter.

When Peter entered the home, he understood the reason for the test about the unclean creatures. It wasn't about eating. It was about changing his attitude towards Gentiles. Peter himself gave this explanation and said, "God has shown me that I should not call any man common or unclean. Therefore, I came without objection [grumbling]" (Acts 10:28-29).

The apostle James also had his test with Gentiles when Paul explained to him how the Gentiles were being called by the Lord without having to become Jews. James agreed. He later wrote, "Do not grumble against one another, brethren, lest you be condemned. Behold the Judge is standing at the door!" (James 5:9).

In the end-times, many people are going to come into the Kingdom of God. They will come from many different backgrounds. They are not all going to like us. We have a tendency to relate to people who are like us. But they will not be like us. They will represent every kind of economic, social, cultural, spiritual, and ethnic background imaginable.

Furthermore, the number of people discovering their biblical Hebraic roots is growing exponentially. And they come from all denominational backgrounds. God has absolutely no interest in our denominational background. He is interested in our relationships. God is going to ask us to open our hearts and our homes to one another beyond our comfort zone of familiar friends. He wants us to receive all of His children to whom we have not related in times past. Like Peter, people we have not been comfortable with. People we have not thought of as being kosher.

Furthermore, we are going to have to learn to get along with everyone because we are going to have to live together in community. God is going to have to do a great work in the lives of American Christians because you can't live in community unless you learn to be submissive, humble, others-centered, and servant minded. We will have to think in term of ours, not mine. We will have to learn to be stewards and not owners.

In addition, the Lord is also calling Christian believers to assist the Jews in North America to make *aliyah*. There is no doubt He is going to give us opportunities to show hospitality to Christians and Jews in these end times. We may have to let a perfect stranger sit in our favorite chair. Or eat what would normally be the second helping of our favorite food. Or pick up someone from the airport at an inconvenient time. Or give sacrificially to help those in need. Or share our home with other families as permanent house guests. May we embrace these opportunities with grace, mercy, and compassion, and as Peter said, without grumbling.

5. Minister Your Gift

Finally, Peter says we should use the spiritual gifts God has given us as good stewards of the manifold grace of God. Now what does he mean by this? God has a wonderful plan for our lives. Jeremiah explains, "For I know the thoughts that I think toward you, says the LORD, thoughts of peace and not of evil, to give you a future and a hope" (Jeremiah 29:11).

As part of God's plan, He calls all of us to some kind of ministry and then anoints us and equips us with spiritual gifts so we can serve Him effectively. All believers are in full-time ministry. While some of us make our living from our ministry, most have a vocational job in the world where they earn money to pay their bills, but their ministry is their calling and purpose of life.

Our ministry is how we serve the Lord. Ministries are the infinite opportunities for us to use our God-given spiritual gifts in His kingdom. The Bible gives us three different categories of gifts. God gives each of us one or more of these gifts and holds us accountable to be good stewards to use them as the Lord enables us.

In Romans 12:3-8, Paul lists what are often called motivational gifts. God gives us these basic motivations when we are conceived. We are hard-wired internally with an inner motivation towards life. They are gifts from the Father. We all have one or more motivational gifts.

Paul lists seven of these gifts. They are:

1. Prophecy
2. Serving
3. Teaching
4. Exhorting
5. Organizing
6. Giving
7. Mercy

Paul gives a second category of gifts in Ephesians 4:11-12. These are equipping gifts, which are often referred to as the five-fold ministry. They are gifts from the Son, given for the purpose of building up the believers and equipping them for ministry. They are not offices but human ministers serving in one or more of these gifts. They are:

1. Apostles
2. Prophets
3. Evangelists
4. Pastors
5. Teachers

Paul gives a third category of gifts in 1 Corinthians 12:1-18. These are the charismatic gifts from the Spirit. Unlike motivation gifts, they are not resident within the believer but are given by the Holy Spirit when there is the need for them to be manifested. They are not human abilities but supernatural manifestation of the Spirit. The nine gifts of the Spirit are:

1. Word of Wisdom
2. Word of Knowledge
3. Discerning of Spirits
4. Faith
5. Healing
6. Miracles
7. Prophecy
8. Tongues
9. Interpretation of Tongues

Manifold Grace of God

Peter says we are to use these all of these gifts as the manifold grace of God. Now what did he mean by that? The Greek word translated as manifold means "multi-colored." It refers to a "big chunk of glass," like a prism. A prism catches the rays of the sun and bends them so that we can see the incredibly beautiful colors in the sun rays that we can't see otherwise.

In Ephesians 3:10, Paul writes that the "manifold wisdom of God might be made known by the church to the principalities and powers in the heavenly places." Paul wants us to understand that we, God's people, are His big chunk of glass. We are God's prism. When the Holy Spirit controls our soul and anoint us with His gifts, people can see in us the life, wisdom, character, fruit, and ministry of God that they would not be able to see otherwise.

I remember years back when I was ministering at a traditional congregation in New England on Sunday morning and only had 30 minutes to speak. Everyone who knows me knows that my introduction to my message can take 30 minutes. I was really praying to the Lord for guidance and wisdom on what to say. When it came time for me to speak, I still didn't know what to say. Now for a minister, that can be frightening.

But as I looked out to the sanctuary, I noticed a large, beautiful, stained glass window in the back of the sanctuary. The church building is listed on the historical society in that community as a landmark building. And the stained glass window was valued at $1 million. The moment I saw it, the Lord impressed on me what I should say. I told them how beautiful was the stained glass window, but it couldn't help anyone. It was only a stained glass window.

But the people were God's real stained glass window. The people were the prism catching the rays of God life and ministry so that, when others who didn't know the Lord, saw them, they would see God in them. And then they would say, "Ah, so that is what God is like? That is what God's love and mercy and wisdom and power are like? Now I see what I could not see otherwise."

People need to see examples of godly living being lived out before them. They would rather see a sermon than hear one. They would rather we walk with them than merely show the way. We instinctively recognize this and often say to one another, "Keep your eyes on Jesus." While I am sure we mean well by that statement, I don't think that is what the Lord has in mind. I think He wants us to live in such a way that we can say with the Apostle Paul, who wrote these words to the believers at Corinth, "Imitate me, just as I also imitate Christ [Messiah]" (1 Corinthians 11:1).

To the Philippian believers he said, "Brethren, join in following my example, and note those who so walk, as you have us for a pattern." (Philippians 3:17).

He reminded the Thessalonian believers with these words, "And you became followers of us and the Lord"(1 Thessalonians 1:6). Also similar in 2 Thessalonians 3:9.

He wrote to Timothy, "Let no one despise your youth, but be an example to the believers in word, in conduct, in love, in spirit, in faith, in purity" (1 Timothy 4:12).

He encouraged the Ephesian believers with these words, "Therefore be imitators of God as dear children" (Ephesians 5:1).

Jesus is physically in Heaven. If people were to look up into the sky to see Him, they would not be able to do so unless God gave them some kind of special vision of Heaven. So how are they going to see Jesus? They are going to see Him as He lives His life in His people. They are going to see Him as His life in us is manifested to those around us.

How will the world around us know about God's holiness unless they see it in us? How will they know about God's righteousness unless we live a righteous life before them? How will they know that

God is love unless His love is flowing out of us? How will they know that God is good unless they see His goodness in us? How will they know that God accepts them unless we show them hospitality? How will people know that God is a giving God if we don't give?

We must live our lives in such a way that people can see Him in us. Our words alone are meaningless. With God's help, we must live out our convictions in our everyday lives in relationships with people. We must endure, we must pray, we must love, we must serve, we must minister. We are God's big chunk of glass. We are His prism.

Amen

Peter closes his comments by saying:

> If anyone speaks, let him speak as the oracles of God. If anyone ministers, let him do it as with the ability which God supplies, that in all things God may be glorified through Jesus Christ [the Messiah], to whom belong the glory and the dominion forever and ever. Amen.

The word "amen," comes for the Hebrew letters "the Aleph, the Mem, and the Nun." It is pronounced in Hebrew as *El/Melech/N'eman*, which means, "God the Faithful King."

God is the faithful covenant-keeping God. He who has called us is faithful. He is faithful to His word. He is faithful to His counsel and decrees. He is faithful to Israel. He is faithful to the grafted-in non-Jewish believers. He is faithful to complete the good work He has begun in us. He is faithful to redeem us to himself. He is faithful to those who endure to the end. He is faithful to raise us from the dead. He is faithful to give us a glorified body that so that we can live forever with Him. He is faithful to establish the fullest reign of His kingdom on the earth at which time we will rule and reign with Him in righteousness.

Because God is faithful, Paul writes:

> But thanks be to God, who gives us the victory through our Lord Jesus Christ [Messiah]. Therefore, my beloved brethren, be steadfast, immovable, always abounding in the work of the Lord, knowing that your labor is not in vain in the Lord (1 Corinthians 15:57-58).

While God's judgment is on the nations and apostate Western Christianity, His glory is for those who seek Him with all their heart. Jude explains:

> Now unto Him who is able to keep you from stumbling [falling], and to present you faultless before the presence of His glory with exceeding joy, to God our Savior, Who alone is wise, be glory and majesty, dominion and power, both now and forever. Amen (Jude 24-25).

The apostle Paul gives us a final word of encouragement:

> For God did not appoint us to wrath, but to obtain salvation through our Lord Jesus Christ [Messiah], who died for us, that whether we wake or sleep, we should live together with Him. Therefore comfort each other and edify one another, just as you also are doing (1 Thessalonians 5:9-11).

About the Author

Dr. Richard Booker, MBA, Ph.D., is an ordained Christian minister, President of Sounds of the Trumpet, Inc., and the Founder/Director of the Institute for Hebraic-Christian Studies. Prior to entering the ministry, he had a successful business career. He is the author of thirty books and Bible study materials that are used by churches and Bible schools around the world.

Dr. Booker has traveled extensively for over thirty years, teaching in churches and at conferences on various aspects of the Christian life as well as Bible prophecy, Israel, and the Hebraic roots of Christianity. He and his wife, Peggy, lead yearly tour groups to Israel where, for eighteen years, Dr. Booker has been a speaker at the International Christian Celebration of the Feast of Tabernacles in Jerusalem. This gathering is attended by over 5,000 Christians from 100 nations.

Dr. Booker and Peggy founded the Institute for Hebraic-Christian Studies (IHCS) in 1997 as a ministry to educate Christians in the Hebraic culture and background of the Bible, build relationships between Christians and Jews, and give comfort and support to the people of Israel. Their tireless work on behalf of Christians and Jews has been recognized around the world, as well as being represented at the Knesset Christian Allies Caucus.

Dr. Booker is considered a pioneer, spiritual father, and prophetic voice teaching on Bible prophecy, radical Islam, Israel, Jewish-Christian relations, and the biblical Hebraic roots of Christianity. His television program, "Sounds of the Shofar," can be seen worldwide on God's Learning Channel. To learn more about his ministry, see his web site and online bookstore at www.rbooker.com or www.soundsofthetrumpet.com.

If you would like Dr. Booker to speak to your congregation or at your conference, you may contact him at ShofarPRB@aol.com.